QNR
(Bel)

READING,
WRITING, AND
REWRITING THE
PROSTITUTE
BODY

0253208599

READING, WRITING, AND REWRITING THE PROSTITUTE BODY

His 10-14
med 41

Shannon Bell

Indiana University Press

Bloomington and Indianapolis

The paper used in this publication meets the minimum
requirements of American National Standard for Information
Sciences—Permanence of Paper for Printed Library Materials,
ANSI Z39.48-1984.

Manufactured in the United States of America

Library of Congress Cataloging-in-Publication Data

Bell, Shannon, date
Reading, writing, and rewriting the prostitute
body/Shannon Bell.
p. cm.
Includes bibliographical references and index.
ISBN 0-253-31166-7 (cl : alk. paper).—ISBN
0-253-20859-9 (pbk. : alk. paper)
1. Prostitution. 2. Prostitution—History. 3. Prostitutes.
4. Feminist theory. 5. Deconstruction. I. Title.
HQ111.B45 1994
306.74'2'09—dc20
93-5447
CIP

1 2 3 4 5 99 98 97 96 95 94

For Gad Horowitz

"And you are the best part. . . . "

CONTENTS

ACKNOWLEDGMENTS

I WOULD LIKE TO thank Gad Horowitz for his interest in this project; for the time he spent theorizing and dialoguing with me and for his editorial assistance. It is a rare privilege to have a postmodern philosopher [king] as an editor; for this I am very grateful.

I am extremely grateful to Isabella Bakker, Janine Brodie, and Michael Kaufman for their many insightful comments and theoretical discernments. I would like to thank Eve Tavor Bannet for her valuable readings and theorizations.

In addition, I wish to extend my appreciation to Ed Andrew, Philippa Berry, Lorraine Code, Asher Horowitz, and Richard Noble for their comments on earlier versions of chapter 2, "Reading the *Hetairae* in Plato's Texts," and to Eleanor MacDonald and Fredrika Scarth for their comments on an earlier version of chapter 4, "Writing the Prostitute Body: Feminist Reproductions."

I wish to thank Julia Emberley for her invigorating discussions with me on chapters 1 through 4; Terry Maley for his theoretical "breakaway" on an aspect of chapter 5; Brenda Cossman, Livy Visano, and Reg Witaker for their engagement of the manuscript.

I would like to thank Annie Sprinkle, Gwendolyn, Scarlot Harlot, Janet Feindel, Veronica Vera, and Candida Royalle for sharing their knowledge with me. There are also friends and colleagues whose work and conversations have been a gift: I would like to thank Sandra Badin, Michael Dartnell, Kath Daymond, Sue Golding, Lise Gotell, Peter Kulchyski, Arthur Kroker, Marilouise Kroker, Rafy Kim Sawchuk and Anne Stretch.

Especially, I want to thank my mother, Mildred Bell, for her wisdom and her support.

Lastly, I wish to thank Idit Dobbs-Weinstein for presenting me with a copy of *The Republic of Plato* many years ago when I had no interest in philosophy. Her inscription read: "For those rare moments when neither laughter nor speech is necessary."

Grateful acknowledgment is made for permission to reprint the following previously published material: excerpts from an interview with

Gwendolyn appear courtesy of *semiotext(e)*; an earlier portion of chapter 2 appears in *Shadow of Spirit: Contemporary Western Thought and Its Religious Subtexts*, ed. Philippa Berry and Andrew Wernick (Routledge, 1992).

READING, WRITING, AND REWRITING THE PROSTITUTE BODY

PROSTITUTION AS a discursive domain has had a marginal place in the cultural exchanges of the West for thousands of years. In two historical/philosophical periods—the pagan and the postmodern—prostitutes have themselves produced discourses. In ancient Greece *hetairae* numbered among the sophistic philosophers. Two such prostitute philosophers, Diotima and Aspasia, are known to us because of the preservation of their memory within the texts of Plato. Thus, what remains for us "pervert" archaeologists to uncover of ancient prostitute discourse is entombed within the "originating" discourse of Western philosophy. Pagan prostitute discourse functions to disturb, destabilize, and undermine our philosophical foundations from within; postmodern prostitute discourse, on the other hand, formed in response to the modern and the feminist productions of "the prostitute," challenges these dominant discourses from their outside.

This work is a genealogy of the prostitute body: it is a discontinuous history written as theory and politics; what Michel Foucault has called "a history of the present,"[1] beginning with a retrospective reconstruction of the *hetaira*, the pagan prostitute, from the vantage point of the postmodern prostitute. The aim is to deconstruct the modernist and feminist construction of the prostitute from both a premodern and postmodern prostitute subject position: to use the presence of postmodern prostitute discourse and performance art to recover and disentomb ancient prostitute voices and knowledges suppressed in and through the narrative of modernity and to use this recovered knowledge to supplement the new position of "the prostitute" of the present moment.

The overarching strategy of *Reading, Writing, and Rewriting the Prostitute Body* is to show how it is that the referent, the flesh-and-blood female body engaged in some form of sexual interaction in exchange for some kind of payment, has no inherent meaning and is signified differently in different discourses. I trace the construction of the prostitute body in five discursive domains: ancient Greece, modern Europe, contemporary feminism (North American and French), postmodern prostitute feminisms (North American and international), and postmodern prostitute performance art (North American).

Modernity through a process of othering has produced "the prostitute" as the other of the other: the other within the categorical other, "woman." At the heart of the foundational metaphysics of Western thought is the logocentric assumption of the binary opposition of masculine and feminine, the masculine being the privileged site and the feminine the disprivileged. This hierarchical opposition is reproduced within each side of the dichotomy. Hegemonic heterosexual masculinity is the privileged site within the category "masculinity" and homosexuality the disprivileged other. I am tracing the descent of a female other doubly disprivileged: inside the feminine and by the hegemonic masculine. Beginning the construction of the contemporary prostitute body as I do in ancient Greece, as opposed to nineteenth-century Europe, is a textual-political act, the intent of which is to displace the more traditional linkage of the contemporary prostitute to the profane, diseased, and excluded female body of the nineteenth century, foregrounding instead its lineage to the ancient sexual, sacred, healing female body.

I will argue that a process of othering runs through the modern and feminist constructions of the prostitute body; that the modern discourse dichotomizes the female into the "good" and "bad" woman in all her manifestations; that modernist feminists, such as Carole Pateman and Catharine MacKinnon, although their theorization is counter-hegemonic, accept and reproduce these dichotomies; that this othering process is fractured with the postmodern theorizations of Luce Irigaray and Gayle Rubin; that prostitute discourse, the reverse discourse, in attempting to break the dichotomies, sometimes slips into them; and, finally, that the overarching dichotomies of "whore" and "madonna," which are applied to all women, are dissolved and unified in prostitute performance art.

The contemporary postmodern is a unique historical moment in which prostitutes, like other others of modernity, have assumed their own subject position and begun to produce their own political identity. The new prostitute identity contains a trace to the pagan prostitute philosophers and political actors who spoke as female others among the sophists; but in postmodernity prostitutes speak from the subject position of prostitute. What has resulted is a politicization of the prostitute body undertaken from its position as experiential body: word-flesh. This politicization has produced a new public site of discourse—prostitute discourse; new political subjects—politicized prostitutes; and a new social movement—local, national, and international prostitute groups.

Reading, Writing, and Rewriting the Prostitute Body is a postmodern text: it is interdisciplinary and intertextual, combining the disciplines of political theory, feminist theory, philosophy, comparative politics, literary theory, the politics of new social movements, and aspects of public policy. My aim is to read other texts, produce new meanings from these texts, and, through intertextual juxtaposition, write a new text. The texts I read include philosophical works, histories of prostitution, medical writings, laws, movement documents, speeches, letters, pamphlets, newspaper articles, interviews, and performance pieces.

Each chapter of this work is a whole in itself and part of the larger project. The text is written to be both continuous and discontinuous. Every chapter will connect in that each is a reading and writing of the prostitute body; each chapter will also stand alone, providing an internal critique of the specific texts at hand. In chapter 2, "Reading the *Hetairae* in Plato's Texts," in addition to tracing the meaning inscribed on the prostitute body in ancient Greece, I provide a critique of feminist scholarship on Plato's texts. In chapter 3, "The Making of the Modern Prostitute Body," in addition to tracing how the modern prostitute body has been produced in five central texts of the nineteenth century, I provide a critique of three contemporary commentators. In chapter 4, "Writing the Prostitute Body: Feminist Reproductions," I examine the works of four well-known contemporary feminists: Carole Pateman, who has explicitly written the prostitute body in her critique of the liberal social contract; Catharine MacKinnon, who produced what became the hegemonic position on prostitution in the women's movement during the 1980s, and Luce Irigaray and Gayle Rubin, who have outlined two very different sexual markings of the prostitute body. I read these feminist writings within the broader context of their understanding of the female body and female sexuality. In chapter 5, "Rewriting the Prostitute Body: Prostitute Perspectives," I examine three different and contradictory prostitute discourses—those of prostitutes' rights groups, WHISPER (Women Hurt in Systems of Prostitution Engaged in Revolt), and Prostitutes Anonymous—which, combined, define the terrain of the prostitutes' struggle. Chapter 6, "Prostitute Performances: Sacred Carnival Theorists of the Female Body," foregrounds the texts of six prostitute performance artists: Candida Royalle, Annie Sprinkle, Veronica Vera, Gwendolyn, Janet Feindel, and Scarlot Harlot; I engage their work in terms of the way it deconstructs the masculinist and feminist inscriptions on the prostitute body.

Until the postmodern moment (chapters 5 and 6 in my text) when prostitutes as new political subjects produce and inscribe their own bodies in diverse and contradictory ways, what is overwhelmingly present in the dominant discourses and even in the feminist counter-discourse is a negative construction and reproduction of the prostitute body that focuses on the undeniable suffering and oppression bound up with prostitution through the centuries. I approach the constituting ancient, modern, and feminist texts from the position of that which is absent—a positive construction of the prostitute body—discovering this position in the very documents that have been employed to construct the prostitute as the negative female other.

As my work is both informed by the postmodern moment and is itself a contributing postmodern artifact, a cursory description of postmodernism is in order.

Postmodernism

Postmodernism, as I use the term—and there are no firmly agreed-upon terms of reference—designates a historically specific social field originating sometime in the 1950s and 1960s in Western capitalist countries.[2] The defining characteristics of postmodernism are fragmentation, discontinuity, indeterminacy, plurality, multiplicity, difference, and ambiguity.

In the cultural-ideological domain the two definitive features of postmodernism are the decentering of the humanist subject of the Enlightenment—the conscious, knowing, unified, rational subject, the site for viewing, creating, and apprehending reality, and the bypassing of meta-narratives and meta-theories aimed at understanding and representing the world. Grand narratives such as the Enlightenment narrative of the gradual but steady progress of reason and freedom, Marx's narrative of the forward march of human productive capacities via class conflict, and Freud's meta-theory of the eternal reproduction of civilization based on the permanent repression of human drives are no longer seen as overarching general theories capable of situating and evaluating all other discourses.

Postmodernism signifies a plurality of discursive formations which produce admittedly partial and interested narratives about the world. The positionality of the historical subject who is constituted as a subject within specific discourses has replaced the Enlightenment epistemology of the knowing transcendental subject who uses reason to establish universal truth. The unitary definition of truth which has since Plato characterized Western thought has been replaced by multiple truths. The postmodern subject is a historical subject constituted by multiple and often conflicting social relations. The postmodern subject is decentered and detotalized, a fragmented subject who is a site of disunity and conflict and who consequently can be seen to engage simultaneously in political change and in the preservation of the status quo.

Postmodernity revalues the aesthetic and the micropolitical: art and minoritarian politics have become sites of resistance to hegemonic grand narratives. In the aesthetic realm—architecture, art, music, and literature—the postmodern appears as a mixture of styles and genres. In architecture this often manifests itself as a collision of the ancient form with the new. Philip Johnson's AT&T highrise on Fifth Avenue, in Manhattan, is an excellent example of postmodern architectural mixing of styles: the building is broken up into a neoclassical midsection, Roman colonnades at the street level, and a Chippendale pediment on top. In literature there has been a move from narrative and developing plot and character(s) to a pastiche of broken narratives, an intermixing of past and present, dream and reality, and sketchy character profiles. Postmodern art is a mixed medium of superimposition and collaging, or a juxtaposition of different media in the same space and as part of the same show, or an intermedia spectacle that combines elements from dance, performance, video, music, and theater in the same piece. For example, Sankai Juku, a Tokyo dance troupe, disharmoniously combines Zen philosophy, Kabuki theater, sculptural art form, and Western music.

Postmodern politics is micropolitics in a global context: a politics of the local and the particular, a politics of racial, sexual, and cultural/subcultural difference brought together in shifting alliances and coalitions. For example, prostitutes' rights groups which operate on their specific local terrains are also members of the international movement for prostitutes' rights; prostitutes and other sex workers from various First and Third World locations gather to develop common strategies every two years at a World Whores' Congress. Prostitutes' rights groups have also formed alliances with gay activists on the issue of safe sex and with feminist groups on the issue of woman's right to control her own body. Postmodern politics extends the political into all spheres, domains, and practices of the lifeworld. Political theory is thus redefined to account for those arrangements of power that devolve upon the body, sexuality, and the unconscious. Radically new political spaces, political subjects, and social movements have emerged in response to the heterogeneity and fragmentation of the social field.[3]

A current debate within feminism hinges on whether to articulate the feminist project with postmodern philosophy. My project does not directly address this theoretical debate; rather, it does some of the concrete work of this articulation. Postmodernism, because it holds the impossibility of a unitary female subject, facilitates feminism(s) of difference(s), differences within the category of "woman" and within the specific social existences of women: positional differences and experiential differences. Postmodernism opens the feminist terrain to prostitute feminist discourse and to differences among prostitute discourses.

The theoretical works of Jacques Derrida, Michel Foucault, and Chantal Mouffe and Ernesto Laclau provide techniques for comprehending the specificity of postmodernism.

Method

In *Reading, Writing, and Rewriting the Prostitute Body*, I apply techniques of post-structuralist analysis that have come to define postmodern scholarship: Derrida's textual deconstruction combined with Foucault's genealogical project, Mouffe and Laclau's concept of radical democracy, plus the materialization of deconstructive theory in the performance medium. I will give a cursory description of each theoretical field and its relevance for my project.

Deconstruction

Deconstruction is a way of reading texts. The deconstructor focuses on the inconsistencies of a text—its ambiguities, gaps, and silences—

to show how the internal logic of the text subverts itself. The deconstructor is interested in "the moment that is undecidable in terms of the text's apparent system of meaning, the moment in the text that seems to transgress its own system of values."[4] The tactic of deconstruction is to show how texts embarrass their own ruling system of logic.

With deconstruction, every act of reading is a new production of meaning: the reader no longer interprets the author's intended meaning but produces meaning and often a new text out of the so-called original[5] text. *Différance,* from the French verb *différer,* which means both to differ and to defer, encapsulates Derrida's most basic premise of deconstruction: that in any thing or moment present there is an absence, a deferral, to another related thing which is both the same and other. This deferral continues interminably along a metonymic chain of association that at some level collapses difference into equivalence.

A plurality of meanings can be appropriated and read from the same text; ultimately, therefore, the text's meaning is undecidable. The meaning of the text is produced by the reader through a process Derrida names "grafting." For Derrida writing and grafting are synonymous: "To write means to graft. It's the same word."[6] The reader's meaning is "grafted" onto the so-called original text, producing a new text and rewriting the "original" text: "Each grafted text continues to radiate back toward the site of its removal, transforming that too, as it affects the new territory."[7] Writing, thus, is the production of a new text through a rereading of the "original"; it is reading as the active production of meaning or, as the literary critic Terry Eagleton calls it, "reading-as-writing."[8] The graft is produced through a process Derrida names "dissemination": the textual practice corresponds to collage/ montage. Collage refers to the transfer of citations from one context and montage to their dispersal in a new context.

Derrida holds that there is no original text, including his own—that all texts are inscribed in the margins of some preexisting texts. "Derrida is, first and foremost, a reader,"[9] claims Barbara Johnson, the translator of his *Dissemination.* He intervenes in the text under study and his intervention produces a new text. In his act of reading, Derrida focuses on peripheral aspects of the work—a footnote, a minor term, a casual allusion—and uses them to take apart—to deconstruct—the logical oppositions upon which the text appeared to rely. "Dissemination" is a word carefully chosen to play on the trace of "insemination." Unlike insemination, dissemination refers to the seed being spilled in vain, an emission that cannot return to its origin, the "original text," but rather changes and alters the meaning of the text from whence it came.

A text has a material existence; it can and must be used in ways which the author did not foresee or intend. Reading is a political act: readers read from positions in the world, whether these positions are acknowledged or not. Readers are socially and historically positioned. How the reader produces meaning is the result of an interaction between all the texts he or she has read in the past, his or her positionality in the world, and the text of the moment.

My deconstructive approach deploys the fourfold rule of deconstruction decoded and developed by Eve Tavor Bannet in her book *Structuralism and the Logic of Dissent*. In a reading of Derrida's famous X, Bannet inscribes four V's in the blank spaces of the X. Derrida uses "X" to signal that the word is "under erasure": He writes the word, crosses it out, and then prints both the word and the erasure. Bannet says "To read this figure [X], one has to focus on the blanks. The blanks in the sign form four V's (or folds) placed back to back so that they intersect with one another."[10] She interprets the four V's as Derrida's method, writing them as DiVision, Articulation, The PiVot, and the Veil of Displacement. These strategies for reading a text, strategies of deconstruction, open the text to the possibility of a subversive reading and to the political project of the reader. DiVision "deconstructs [the] notion of the text as a single, coherent and identifiable entity by seeking out each text's inconsistencies, incoherences and obscurities and by developing them into full-scale contradictions."[11] Articulation dissolves the boundaries between the inside of the text and its outside and grafts different texts onto one another.[12] The PiVot reverses accustomed hierarchies that structure Western writing, such as presence/absence, speech/writing, concept/metaphor, philosophy/rhetoric, soul/body, reproduction/libidinal, and masculine/feminine. It does so by making the term which is customarily the minor term of the couple the condition of operation of both terms. "In the pivot . . . the critical text actively intervenes in the text which is being read by reversing its assumptions."[13] The Veil of Displacement is what Bannet claims distinguishes Derrida from other critics who also have engaged in textual operations that correspond to DiVision, Articulation, and The PiVot. Derrida, she suggests, displaces in two ways these textual operations that others engage in:

> First, . . . he divides, articulates and pivots in a different place from everyone else: he divides what we are accustomed to thinking of as connected, articulates what we are accustomed to thinking of as distinct, and pivots hierarchies that we have not previously noticed, much less questioned. And secondly, he gives these operations new names. . . .[14]

The political project underpinning this fourfold rule of deconstruction is the destruction of the ethnocentrism and self-referentiality of the West based on the logos of the white heterosexual man who reproduces what has been termed in some literary circles as "white-guy theory," exploding the closure of repetitive texts (the canon texts) that refer only to one another and represent only themselves. Perhaps the most important political result of these four strategies is the exposure, in all the "white-guy" canon texts defining the various disciplines that constitute knowledge, of the gaps, spaces, and traces which escape mastery. And these constitute the ethical space where different readers producing different meanings and different critical texts can intervene in the canon text.

I apply these four stategies of deconstruction in the following ways. First, by the particular combination of texts that I choose to produce my new critical text: Plato's *Symposium*, *The British Royal Commission on the Contagious Diseases Acts*, and Gayle Rubin's "Thinking Sex. Notes for a Radical Theory of the Politics of Sexuality" have not previously been intertextually read. Second, by the texts and the parts of texts that I emphasize: when reading Plato, for instance, I focus on texts and parts of texts that have been marked out by the canonizers of Western philosophy as the not-serious portions of Plato's writings. And third, by the position from which I read: I read and write from the position of the clitoris, implicitly throughout my text and explicitly in chapter 2. This is a position which has been carefully constructed to reframe Derrida's employment of "the hymen," a term which he uses to indicate textual operations that give way to the infinite mystery at the opening of other texts and that give entrance into the hole, the gap, the blank space of the text under investigation. The clitoris, from this position, is the presence, rather than the Derridean absence, at this opening; it is the site of excess and of pleasure. The clitoris represents that part of female sexuality—pleasure—that is superfluous to (re)production and is capable of structuring the (w)hole female sexual organ (the clitoris, urethra, vagina, and womb) as an unfragmented conduit of pleasure. That is to say I read from a female position of power and pleasure, a position outside or in excess to the phallic or male-defined feminine.

The Genealogical Project

Michel Foucault can be said to apply methods somewhat similar to deconstruction in his historical analysis of various phenomena: Foucault, like Derrida, focuses on the apparently incidental, detotalizing history into discontinuous events and concentrating on phenomena and populations which have been ignored.[15] Genealogy is what Foucault, following Nietzsche, calls the construction of noncontinuous history and lineages of descent. A genealogical approach foregrounds that which has been omitted, those who have been excluded or marginalized, by the grand historical projects. Foucault writes the histories of marginal, unknown, and excluded discourses, a history of "subjugated knowledges,"[16] against what he refers to as "the tyranny of globalizing discourses."[17] Central to his concept of genealogy is the interrelationship between the production of knowledge, power, and the body: a genealogy maps the interconnection between knowledge, power, and the body.

In his 1970 inaugural lecture to the College de France, "The Discourse on Language," Foucault sets out four strategies that had implicitly informed his work up to that point and were to overtly inform his emergent genealogical project: reversal, discontinuity, specificity, and exteriority.

Foucault's strategy, when tradition gives a particular interpretation of an event or a historical development, is to examine the implications of the reverse or opposite interpretation; he does this in his study of madness and in his studies of the development of the hospital and the prison. Foucault uses the strategy of historical reversal in his critique of the "repressive hypothesis" in his first volume of *The History of Sexuality*. The "repressive hypothesis" holds that beginning with the Victorian era human sexuality has increasingly been repressed. Foucault contends that this reading of the history of modern sexuality is mistaken; from the nineteenth century on there has been "a steady proliferation of discourses concerned with sex."[18]

The strategy of reversal directly informs three of my chapters and underpins my work as a whole. In chapter 2, reversal is doubled in two respects: While Plato is usually read from the position of the male Athenian citizen, I read him from the position of the female noncitizen; unlike most feminist critics, however, I do not approach the Athenian polis through the position of the citizen's wife but from the position of "the other woman," the philosopher/whore, the embodiment of the philosophical clitoris. I read Plato in the space of those who have been made to appear in both phallic and gynic historiography as the patriarch's collaborators. In chapter 3, I trace the socio-historical construction of the prostitute body, showing and questioning the ambiguity of the assumptions of the medical-moral, legal-political, and psychoanalytic-sexological discourses. In chapter 4, I approach the writings on the prostitute body in contemporary feminism from their reverse implications: for example, I present prostitutes as not only victims of the male body politic but also as social agents acting with relative autonomy within the presently insurmountable restrictions and confines of the male body politic.

Foucault views history as "discontinuous"; he looks for and focuses on ruptures, breaks, gaps, displacements, interruptions, thresholds, and shifts. Yet the breaks are never seen as complete: within discontinuity there is "overlapping, interaction, and echoes"[19] of what came before. Like its object—the historical development or construction of the prostitute body—my thesis is discontinuous. I pinpoint five thresholds in the construction of the prostitute body: ancient Greece, modern Europe, contemporary British, French and North American feminism, the North American and international prostitute movement, and North American prostitute performance art. Yet each discursive domain interacts with and contains echoes of its predecessors and some premonitions of its descendants.

Foucault assumes the specificity of particular discourses: historical periods are radically different and the object of a discourse is different in each specific discursive formation. For example, the signifier "prostitute," in spite of the behavioral consistencies at the level of the body, means something different in different discourses. Discourses therefore need to be presented in their specificity.

Foucault's strategy of exteriority refers to taking the surface of events as the fundamental reality and not as mere "manifest content" referring to a more fundamental hidden reality: "The body is the inscribed surface of events[.]"[20] The task of genealogy is "to expose a body totally imprinted by history and the process of history's destruction of the body."[21]

The human body is the only irreducible in Foucault's theorizing: it is the site at which all forms of domination are ultimately inflicted and registered and it is the site of resistance. The human body is simultaneously a biophysical given and a cultural construct; what has come to be recognized as female is a cultural construct right down to the biosocial level of the body.[22] The body as imprinted by history is a text on which are inscribed the forces of socialization, discipline, and punishment. The body is contextualized and given meaning in discourse.

> Everything we know about the body . . . exists for us in some form of discourse; and discourse, whether verbal or visual, fictive or historical or speculative, is never unmediated, never free of interpretation, never innocent.[23]

The body is given different meanings in different discourses and the meanings of the body in discourse shape the materiality of the real body: "deployments of power are directly connected to the body—to bodies, functions, physiological processes, sensations, and pleasures."[24]

In applying the task of genealogy to the prostitute body I expose the prostitute body as a cultural construct: in chapter 3 I show how the modern prostitute body was produced as an identity and prostitution as a deviant sexuality; chapters 5 and 6 document how prostitutes collectively and in the realm of art deploy their bodies as sites of resistance to undermine both the hegemonic production of the prostitute body in modernity and the modernist feminist reproduction of the prostitute body.

In the modern period sex has become a focal point for the exercise of power through the discursive constitution of the body. Sex has no essential nature or meaning and never exists outside discourses of sexuality. Sexuality is, for Foucault, historically and socially constructed: sexuality "must not be thought of as a . . . natural given which power tries to hold in check, or as an obscure domain which knowledge tries to uncover."[25] Foucault distinguishes between sexual practices that have always been with the human body and "sexuality," which names these practices, constructs them, and assigns them values, meanings, and positions in the sexual hierarchy:

> Sexuality . . . is the name that can be given to a historical construct: not a furtive reality that is difficult to grasp, but a great surface network in which the stimulation of bodies, the intensification of plea-sures, the incitement of discourse, the formation of special knowl-

edges, the strengthening of controls and resistances, are linked to one another, in accordance with a few major strategies of knowledge and power.[26]

Although different sexual populations have existed in all historical periods, it wasn't until the Victorian period that they were systematically marked and identified: mapped like a geographical terrain. Scientific knowledge produced sexual/social identities, such as the prostitute, through regulation, surveillance, and the labeling of human activity.[27]

Foucault calls the dominant form taken by sexual discourse *scientia sexualis*, beginning in the eighteenth century and multiplying and proliferating in the nineteenth century. The science of sexuality was produced by a fusion of the traditional procedures of the Roman Catholic confessional and the more recent techniques of science that have become the backbone of psychoanalysis and sexology: questionnaires, interrogation, hypnosis, free association, case studies. Foucault contrasts *scientia sexualis* with ancient *ars erotica*, studies in the erotic arts that enhance pleasure:

> In Greece, truth and sex were linked, in the form of pedagogy, by the transmission of a precious knowledge from one body to another; sex served as a medium for initiations into learning. For us, it is in the confession that truth and sex are joined, through the obligatory and exhaustive expression of an individual secret. But this time it is truth that serves as a medium for sex and its manifestations.[28]

In Greece *ars erotica* extended to include learnings of the mind and soul as well as of the body. I begin my study with the *hetairae* of ancient Greece who acted as teachers of erotics, philosophy, and rhetoric. In the modern period *scientia sexualis* absents the prostitute as anything other than a clinical subject; the postmodern discourse of prostitutes recovers the prostitute's ancient role as erotic teacher.

Two additional Foucauldian concepts are important to my study: discourse and identity. Discourse is a way of constituting knowledge and identities: a discourse combines and is a combination of social practices, forms of subjectivity and power relations and the interrelations among these. All experience is constituted by discourse. Discourses create subjects as well as objects. Foucault's subjects are concrete historical and cultural subjects. Knowledge and power, for Foucault, are interfaced: "There is no power relation without the correlative constitution of a field of knowledge, nor any knowledge that

does not presuppose and constitute at the same time power relations."[29] Power is productive—power produces knowledges, institutions, bodies, pleasures, desires, and truths. Power operates through
the construction of particular knowledges which become accepted as
truth and reality. At the same time power produces resistances. A
discourse deploys a hegemonic form of subjectivity; its very existence
and organization, however, posit other subject positions and the possibility for reversal. Reverse discourse is the discourse of the subjugated subject of the hegemonic discourse; in it the meaning and power
of the dominant discourse are to some extent challenged. Prostitute
discourse is the reverse discourse of both the hegemonic (phallocentric) and counter-hegemonic (gynocentric) discourses; it responds to,
challenges, and transgresses these.

Identification is the discursive process through which subjects assume the identities set up in the dominant discourse; counter-identification is a process in which the identity constructed by the dominant
discourse is rejected while the subject remains complicit in that rejection, countering the meanings but unable to go beyond or transgress
them; the gynocentric feminist discourse is counter-hegemonic. Dis-
identification[30] is the process in which the identities set up in the
dominant ideology, rather than being merely countered, are perverted
and displaced through the inscription of unexpected new meanings. In
chapter 5, I argue that prostitute discourse encompasses both a counter-identification and a dis-identification; that some components of
prostitute discourse counter and challenge the dominant ideology in
line with gynocentric counter-identification, while others are transgressive, moving the discourse to a different terrain of meaning. When
it is transgressive, resistance not only opposes the hegemonic categories and inverts them but takes them apart and puts them together
in ways that shake up their original meanings. Thus some elements
of prostitute discourse are transgressive of both phallocentric hegemony and gynocentric counter-hegemony.

Radical Democracy

Ernesto Laclau and Chantal Mouffe have reconceptualized the theory of liberal democracy to account for new political actors such as
prostitutes. What sets radical democracy apart from liberal democracy
are two main distinctions. First, equality is premised on difference
rather than sameness. The field of influence of democratic discourse
is extended from the abstract equality of citizens in a political democ-

racy to specific social relations: the sexual, the racial, the generational, the regional, the cultural. The politics of difference has its foundations in the emergence of new political subjects and subject positions out of these relations. The politics of difference is therefore identity politics: political engagement and mobilization based on the construction of collective political and cultural identities. Second, although radical democracy retains the concept of rights, it presents them as simultaneously individual, collective, and plural: "[D]emocratic rights . . . while belonging to the individual, can only be exercised collectively and presuppose the existence of collective rights for others."[31]

The work of Laclau and Mouffe provides resources for theorizing how prostitutes as a collective subject enter the postmodern scene in the 1970s and also for understanding the diversity of the sites of prostitute struggles. In their book *Hegemony and Socialist Strategy: Towards a Radical Democratic Politics*, Laclau and Mouffe explore the incapacity of that form of socialist discourse which is premised upon the universal subject position of "the worker" to theorize mobilizations centering upon a multiplicity of other subject positions. They state:

> What we are witnessing is politicization far more radical than any we have known in the past, because it tends to dissolve the distinction between the public and the private, not in terms of the encroachment on the private by a unified public space, but in terms of a proliferation of radically new and different political spaces. We are confronted with the emergence of a *plurality of subjects*, whose forms of constitution and diversity it is only possible to think if we relinquish the category of "subject" as a unified and unifying essence.[32]

Laclau and Mouffe use the conception of multiple subject positions to refer both to the new political spaces and to indicate that each individual's subjectivity is sutured at the intersection of various discourses. Mouffe says:

> I affirm . . . the existence in each individual of multiple subject positions corresponding both to the different social relations in which the individual is inserted and to the discourses that constitute these relations.[33]

The political prostitute as a collective subject is sutured at the intersection of four discourses: *ars erotica, scientia sexualis*, new feminist theory, and the lesbian/gay movement.

Political subjects emerge in response to two processes which can elicit antagonism: the withdrawal of legal or *de facto* rights previously enjoyed, and the positing of equality in one set of discourses for subjects who are subordinated in another set. These two processes mobilized prostitutes as political subjects: in Canada and the United States the state stepped up its intervention into prostitutes' private and public existence, taking away the *de facto* right to solicit through the tactic of mass arrests beginning in the late 1970s and intensifying throughout the 1980s. In the seventies, there was the new feminist movement's demand for equality for women in all aspects of life and for women's control over their own bodies combined with the emergence of gay liberation groups that formed an international movement for the equal rights of sexual minorities. In each of these developments, prostitutes were interpellated/constituted as equal: prostitutes were women, and they were a sexual minority which engaged in sexual activity for a living. It is this contradictory positioning created by the state's intensified criminalization of the prostitute and the women and gay movements' demand for equality that has produced the prostitute as a political subject.

Difference, coming out of the Derridean project and informing Laclau and Mouffe's concept of radical democracy, is crucial for *Reading, Writing, and Rewriting the Prostitute Body.* I use "difference" in two ways which are conflicting but necessarily inseparable for a project such as mine, which is concerned not only with challenging masculinist and feminist textual systems of domination and opening these texts to their absences but also with tracing the identity construction of those othered by the presence of the texts. The two modalities of difference are positional meaning and standpoint epistemology.

Différance as positional meaning is the basis of the Derridean deconstructive project which at its simplest is the revelation that in any apparent presence there is also an undermining absence, a deferral to another place. Meaning, then, arises always as the interrelationship of presence and absence. That which is present is structured by its absence and that which is absent determines presence.

Difference in terms of standpoint epistemology is at one and the same time a modernist and a postmodernist concept. Standpoint epistemology is modernist when it is used to posit a subject position in the world and to link theorizing directly to this position; it is modernist when it claims that certain standpoints are epistemically superior to others and when it entertains the totalizing ambition to occupy the dominant alternative position to hegemonic views. But standpoint epistemology is postmodernist when it is employed to open subject space to include others, when it takes into account a multiplicity of standpoints linked to a number of different subject positions with no privileging of one subject position, and when it facilitates the theoretical space for new marginal political subjects. The modern and postmodern aspects often coexist. For example, feminist standpoint epistemology is a theory of knowledge based on the experiential positions of flesh-and-blood women, and in this sense it is modernist. Postmodernist feminist standpoint epistemology emphasizes the differences within the category "woman" and within the specific existences of women. The female subject, always constructed in gender, is engendered as other across representations of class, race, language, national boundaries, sexual orientation, and age.

I consciously reproduce the tension in postmodernism between the disengagement from systems of textual domination found in Derrida's deconstructive project and in Foucault's genealogical project, on the one hand, and the concept of a new social agency of the absented other of modernity found in the political project of Laclau and Mouffe, on the other.

Performing Theory

Performance art is at the forefront of postmodern theorizing. Artists are performing theory: acting out theory. Performance art destabilizes the established conception of what is considered theoretical engagement and broadens the concept of theory to include new areas of life and new political subjects. In the performance medium one can actually witness the theories of Derrida, Foucault, and Laclau and Mouffe, among other postmodern theorists, applied by individuals who would not be considered theorists in any conventional modern discourse. For instance, the performance medium is the home of such new sexual political subjects as the dyke, the drag queen, the transvestite, and the whore. Those previously coded as merely "obscene" and contained as carnivalesque transgression are using artspace to reconstitute themselves as living artifacts of resistance. The main site of resistance is their own bodies. Foucault's claim that the body holds a transgressive potential and can act as a site of resistance is their point of departure for doing theory. Performance artists such as dykes, fags, and whores use their marginalized and "obscene" bodies as sites of resistance to reclaim and remap their own identities, to deconstruct the masculinist, feminist, and heterosexual inscriptions on their bodies, and as a consequence to destabilize the hegemonic discourse itself. Chapter 6 documents the manner in which prostitute performance artists use artspace to reclaim and redefine the prostitute body and to educate the public. Prostitute artspace acts as a postmodern salon reminding the viewer/reader that in ancient Greece *hetairae* had salons in which they practiced and taught the arts.

Methodological Summary

Although I use the techniques of deconstruction, as explained above, throughout my text, especially in the sense of pinpointing absences in the modern and feminist discourses on prostitution, deconstructive tactics are most overtly used in chapter 2. Foucault's genealogical project informs the whole of my study while his concepts of discourse and identity construction more directly structure chapters 3 and 4. Chapter 5 is influenced both by Foucauldian theory of discourse and identity construction and by Laclau and Mouffe's work on new political subjects and new democratic struggles. And chapter 6 witnesses a merging of the theoretical frameworks of Derrida, Foucault, and Laclau and Mouffe more or less unknowingly deployed in the space of the performance artists.

2

READING THE *HETAIRAE*
IN PLATO'S TEXTS

Postmodern prostitute performance artists have traced their lineage back to the sacred prostitute; in so doing they have produced a strategic genealogy that undermines and displaces the modern construct of the prostitute. Following their example, this chapter reclaims Diotima and Aspasia, the first women of Western philosophy, as *hetairae*: the secularized remnant of the ancient sacred prostitute. This leads to a different reading of Plato, the first canon author of Western philosophy, from the position of the subterranean presence of the *hetairae* of ancient Greece in two of his dialogues: the *Symposium* and the *Menexenus*.

My aim is twofold: not only to retrieve the *hetairae* in Plato's texts but also to reintroduce Western thought to their ancient disturbing element. In the context of this project, I will provide a rereading of the two dialogues as well as a cursory rereading of Book V of the *Republic* in which Socrates establishes the equality of the female and the male. The purpose is to destabilize Western philosophy at its founding moments.

My reading of the *Symposium* disentombs the ancient priestess Diotima, whose shadowy presence has haunted the phallic representations of woman in Western thought and the masculine imaginary. My reading of the *Menexenus* recovers Aspasia—a burlesque treasure and a philosophic presence: a female interrupter of the male political narrative. It is in the space of postmodernity where the body boundaries of sex and gender, inside and outside, are losing definition that the first women of Western philosophy can be reclaimed: Diotima as spiritual teacher and whore; Aspasia as secularized political prostitute philosopher. I read Diotima as a manifestation of the goddess whose flesh is not radically distinguished from spirit, who teaches simultaneously the receiving and giving of pleasure and the receiving and giving of knowledge. I read Aspasia as a sophistic educator and teacher of rhetoric, a political actor who played an unofficial role in the politics of Greece.[1]

This reclamation of Diotima and Aspasia as sexual/sophistic philosophers could only be undertaken at this postmodern moment, the historical moment in which prostitutes are collectively constructing their own political identity. It is precisely prostitutes' assumption of their own subject position that has facilitated my sighting of the Greek prostitute, the *hetaira*, inscribed in Plato's texts. Diotima and Aspasia are the ancient precursors who telegraph the postmodern prostitute body as a sexual/sophistic body. Their discourse, the pagan discourse of the sophists, contains premonitions of the feminine sophistry of prostitute performance artists in postmodernity.[2]

Reading from the Position of the Philosophical Clitoris

My approach is that of the deconstructor. Focusing on textual gaps, traces, and extraneous details that have escaped the mastery of the canonizers, I read between the lines and discover ways in which the text subverts itself. A plurality of meanings can be appropriated and read from the same text; its meaning is ultimately undecidable. For the deconstructor, the emphasis has shifted from the search for the "true" authorial intention to the concerns of the reader approaching the text. Mine is an unfaithful reading: a reading that "strays from the author, the authorised, producing that which does not hold as a reproduction, as a representation."[3] My infidelity arises out of a particular female position from which Plato has never yet been read.

I read and write from the position of the clitoris; Plato, many have argued, wrote from the position of the phallus. Gayatri Spivak names the clitoris a "short-hand for woman's excess in all areas of reproduction and practice, an excess that must be brought under control to keep business going as usual."[4] The clitoris represents that dimension of female sexuality—pleasure—which is superfluous to reproduction: a site of radical excess that provides a point of departure for an affirmative feminism. The physicality of the concept of the "radical excess" of the clitoris, its immediate and powerful relation to physical pleasure, seems radically at odds with Plato's attempt to orient the philosophic eros away from the body toward the Idea. Yet the sexual body is the underside, the shadow of the spirit, that had to be mastered: a subtext always present, insistent in the text's denial of the body.

I read classical antiquity as carnivalized antiquity. Carnivalization is the intrusion of play, humor, and folk culture into high discourses such as philosophy.[5] I focus on mimicked speech, rhetoric, and the sexual body. These are embodied in Plato's works in the *hetaira*—the female body at the occluded center of patriarchal Greek philosophic and political discourse. Carnivalization gives rise to a transcoding and displacement between idealized and degraded images of the physical body, between philosophic and vulgar discourses, and between high and low status locations in the social domain.

To read from the position of the philosophic clitoris is to read from the space between two contending discursive approaches to the history of philosophy: the phallocentric tradition upholding the classical canon, and the gynocentric strategies opposed to it by many feminist political theorists and philosophers. The latter have tended to appropriate feminine difference in the texts solely as difference in relation to the male subject. They have neglected the inscription of difference within the category "woman" (the maternal female body/the libidinal female body) found in the texts. Consequently, they have privileged the reproductive in the couple maternal/sexual that has come to delimit the female. I reverse or pivot the hierarchy, making the libidinal the ground or condition of my reading. The subordinate term in the couple male/female and the subordinate terms in the couples maternal/sexual, reproductive/libidinal, and womb/clitoris are my points of departure for approaching the text not merely to invert the hierarchy but ultimately to displace these dichotomies.

In reading from the standpoint of the philosophical clitoris and reappropriating the sophistic-sexual female subject one must be cognizant of three things: First, that the excess of the clitoris does not permit any radical distinction between the physicality of female pleasure and the activity of philosophy itself. So-called physical pleasure is the conduit for so-called spiritual pleasure. This is why I substitute the concept "philosophical clitoris" for Spivak's clitoris. The excess of the clitoris is no simple other of the thinking mind. This will be crucial in rereading the logocentric element of Diotima's speech in the *Symposium*. Second, patriarchy will make every effort to split off the "mere physicality" of clitoral excess and to bring it under control as Plato does in Book V of the *Republic*. Finally, the uterine social organization, the punctuation of the world in terms of the reproduction of future generations, where the uterus is the chief agent and means of production, cannot simply be written off in favor of the clitoral. "The uterine social organization should, rather, be 'situated' through the understanding that it has so far been established by *excluding* a clitoral social organization."[6]

Feminist Readings of Plato

Feminist philosophers and theorists have tended to take up and counter-theorize what they read as the dominant image of woman in the canon texts of Western philosophy: that of woman as reproductive body. In so doing they have silenced and othered another female body written in those texts—the libidinal female body—and (re)inscribed a binary opposition within the category "woman," polarizing the reproductive and the libidinal, reducing difference to this opposition, and privileging one side—reproduction—as essentially female and therefore as superior. The readings of two innovative feminist philosopher/ critics, Wendy Brown and Page du Bois, will serve as examples. I choose the writings of Brown and du Bois as exemplifications of feminist textual strategies that approach the "original" text from the position of the maternal body because I consider their work to be the most innovative in this discourse of the womb.[7]

Wendy Brown, in her article "Supposing Truth Were a Woman . . . Plato's Subversion of Masculine Discourse"[8] and her book *Manhood and Politics: A Feminist Reading in Political Theory*,[9] reads Plato's personification of philosophy as female and Socrates' equation of philosophy with procreation as a "feminine" critique of the dominant masculine ethos of the Athenian polis. Brown cites Socrates' discussion of philosophy's lovers in the *Republic*:

> [M]en for whom philosophy is most suitable go . . . into exile and leave her abandoned and unconsummated . . . while . . . other unworthy men come to her . . . and disgrace her . . . of those who have intercourse with her, some are worthless and the many worthy of bad things. . . . When men unworthy of education come near her and keep company in an unworthy way, what sort of notions and opinions will we say they beget? Won't they be truly fit to be called sophisms[?][10]

For Socrates, philosophy is simultaneously sexual and maternal. Yet Brown appropriates only the maternal metaphor and marks the Platonic female body as the maternal body. She misses that for Plato philosophy was on occasion simultaneously cognitive and carnal. Du Bois, in *Sowing the Body*,[11] argues that Socrates' incorporation of the female activities of procreation, generation, birthing, labor, and nurturance into his own body—that of the male philosopher—opened the way to the subsequent production of woman herself as *lack*. One can only hang this on Socrates/Plato if his "maternal" metaphors are read absent of libidinal content and if Socratic philosophy is understood as strictly a male activity.

I read the maternal body in Socrates' speech as a trace[12] for the body of the *hetaira*; this trace has been lost in contemporary phallocentric and gynocentric readings. Socrates, identifying his philosophic powers with the midwife's skills, says in the *Theaetetus*:

> [W]ith the drugs and incantations they administer, midwives can either bring on the pains of travail or allay them at their will[.][13]

"Midwife" can be read with awareness that many *hetairae* worked as midwives, perpetuating the simultaneity of the procreative and sexual aspects of the sacred prostitute. William Sanger, in *The History of Prostitution*,[14] connects the skills of midwifery with sorcery and both with the *hetairae*: "[R]etired courtesans often combined the manufacture of . . . charms with the business of a midwife."[15]

Socrates incorporates the female body into his speech as the mimicked speech of his teachers and as metaphoric identification with the midwife. Socrates' only cited teachers were sophist *hetairae*: Aspasia, in the *Menexenus*, is given voice, mimicked, by Socrates, as is Diotima in the *Symposium*. To read this appropriation solely as maternal, as Brown and du Bois do, is to overwrite the other aspect of the female body present in Socrates' speech and thus in Plato's writing: the philosophic clitoris. Brown's and du Bois's readings occlude the weighty presence of an active speaking sexual female subject doing philosophy; she is reduced to a spiritualized, maternal referent for desexualized philosophy.

This is, as well, the error of David Halperin, who poses the questions "Why is Diotima a woman?" "Why did Plato select a woman to initiate Socrates into the mysteries of a male, homosexual desire?" "What qualifies . . . her to be a professor of (male) desire?"[16] Why does Plato introduce a woman "to enlighten a group of articulate paederasts about the mysteries of erotic desire?"[17] These are well-posed questions. And Halperin, writing from a homosexual/feminist subject position, provides an interesting twist on feminist readings of Diotima. Yet he writes the same female body. He argues that "woman" is a trope in the representational economy of Plato's text: she is the figure by means of which Plato images male philosophical values. Halperin claims that a double movement underlies Plato's erotic dialogue: "men project their own sexual experience onto women only to reabsorb it themselves in the guise of a 'feminine' character."[18] Thus, the woman is a "pseudo-Other" constructed as "a masked version of the same":[19] the male. The crux of Halperin's reading is that the interdependence of the sexual and reproductive capacities contained in Diotima's metaphors of erotic doctrine can refer only to male physiology; in women, he argues, the sexual and the reproductive are separate; therefore, the unified sexual and reproductive allegory in the *Symposium* must be read figuratively, not literally. Halperin's, like other hysterocentric feminist readings, forgets that the sexual, the reproductive, and the spiritual were simultaneously embodied in the sacred prostitute in the ancient world. He takes the contemporary dichotomization of the female body for granted and reads it back into Diotima's body.

The Sacred Prostitute and Her
Secularized Successor: The *Hetaira*

Embodied in the sacred prostitute, in practice and in representation, is the unity of womb and clitoris. The temples of sacred prostitution, the best known of which were the temples of Aphrodite in Corinth, were oriented simultaneously to clitoral, uterine, and spiritual purposes: sexuality, fertility, and spirituality were not radically distinguished. The temple prostitute was the embodiment of the sacred unity of the sexual and maternal bodies, which had by the classical age been split by Solon's legal code that identified women either with a private and secluded reproductive function, as wives and mothers, or with a sexual function, as prostitutes.[20]

The female sexual body itself was split into high and low bodies. There were three classes of prostitutes in fifth- and fourth-century Greece: the *hetairae* (high-status prostitutes, including courtesan philosophers and political actors), the *auletrides* (flute players, dancers, and acrobats), and the *dicteriades* (common prostitutes: brothel inmates and streetwalkers). Unlike the *hetairae* and the *auletrides*, the *dicteriades*, the great majority of prostitutes in classical Greece, occupied a low status in society. The plight of the *dicteriades* and the wives and daughters seems to have been the same: exclusion from the polis and restriction to functioning as the medium of exchange for men.

Marriage posited women as a medium of exchange between men of different households; the dicteriades, by means of brothel taxes, financed the ships and arms of government. "[O]rdinary prostitution in Greece developed out of the practice of sacred prostitution."[21] The *hetaira* can be seen as a surviving remnant of the archaic prostitute/priestess. The *hetairae* functioned outside the restrictions that the male state imposed on the *dicteriades*, wives, and daughters. Among them were female sophists who functioned at the margins of male public space, exchanging teaching, conversation, and sexual interaction for payment. Jess Wells, in her feminist pastiche history *A Herstory of Prostitution in Western Europe*, provides the following description of the *hetairae*. She writes:

> The Athenian women with the most exalted position and the most freedom were . . . the hetairae. They were intelligent, witty, articulate and educated, the only women in Athenian society allowed to manage their own financial affairs, stroll through the streets anywhere at any time. They were free to attend plays, ceremonies and speeches, to speak with whomever, whenever they pleased, to share the intellectual activities of Greece. They could take the sexual or romantic initiative with men. . . . [T]he hetairae were accomplished conversationalists, the intellectual equals of the men they entertained. They were herbalists and midwives, the mothers and lovers of kings, statesmen, artists and poets. They demanded enough money for their sexual services to keep themselves and the prostitutes in their homes ostentatiously.[22]

It has been argued that the sexual function of the *hetairae* was defined exclusively in terms of male desire; yet *hetairae* were able to experience and express desire with one another. Aristophanes, in his speech in Plato's *Symposium*, makes reference to lesbian love: "the woman who is the slice of the original female is attracted by women, rather than by men—in fact she is a Lesbian[.]"[23] A link can be made between the *hetairae/auletrides*[24] and lesbianism. Alciphron, a third-century Athenian rhetorician and epistolographer, puts a letter in the hand of Megara to Bacchis in which Megara chides Bacchis for being unable to leave her male lover for a minute to attend Glycera's sacrificial feast. Megara scolds: "You have become a virtuous woman and are devoted to your lover. I congratulate you on your respectability— we are just wanton harlots." Megara, stating "we were all there," lists the *hetairae* and *auletrides* who attended: Thessala, Moscharion, Thais, Anthrakion, Petale, Thryallis, Myrrhina, Chrysion, Euxippe,

Philumena. No men were present. The *auletrides/hetairae* festivals were often limited to women. The feast appears to be very similar to the male symposium:

> Oh, what a party we had! . . . Songs, jokes, drinking till cock-crow, perfumes, garlands, and a delicious dessert. . . . We have often had a drinking party before, but seldom such a pleasant one as this.[25]

In Sappho's poem "To Hera, the Great Goddess, who succoured Agamemnon, a prayer for safe journey" we read: "I may do lovely things in Mytiline, / among the girls whom I once led in dancing."[26] These two lines are followed by "And whom so often, on your holy feast days I lead in singing!"[27] In Sappho's "house of the muses" the "girls" were instructed in all the musical arts—playing, singing, dancing.[28] It does not take much of a conceptual leap to connect Sappho's training in music, dance, and singing with houses where *auletrides* were trained, and the *auletrides* feast days with the feast days mentioned by Sappho. Even if one concedes that the *hetairae* were primarily objects of male desire, the excess of the clitoris survives in their pursuit of philosophy, which itself was excess to the political realm, the city.

Tomb of the Sacred Prostitute: The *Symposium*

Both the male philosophical tradition and the feminist anti-tradition account for Diotima's presence in the *Symposium* as the teacher of Socrates on the grounds that she is not an ordinary woman but a desexualized, spiritualized, religious priestess. Socrates introduces Diotima as

> . . . a woman who was deeply versed in . . . many . . . fields of knowledge. It was she who brought about a ten years' postponement of the great plague of Athens on the occasion of a certain sacrifice[.][29]

Robin May Schott, in *Cognition and Eros*, writes

> Diotima is not merely a woman; she is a priestess. According to Greek religious practices, those women eligible to serve the gods were either virgin or past child-bearing years. . . . Plato admits into the dialogue the role of the priestess as a mouthpiece for the gods, along with the presupposition that she had become desexualized, in order to transform her into the mouthpiece for philosophy. . . . [I]t is the abdication of her sexuality that allows Diotima access to wisdom.[30]

Andrea Nye, in her radical reading "The Hidden Host: Irigaray and Diotima at Plato's *Symposium*," rejects Irigaray's view of Diotima as the feminine absence underpinning and destabilizing Platonism; she argues that Diotima is the host of the *Symposium*.[31] Diotima in Nye's reading represents the Minoan heritage of female spiritual leaders, and thus is a "spokesperson for ways of life and thought that Greek philosophy feeds on, ways of thought whose authority Plato neutralized and converted to his own purpose."[32]

It occurs neither to the phallocentric reader nor to feminist critics such as Schott and Nye that it is precisely Diotima's sacred sexuality that allows her access to Platonic divine paederasty or wisdom. Schott can equate female sexuality with childbearing, and portray the priestess as a mouthpiece for the male gods rather than the divine Aphrodite, only because she ignores the *hetairae* who practiced philosophy in ancient Greece; *hetairae*, hardly "desexualized" women, practiced as both midwives and priestesses. Nye, like Schott, absents the sexual in Diotima's speech, reducing it to abstract generativity:

> Diotima's theory of love does not focus on pleasure; genital pleasure in the sense of a private sensation is not mentioned in her philosophy. . . . Although Diotima grounds sexual desire in a principle of nature, that principle involves neither women's reproductive organs or men's penises. Instead, it has to do with the fact of mortality and the impulse of living things to perpetuate themselves.[33]

I read Diotima as a sophistic *hetaira*—a sophistic teacher of love, a trace to the sacred prostitute, servant of the divine Aphrodite. The very name "Diotima" is a trace to the temple prostitute or priestess; "Diotima" means "one who honours God,"[34] one who works in the "service of the god or goddess."[35] There is textual and contextual evidence to mark Diotima a *hetaira*. The symposium was a central part of Athenian social and sexual life. It was a gathering dedicated to eating, drinking, games, philosophic discourse, and sexual intercourse among men and between men and hetairae: carnal and psychic paederasty, the spilling of the seed in vain. There are two women present in the *Symposium*: the flute girl or *auletris*, hired to perform musical and sexual services for the host and his guests, whose absence is requested at the beginning of psychic paederasty, high philosophical discourse; and Diotima, the absence made present as mimicked speech.

Diotima was Socrates' "instructress in the art of love."[36] The context of Diotima's speech in the *Symposium* and its location in the text gives a dual meaning to the art of love: philosophy and sexuality. Diotima prefaces her discussion of the function love performs among men with a parable of Eros' birth. Eros was conceived on Aphrodite's birthday at the festival of Aphrodite. Aphrodite, the Greek goddess of love, beauty, and fertility, was originally the Great Mother Goddess. In *Prostitution and Society*, Fernando Henriques has contended that in the archaic world the goddesses of fertility were also goddesses of prostitution.[37] If so, then Aphrodite later became fragmented. In the Greek pantheon of gods, fertility was identified with the goddess Demeter, sexuality with Aphrodite:

> The sexual functions of women were concentrated in the various manifestations of Aphrodite . . . especially the persona called Aphrodite Pandermos (of All the People) and Aphrodite Hetaera, who was neither wife nor mother.[38]

"Festivals of Aphrodite . . . were celebrated in honour of the goddess by the *hetairae* in numerous places in Greece."[39] "For the *hetairae* . . . there was the evocative name 'foals of Aphrodite.' "[40]

Diotima's Aphrodite is unfragmented, a deity who unites the reproductive and the libidinal. In Diotima's construction Eros similarly combines the sexual and reproductive and like the sacred prostitute he mediates between the gods and man. Diotima's Eros is "a very powerful spirit," a *daimon*, "half-way between god and man."[41] The sacred prostitute was in a sense the human manifestation of Eros: the real body through which man could have intercourse with the gods. Eros, like the *hetairae*, was "adept in sorcery, enchantment, and seduction."[42] Walter Hamilton, in his translation of Plato's *Symposium*, marks Eros "a true sophist."[43]

Diotima's speech[44] contains the major contradiction out of which Plato's philosophy is produced: the relationship between the body and the soul. There are two moments in Diotima's speech: the sophistic moment which puts forth an ancient pluralist understanding of love and the Platonic moment in which love and wisdom are hierarchized. The first part of Diotima's speech can be read as the teaching of a sophist: here she advocates a plurality of forms of love, attributing to none more importance than another, and the unity of the body and soul.

Socrates says at the beginning of Diotima's speech that what he is about to convey is a composite of "some lessons"[45] that he was given by Diotima. Perhaps the most important of these lessons is her method of question and answer, which Socrates studiously follows. The aim of Diotima's method is to undermine the dualism of logocentrism, to uncover and hold the middle between two opposites, to attain the state halfway between such conceptual opposites as mor-

tal/immortal, wise/ignorant, good/bad, ugly/beautiful; this state she
attributes to Eros, establishing at the heart of her philosophy of love[46]
the discourse of the intermediary.

In another lesson Diotima teaches Socrates that there are many
equally valuable types of love: longing for happiness and for the good
in athletics, business, philosophy, and so on. In another teaching Diotima instructs Socrates: "To love is to bring forth the beautiful in both
the body and the soul";[47] and we know that the sacred prostitute was
the one through whose body one entered the sacred and attained the
beautiful. Then following the image of the unified body/soul, the body
and soul are separated:

> [T]hose whose procreancy is of the body turn to woman as the object
> of their love, and raise a family. . . . But those whose procreancy is of
> the spirit rather than the flesh . . . conceive and bear things of the
> spirit.[48]

Mortals desire to generate because they desire immortality of the flesh
and/or of the spirit. Diotima now privileges offspring of the soul.

Diotima's speech becomes logocentric, at least as quoted by Socrates, as quoted by Plato, in proclaiming a hierarchy of love upward from
the body to the soul, and phallogocentric in privileging correct psychic
paederasty—philosophical intercourse among male lovers. It is this
logocentric moment of Diotima's speech that is appropriated by philosophy as truth. Diotima sets out an ascending ladder of love that any
candidate studying the philosophy of love must master:

> [T]he candidate for this initiation cannot . . . begin too early to devote
> himself to the beauties of the body. First of all . . . he will fall in love
> with the beauty of one individual body, so that his passion may give
> life to noble discourse. Next he must consider how nearly related the
> beauty of any one body is to the beauty of any other . . . he must set
> himself to be the lover of every lovely body. . . . Next he must grasp
> that the beauties of the body are as nothing to the beauties of the
> soul, so that whenever he meets with spiritual loveliness, even in the
> husk of an unlovely body, he will find it beautiful to fall in love with
> and cherish it. . . . And from this he will be led to contemplate the
> beauty of laws and institutions . . . his attention should be diverted
> from institutions to the sciences, so that he may know the beauty of
> every kind of knowledge . . . until, confirmed and strengthened, he
> will come upon one single form of knowledge, the knowledge of the
> beaut[iful]. . . .[49]

Standard phallocentric readings of Diotima's famous construction
of truth are based on the conception of the body as contamination, or

as mere resource, which the soul must control and transcend in order to attain the purity of thought necessary for true knowledge. However, if one reads from the position of the philosophic clitoris, the body/ mind/soul are not radically distinguished, even in the logocentric moment of her speech. Through the holy prostitute one came to the gods; her body was a conduit to the Divine Body. The entire passage beginning with one body and culminating in knowledge of the beautiful (truth) is a metaphor for the sacred prostitute. Of course, Plato presents Socrates' mimicry of Diotima as making no reference in speech to the philosophic clitoris—that is, to the sophistic-sexual body—in her outline of the hierarchy of forms of love. Diotima does not speak of her own body; yet she is powerfully present as the active speaking body, simultaneously presenting and undermining the foundational moment of Western philosophy. She is presenting the same hierarchical progression from the body to the soul to Beauty found in Socrates' discussion of the relation of the body to the soul in the *Phaedo* and the Form of Beauty in the *Phaedrus*. This leads the reader to question whether Plato is usurping Diotima's authority to found hierarchical philosophy and having her mimic Platonism as he is mimicking her. But her mimicry is pseudo-mimicry, an overlay of Platonism rather than an acceptance. The overlay is incomplete; there is a glimpse of the sophistic moment. The Platonic body is a "contaminating" body,[50] a body that must be got rid of, overcome, in order to attain pure knowledge; the Platonic body is a "walking sepulchre" which "pollutes" beauty.[51] Diotima's body is a sacred body through which one comes to beauty. The logocentric moment as Diotima presents it holds the middle between two extremes: the Platonic position which understands the body as contamination and pollution and the position of the ancient sacred prostitute for whom the sexual body is sacred and not distinguished from spirit.

Entombed within the *Symposium*, then, is the body of the sacred prostitute. The sacred prostitute materializes here at the heart of Platonist idealism as the body which acts as a conduit to the spirit—from one lovely body to many lovely bodies, to every lovely body, to all bodies lovely and unlovely, to the beauty of the spirit: truth.

In Diotima's speech homosexuality is proclaimed a higher form of love than men's love of woman.

[H]e and his friend will help each other rear the issue of their friendship—and so the bond between them will be more binding, and their communion even more complete, than that which comes of bringing children up, because they have created something lovelier and less mortal than human seed. And I ask you, who would not prefer such fatherhood to merely human propagation. . . . [52]

However, only if Diotima is perceived as desexualized can she be taken as simply colluding in a "male identified" fashion with the Platonic privileging of homosexuality. If Diotima is recognized as the sacred priestess, "servant of Aphrodite," then the absence of any reference to her own body, her form of love—sophistic/sexual intercourse —is a pregnant silence. Diotima's speech about homosexual love is a referent for the other form of love in which the seed is spilled in vain, taken from dissemination, as it were: sophistic-sexual love.

As Socrates concludes Diotima's speech, the sliding between the earlier sophistic non-logocentric and the later Platonic positions is recycled with the entrance of drunken Alcibiades, who displays in speech and action his desire for Socrates. Alcibiades enters with a flute girl; the *auletris* reenters the symposium, marking the end of correct paederasty. The logocentric part of Diotima's speech which concludes with the privileging of the soul, the part which entombs the sacred prostitute, is the textual space between the sexual body of Aphrodite, the unfragmented goddess of sex and reproduction, and the sexual body represented both by the *auletris* and by Alcibiades—the desiring homosexual body.

If we briefly take a look at another *hetaira* connected with Socrates in Xenophon's *Memorabilia*, Theodote, who was a disciple and companion of Socrates rather than his teacher, we find a trace to Diotima. When Theodote invites Socrates to come and see her often, he replies that it is difficult for him to find the time, saying: "I have the dear girls, who won't leave me day or night; they are studying potions with me and spells."[53] Leo Strauss, unable to believe that Socrates could have female friends, reads this as a closeted reference to Socrates' male companions:

By his female friends he probably means his companions who seek him for the sake of philosophizing; he calls them female for the same reason for which he sometimes swears by Hera.[54]

I, on the other hand, read this as a straightforward and "out" reference: Socrates is taught by *hetairae* and learns from them; he exchanges the teaching of potions and spells with *hetairae*. This would reinforce, in turn, my reading of Diotima—she who was able to prevent a plague on Athens by a sacrifice—as a trace to the sacred prostitute.

For Strauss, "female friend" is a cover for "young man." From my point of view, Plato's privileging of homosexuality in the *Symposium* is also a referent for Socrates' connection with *hetairae*. Diotima's teaching is immortalized through her friendship with Socrates. The presence of Diotima, the prostitute priestess in Platonic drag, queers Strauss's way of looking at "friend." "Female friend" could mean female friend; it could be a referent for "beautiful young man"; and "beautiful young man" could be an inverted referent for *hetairae*, by Hera.

Burlesque Treasure: The Prostitute Rhetorician in the *Menexenus*

Unlike Diotima, whose possible identity as a sacred prostitute has been obscured, Aspasia has been marked in history both as a well-known female sophist and as a well-known *hetaira*. Aspasia ran a "gynaeceum" for prostitutes where she taught rhetoric, philosophy, religion, poetry—not only to prostitutes but also to statesmen, including Pericles and Alcibiades, and philosophers, including Socrates. Her famous salon has been immortalized in a fresco over the library entrance to the modern University of Athens. Among other notable Athenians represented in the fresco are Socrates, Pericles, Plato, Alcibiades, Sophocles, and Antisthenes.[55] Socrates openly cites Aspasia as his teacher of rhetoric and politics in the *Menexenus*. Alciphron writes these words in the hand of Thais, another well-known Greek *hetaira*:

> Do you suppose that a professor is any different from a courtesan?
> . . . As for teaching young men we do quite as well as they. Compare a courtesan like Aspasia with a sophist like Socrates, and consider which produced the better pupils: the woman trained Pericles, the man Critias.[56]

The *Menexenus* is considered by both phallocentric and feminist critics alike as a not very serious work: a "baffling dialogue,"[57] a "puzzling piece of work."[58] Feminist and traditional male philosophers as diverse as Nicole Loraux and Karl Popper read the *Menexenus* as a parody of both the Athenian tradition of funeral oration and of Pericles.

Plato has Socrates, in the *Menexenus*, identify Aspasia as his teacher and as the real author of Pericles' "Funeral Oration." Socrates says:

> I have an excellent mistress in the art of rhetoric—she who has made so many good speakers, and one who was the best among all the Hellenes, Pericles.[59]

The dialogue is most often taken as an aristocratic denigration of the democrat Pericles and his hagiographer, Thucydides. It is largely because Pericles' words are attributed by Plato to a woman, Aspasia, that the dialogue is considered an ironical work of Plato. Nicole Loraux, in *The Invention of Athens*, provides an illuminating twist on those readings that present the *Menexenus* as ironical. She reads the *Menexenus* as "comic parody and Platonic pastiche";[60] she documents it as a pastiche of the whole genre of funeral oration: "the systematic application of the topoi of the genre."[61] Loraux situates the *Menexenus* by pointing out that it contains many traces to the comic poet Aristophanes' play *Wasps*.[62] More important than her documentation of Plato's heavy borrowing from Aristophanes[63] is Loraux's disclosure that the funeral oration is nothing but a simulacrum, a copy for which the original is lost, merely "an imitation of itself."[64] This being the case, then, the one inconsistency in Plato's replication is the position from which the oration is narrated: Socrates is mimicking Aspasia, a female philosopher/rhetorician. Loraux contends that Plato, by his attribution of the funeral oration to Aspasia, is "using the resources of comedy."[65] Loraux continues: "There can be no doubt that the introduction of a feminine element into an eminently male procedure is yet another way of discrediting the funeral oration."[66] Most readings of the *Menexenus*, including Loraux's, have approached the dialogue by privileging the funeral oration: questioning what Plato does to the funeral oration and hypothesizing about what is meant by his treatment of it.

But as I am reading the *Menexenus* from the position of the philosophic clitoris, I have no investment in deciphering Plato's intent. Rather, I am interested in that which is different, that which interrupts and breaks the simulacrum of the funeral oration genre. What is different in Plato's representation of the genre, needless to say, is Aspasia's absent presence: her speech is given voice, mimicked by Socrates. She is the force of the dialogue, the teacher; yet, like Diotima, who is the force of the *Symposium*, Aspasia is absent. She is present through the speech of Socrates. Socrates is teaching Menexenus the art of rhetoric, which he learned from the prostitute-sophist Aspasia; later, we find out that Menexenus has met Aspasia often, perhaps frequented her salon and taken pleasure in her tutelage as Socrates had done.

My reading of the *Menexenus* is at three levels: (1) the presence—the dialogue between Socrates and Menexenus; (2) the absence made present—Aspasia's speech absent but made present by Socrates' voice; and (3) the absent trace—the speech under erasure in Aspasia's speech—that is, Pericles' "Funeral Oration" as reported by Thucydides.

R. E. Allen, a representative of "canon" commentators, marks Aspasia's speech as "sandwiched between two puzzling pieces of dialogue which seems to deny its seriousness."[67] The pieces of dialogue Allen is referring to are those which set the context of the speech. Menexenus has returned from the agora where the Council of the Assembly was going to choose a funeral orator. When questioned by Menexenus as to what he would say if he had to make a speech praising those who died in battle, Socrates claims:

> Of my own wit, most likely nothing, but yesterday I heard Aspasia composing a funeral oration about these very dead. For she had been told, as you were saying, that the Athenians were going to choose a speaker, and she repeated to me the sort of speech which he should deliver—partly improvising and partly from previous thought, putting together fragments of the funeral oration which Pericles spoke, but which, as I believe, she composed.[68]

Socrates' statement does confirm Loraux's representation of the funeral oration as "scraps of epitaphios stuck together; . . . an imitation of itself";[69] but it also interrupts the imitation by inserting Aspasia as an author of an authorless genre. I am not concerned about why Plato does this, nor am I interested in his intended meaning. My concern and investment is that this accreditation positions Aspasia, the *hetaira*, as a teacher within the male narrative of praise for military valor, and that it connects her to civic discourse. Wendy Brown has argued that the "sophistic mode of speech and the heroic ethic of political deed comprise a specifically masculine ethos in Greek popular ontology."[70] Not only her appropriation but particularly Aspasia's mastery of this discourse interrupts, collapses, and undercuts the male presence at the foundation of Western philosophic thought.

Socrates recounts that Aspasia was a firm teacher, "ready to strike"[71] him whenever he forgot his lines. Menexenus, at the end of the dialogue, says: "Truly, Socrates, I marvel that Aspasia, who is only a woman, should be able to compose such a speech—she must be a rare one."[72] Menexenus expresses his surprise, surprise that a woman is able to interrupt his male genre by adopting and applying to the genre precisely the technique it is based on: mimesis. We quickly realize that Menexenus is feigning surprise at Aspasia's authorship; perhaps parodying for Socrates' enjoyment the "official" male response. After all, Socrates was far from representing the conventional Athenian male: he learned from women, acknowledged his philosophic debt to the female, and employed female metaphors in his own teachings. To Socrates' invitation "if you are incredulous, you may come with me and hear her," Menexenus concedes: "I have often met Aspasia, Socrates, and know what she is like."[73] Socrates warns Menexenus not to tell on him, and he promises to "repeat . . . many other excellent political speeches of hers."[74] This indicates that Socrates was a regular student of Aspasia's and that Aspasia spoke and taught many political speeches. Arlene Saxonhouse reads Socrates' swearing of Menexenus to silence as a sign that "Aspasia's education of Socrates must not be talked of, not be part of the public discourse."[75] In view of Socrates' open acknowledgment of Diotima as his teacher in the *Symposium*, Socrates' warning could just as easily be read as a warning to Menexenus not to reveal the origin of Pericles' speech and similar speeches, not to subvert the masculine ethos by publicly disclosing Aspasia's mastery of it in sophistic discourse.

The speech itself can be read as the absent portion of Pericles' speech as reported by Thucydides. Aspasia, according to Socrates, pieced her speech together from the speech she composed for Pericles. The two speeches are not read in this manner because the dialogue has been read either as making fun of the rhetoricians, in particular Pericles, or as an ironic depiction of Athenian political rhetoricity in general. If one takes seriously Socrates' claim that Aspasia was his teacher and the teacher of Pericles and that Aspasia composed Pericles' "Funeral Oration," then the speeches can be read as filling in each other's gaps. The structures of the speeches are, of course, parallel: in adherence to convention, they praise the Athenian dead by linking their heroic deeds with past heroic deeds and provide consolation and civic advice to the living. The contents of the speeches differ: one dialogue can be read as filling the gaps and spaces of the other. Aspasia's speech fills in three omissions in Pericles' speech: she narrates the deeds of the male military body and she writes two female bodies: the reproductive body and the civic body.

Pericles, after establishing that the law requires a speech to praise the dead, skips over their warlike deeds and focuses on the adventurous Athenian spirit, the democratic constitution, and the cultured Athenian way of life. Pericles specifically states:

> I have no wish to make a long speech on subjects familiar to you all: so I shall say nothing about the warlike deed by which we acquired our power or the battles in which we or our fathers gallantly resisted our enemies, Greek or foreign.[76]

Aspasia provides an itinerary of the war deeds alluded to but written out of Pericles' speech: in fact, the bulk of her speech (239d to 246a) is a documentation of Athenian glories of battle from the Persian Wars, through the wars with the other Greek states, to the Peloponnesian War. Aspasia speaks the classical male body in ancient Greece: the body as a supreme instrument of war. But she decontextualizes this representation by prefacing it with two more powerful female bodies: the mother body, the earth, and the civic body, Athena.

Aspasia begins her praise of the ancestors with their nobility of birth; noble because they were born from the Athenian land. She personifies the land as their mother:

> [S]he bore them and nourished them and received them, and in her bosom they now repose. . . . [A] great proof that she brought forth the common ancestors of us and the departed is that she provided the means of support for her offspring. For as a woman proves her motherhood by giving milk to her young ones . . . so did our land prove that she was the mother of men, for in those days she alone and first of all brought forth wheat and barley for human food, which is the best and noblest sustenance for man, whom she regarded as her true offspring. . . . [T]he woman in her conception and generation is but the imitation of the earth, and not the earth of the woman.[77]

Aspasia's equation of the land with the human mother is a significant interruption of the traditional Athenian autochthony myth which has the male born from the land without a human mother. "The male seed was simply planted in the soil, and thus the woman could be left out of the origin of cities."[78] By equating the land with the human mother, Aspasia locates woman as the foundation of the political community. Aspasia interrupts her mother-land metaphor with a trace to Athena, the political and warring female goddess. The "strife and contention of the gods respecting her"[79] is a fleeting reference to the myth of the dispute between Athena and Poseidon over the naming of the land. This myth was used by the Greeks to explain the exclusion of women from public life. Athena won the contest between herself and Poseidon to name the city Athens. Athena won because the women who then voted had a majority of one. To ward off Poseidon's revenge, women were not allowed to vote anymore;[80] they were excluded from the public/political realm. For Pericles, Athens is a lover, the erotic libidinal female body. He invites the citizenry to "fix your eyes every day on the greatness of Athens as she really is, and . . . fall in love with her."[81] The fragmented female body—the libidinal body, the reproductive body, and the political body—is unified in the two speeches read as one. The political female body named the city, the libidinal body symbolized the city—"fall in love with her"—and the maternal body regenerated and supported the city.

Both speeches appeal to the relatives of the dead to "be like them"[82] and "make this your . . . aim—to exceed . . . not only us but all your ancestors in virtue."[83] Aspasia claims to speak the voices of the men themselves. They speak silently through her voice while she explicitly speaks with theirs. She says:

> I ought now to repeat what your fathers desired to have said to you who are their survivors, when they went out to battle. . . . I will tell you what I heard them say, and what, if they had only speech, they would fain be saying. . . . And you must imagine that you hear them saying what I now repeat to you.[84]

The implication, outside the text, is that Aspasia consorted with the leaders of the military at her salon. The association of the political actors and philosophers of the day with Aspasia is, of course, no secret.

Pericles closes his speech with words of advice to the women widowed. He says:

> Your greatest glory is not to be inferior to what God has made you, and the greatest glory of a woman is to be least talked about by men, whether they are praising you or criticizing you.[85]

There are two conflicting readings of Pericles' statement: one is that since it is not found in Aspasia's speech, Pericles alone is responsible for it;[86] the other is that Aspasia was indeed responsible for the recommendations but that they were, obviously, for married women, not for women such as herself.[87] If one reads Aspasia as the writer of both speeches, as is claimed by Socrates, then these are her words and the second interpretation is accurate. Pericles' admonition is to the official reproductive body: wives of citizens. Both speeches end with the declaration that a speech has been made "according to the law."[88] The law demanded the exclusion of the Athenian reproductive body from the polis. The *hetairae* were outside the law, remnants of the pre-legal archaic institution of sacred prostitution, before male law encoded the splitting of the female body into reproductive and sexual bodies and the female sexual body into high and low bodies. Aspasia's subversion of this division is to base the existence of the city on female generation.

Book V of the *Republic*: Reread

Socrates' career as a student of two *hetairae*, Diotima and Aspasia, suggests a new reading of the teaching of gender equality in Book V of the *Republic*. Book V has been read as a masterpiece of ironic discourse by Leo Strauss and his followers,[89] or it has been accepted at face value only if woman is desexualized and degendered. Read from the position of the philosophic clitoris, Socrates' much cited statement "[T]here is no practice of a city's governors which belongs to woman because she's a woman, or to man because he's man; but the natures are scattered alike among both animals; and woman participates according to nature in all practices, and man in all[.]"[90] can be removed from the realms of irony and logocentrism. Socrates and Plato[91] had a model, an experience of women behaving as prescribed in Book V of the *Republic*, and that lived body was the *hetaira*.

Plato's community of wives provides a secularized trace to the community of priestesses serving the temples of Aphrodite. The "sacred marriages,"[92] as Plato names the unions of male and female guardians, can be read as a trace to the sacred marriages of sacred prostitutes to the god/goddess and to man.

Plato contends that women's function and role in reproduction is irrelevant in terms of her participation in the public sphere. Once Plato has admitted women to the guardian class, however, they become subject to uterine sexual organization: the best women and men have intercourse with each other as often as possible to beget the best children; only when women and men are beyond the age of procreation are they free to have intercourse with whoever they want. When Plato, in the *Republic*, brings philosophy and the city (politics) together, he brings the excess of the clitoris, which allows him to write an intellectual sameness between male and female and to include men and women in the guardian class, under a uterine reproduction-oriented organization.

Conclusion

What is the purpose of an unfaithful reading such as I have carried out here, aside, of course, from the pleasure of carnival? It is to over-write the closure of authority: authority of meaning, authority of the author, authority of the canon interpretations constructing the history of philosophy. It is to reinscribe and reincarnate in Western thought the maternal, the sexual, and the spiritual female body: the divine Aphrodite unfragmented. It is to present a moment when prostitutes were spiritually and politically powerful, a moment which recurs in postmodernity. The recurrence, however, is a repetition with a differ-ence, since it is punctuated by the construction of "the prostitute" as an identity in modernity. Diotima and Aspasia are pagan prostitute philosophers (un)mastering the foundations of Western philosophical discourse; however, they speak within the dominant patriarchal dis-course; their postmodern descendants speak from a prostitute subject position, a politicized counter-identity that emerged through the pro-cess of othering which culminated with the codification of "the pros-titute" in modernity. The next chapter will record the production of the modern prostitute body in all of its ambiguity.

3

THE MAKING OF THE MODERN
PROSTITUTE BODY

THE PROSTITUTE body was mapped—marked out and defined—as a distinct body, and "the prostitute" was actively produced as a marginalized social-sexual identity, particularly during the latter half of the nineteenth century and the beginning of the twentieth century. This chapter will document the production of the prostitute as an entity and identity.

The territorialization of the prostitute body took place within the most general of the dichotomies at the heart of Western thought: identity (sameness)/otherness (difference), the foundation of the masculine/feminine opposition which places the phallic "I" at the positive center of the philosophical system and constitutes "woman" as the negative other. The identity/otherness dichotomy is duplicated inside the category "woman" to produce an internal dichotomy: virtuous woman/whore.

Prostitutes were analyzed and categorized in relation to the bourgeois female ideals: the good wife and the virginal daughter. The prostitute might be the same, she might be different; often she was located on a continuum somewhere between sameness and difference, but she was always the disprivileged other in relation to the determinant site: wife, mother, daughter. The sameness/difference opposition provided the framework for derivative couples inside the category "woman": good girl/bad girl, madonna/whore, normal/abnormal, licit/illicit, wife/prostitute, as well as the high and low images that have fragmented and categorized the female body. The first in the couple is the determining site, the site of presence; the second is the determined site, the site of the other. The site of presence posits and produces the other: that which is absent, those who are excluded. Yet that which is articulated as the other generates presence. Both elements of the couple inhabit each other: the privileged site bears traces of the disprivileged just as the disprivileged or secondary concept carries traces of the first. Each is conditional and dependent upon the other. The virtuous woman was constructed in relation to the production of the unvirtuous prostitute woman, just as the opposite was the case.

The modern discourse on prostitution was part of a broader discursive production of female sexuality which separated the female body into the reproductive body and the un(re)productive body: normal female sexuality was defined in terms of woman's reproductive functions; deviant female sexuality was defined in terms of prostitution. Reproductive sexuality, which denied woman active sexual desire and pleasure, was the respectable norm; prostitution was its inversion. And it was the mapping of prostitution which made possible the delimitation of this respectable norm.

The processes of societal exclusion and inclusion of women working as prostitutes in the medieval and renaissance periods, moving through the shifting policies of repression, tolerance, and institutionalization, set prostitutes apart from other women. There are two conflicting views in current literature on the position of prostitutes in the medieval and early modern period: that prostitutes were integrated into society and constituted something like a professional guild, and the contrary view that prostitutes were marginal others along with criminals and beggars.[1] It wasn't until the nineteenth century, however, and its obsession with science, statistics, and the medicalization of the body that the prostitute was territorialized as an "object of inquiry" and defined as a distinct female body. The methods brought to bear on defining the prostitute were those used on all human objects of science in the nineteenth century: social anthropology, statistical inquiry, empirical survey, phrenology, and physiognomy. In addition, the discourse on prostitution was strongly influenced by the language of the public health debate on sanitation and hygiene.

Informed by Michel Foucault's theories of knowledge production and identity construction and Bakhtin's concept of carnivalization, and making use of the primary premise of deconstruction—that each text contains its own contradictions—I retrace, in this chapter, the construction of the modern prostitute body, showing how the bourgeoisie formulated its own identity by producing the prostitute as other. Michel Foucault, in his *History of Sexuality*, documents how "sexuality" emerged in the nineteenth century as a discursive domain[2] differentiating sexual behaviors as normal and deviant. Focusing on one of the "peripheral sexualities," Foucault shows how homosexuality was defined as a specific sexual syndrome and "the homosexual" categorized as an identifiable type of person in the nineteenth century. Like "homosexual," the term "prostitute" is "an historical construction[; it] works to define and categorize a particular group of women."[3] According to Foucault the nineteenth-century public discourse on sexuality had three centers: medical, legal, and psychiatric, all informed by an underpinning Christian moralism.

The nineteenth-century public debate on prostitution was extensive. This entire body of knowledge, save for the voice of the Ladies National Association, was produced by the hegemonic male voice: the doctor, the lawyer, the judge, the policeman, the administrator. From a plethora of nineteenth-century texts on prostitution, I have selected five that were instrumental in marking and making the modern prostitute body. These are Alexandre Parent-Duchatelet's *De la prostitution dans la Ville de Paris* (1836), William Acton's *Prostitution Considered in Its Moral, Social, and Sanitary Aspects in London and Other Large Cities and Garrison Towns* (1857), the *British Royal Commission on the Contagious Diseases Acts* (1871), Havelock Ellis's *Sex in Relation to Society* (1910), volume six of his *Studies in the Psychology of Sex*, and two essays of Freud, "Infantile Sexuality" (1905) and "A Special Type of Object Choice Made by Men" (1910). These texts were chosen for the following reasons: Parent-Duchatelet initiated the modern discourse on prostitution; his text was the prototype for most nineteenth-century knowledge production of "the prostitute." Acton's text is a good collage of medical and moral writings and studies supporting the regulation of British prostitution. The Contagious Diseases Acts created the prostitute as a distinct legal category. And the sciences of sexuality (sexology and psychoanalysis) marked a turning point in the conceptualization of "the prostitute": I have chosen Ellis and Freud because their specific depictions of the prostitute have contributed a great deal to contemporary images of "the prostitute."

I will argue that these writings are characterized by a bizarrely high degree of ambiguity in the presentation of the prostitute body, an ambiguity which results from processes of transcoding and displacement among the high and low images of the female body associated with the sameness/difference dichotomy. One finds a sliding between the prostitute body and the mother body; between the prostitute as different, as contaminated other, and as the same, the same as "our" mothers, daughters, and wives—"honest women"; a sliding that Freud suggests originates in the unconscious mind of the son. Contemporary commentators have tended to appropriate from these texts primarily one narrow aspect of this ambiguity: Judith Walkowitz finds a working-class body; Alan Corbin and Sander Gilman discover a "grotesque" diseased body. These cultural interpreters overlook the striking ambivalence, highlighted by Bakhtin's notion of carnivalization, in the representations of the marginalized body: the "low" is "the primary site of contradiction, the site of conflicting desires and mutually incompatible representations."[4]

Bourgeois Identity and the Not-I

The nineteenth-century bourgeoisie constituted itself as a social class and constructed its self-identity by extruding the carnivalesque. "[T]he bourgeoisie consolidated itself as a respectable and conventional body by withdrawing itself from the popular, [and] . . . construct[ing] the popular as grotesque otherness."[5] Carnival, the ritualized practice of inverting social hierarchies, the transcoding and displacement between high and low bodies, which in pre-bourgeois society had served the function of social cohesion, was rejected as irrational; the carnivalesque came to be fragmented from the social body and marginalized as the grotesque other. Desire for the carnivalesque, embodied in the prostitute, was sublimated by the male and female bourgeois subject into the codification, surveillance, regulation, and control of this body. The repressed desire for the carnivalesque surfaced in the fantasy life of the bourgeoisie. "The carnivalesque was marked out as an intensely powerful semiotic realm precisely because bourgeois culture constructed its self-identity by rejecting it."[6] The bourgeois subject defined itself through the exclusion of what it marked out as low—as dirty, repulsive, noisy, contaminating. The act of exclusion was constitutive of its own identity. The low was externalized under the sign of negation and disgust. The prostitute identity was produced as the negative identity of the bourgeois subject: the "not-I."

Charles Baudelaire: The Prostitute as the Allegory of Modernity

Charles Baudelaire, who was the theorist *par excellence* of modernity according to Walter Benjamin, writes the prostitute body as the allegory of modernity. Baudelaire, according to Benjamin, captures the new form that prostitution took in "the great cities" of modernity: "the prostitute appears as a commodity and as a mass-produced article," a presence on the urban cityscape "framing" "the labyrinthine character of the city."[7] The modern prostitute comes into being only when woman becomes a commodity, subject *en masse* to the wage relation, inserted into commodity production, massified on the urban landscape.

For Benjamin, the modern prostitute is a new anthropological figure. She manifests the end of aura: her religious and cultic presence, her feminine body as a manifestation of celestial beauty, have been made to vanish. The link to the sacred prostitute that was present in the *hetairae* and even to some extent in the medieval prostitute is severed in the modern prostitute body. Eros is subjugated by Thanatos; the prostitute body is written as the death body, the putrified body, the profane body. At the same time, however, a process that Benjamin calls "spleen" operates in an insistent unconscious mapping of the lost past onto the prostitute body. Spleen is a "mental process in which the preserved image of the originally lost object is projected onto other objects so as to repeat . . . the experience of the lost other via a fantasy image."[8] The modern prostitute body acts as a hieroglyph providing a trace to the sublime body, promising a connection with the sacred which can, however, be maintained only for a fleeting moment.

Baudelaire's poetry captures this moment: "There is . . . no exalted pleasure which cannot be related to prostitution."[9] His poetry is cognizant of the modern prostitute body as simultaneously a site of death and destruction and a site of pleasure. In Baudelaire's poem "Allegory" the prostitute operates as a hieroglyph, a trace to the sublime body, through resistance to the physical and moral disfigurement of the sublime body which it simultaneously manifests:

> It is a lovely woman, richly dressed,
> who shares her wineglass with her own long hair;
> the brothel's rotgut and the brawls of love
> have left the marble of her skin unmarred.
> She flouts Debauchery and flirts with Death,
> monsters who maim what they do not mow down,
> and yet their talons have not dared molest
> the simple majesty of this proud flesh.[10]

Unlike Baudelaire's poetic inscriptions, the hegemonic discourse of the Victorian period, the medical-legal-moral discourse, absented the prostitute body as a site of pleasure and as an allusion to the sublime body. Instead it produced two master images of the prostitute, both profane: one a ruined, destroyed, victimized body; the other a destroying body, a disease that spreads and rots the body politic. These images are inversions of one another. Within this composite picture we shall find a number of ambiguous features. The rest of this chapter will survey the five selected texts, following the major deconstructionist theorem: all discourses are ambiguous; texts contain their own contradictions and opposing possibilities.

Parent-Duchatelet: The Production of the Prostitute as a New Anthropological Figure

Dr. Alexandre Jean Baptiste Parent-Duchatelet's anthropological study of Parisian prostitutes, *De la prostitution dans la Ville de Paris*, was the prototype for most nineteenth-century knowledge production of prostitution in Europe. Parent-Duchatelet constructed the characteristics of the prostitute body that many others subsequently reproduced either through incorporation or rejection. Jill Harsin states of Parent-Duchatelet that "his analysis of prostitutes was almost immediately granted the status of truth."[11] Harsin claims

> The nineteenth-century view of the prostitute was essentially that of Parent-Duchatelet; few duplicated or added to his detailed research, preferring simply to copy his assertions (whether credited to him or not) as fact.[12]

Judith Walkowitz indicates that Parent-Duchatelet's study served as a model for the British investigation of prostitution from the 1840s to the 1880s.[13] Alain Corbin describes Parent-Duchatelet's influence as predominant both in the social construction of the prostitute and in the identity formation of the prostitute herself:

> Parent-Duchatelet's portrait of the prostitute was repeated so often in the literature on prostitution and inspired so many novelists that, in addition to distorting the vision of later researchers . . . it determined to some extent the behavior of the prostitutes themselves.[14]

Parent-Duchatelet's expressed purpose was to provide a scientific study of prostitution. He gathered data by using what were to become standard social science procedures: personal observation, professional testimony, interviews with prostitutes and administrative officials, archival research—prison, police, and hospital archives.

Parent-Duchatelet designed a taxonomy of the prostitute—physiognomy and physiology, producing her as a new anthropological figure. He presents the reader with a statistical description of the physical

types of prostitutes, the quality of their voices, the color of their hair
and eyes, their physical abnormalities, their sexual profiles in relation
to childbearing and disease, their family background and education.
Parent-Duchatelet shrouds the study in his "love of precision," which
he claims is a "veritable religion" for him.[15] Perhaps one of the best
representations of his love for numerical results and precision was his
hair/eye/eyebrow chart of all prostitutes (12,600) registered in Paris
from 1816 to 1831. He tried, although failed, to establish a correlation
between prostitutes' coloring and their place of origin in cities, towns,
or the countryside. He assumed that the different environments would
produce different physical coloring.[16]

Parent-Duchatelet's demographic study of registered prostitutes in
Paris enabled him to mark prostitution a transitory occupation and the
prostitute a working-class woman. He composed statistical tables on
the ages of the 3,517 prostitutes known to the authorities on December
31, 1831, and their length of time working in prostitution. Of those
3,517 prostitutes, 2,100 had been working for four years and under;
704 for nine to twenty years.[17] Half of the 3,230 prostitutes for whom
birth certificates were available were between the ages of twenty and
twenty-seven; only 128 were under eighteen, and of these only twenty-
seven were between the ages of twelve to fifteen inclusive.[18] One was
twelve, thirty-four were fifty and over, and two were over sixty.[19] The
majority of prostitutes' fathers were artisans—what Judith Walkowitz
calls the "working poor."[20] Of the fathers of prostitutes born in Paris,
828 for whom statistics were available, most either worked as day-la-
borers (113), were persons without trade or calling (64), or were shoe-
makers (50). Only four were surgeons, physicians, or lawyers, three
were teachers, and nine were musicians.[21] Occupational data on the
fathers of prostitutes born in the departments substantiates these findings. Prior to prostitution by far most women were employed as domestic and factory workers.[22]

Parent-Duchatelet's social science discourse is ambiguous: it contains many tensions and opposing possibilities. It has been claimed
that Parent-Duchatelet marked out the prostitute body as nonpatho-
logical in the somatic "degenerate" sense—as pathological only in the
social-environmental sense. To a large extent he did. Sexologists who
followed Parent-Duchatelet, such as Havelock Ellis, reinvested the
prostitute body with "degenerate" somatic and sexual characteristics.
On the other hand, Alain Corbin and Sander Gilman correctly observed that "Parent-Duchatelet's use of the public health model re-

duces the prostitute to a source of pollution in much the same class as the sewers of Paris."[23] The public hygiene discourse informs Parent-Duchatelet's work directly. His previous scientific work had been on sewers, and he frames his prostitution study within this context. A reference to sewer and public hygiene discourses at the beginning of his study provides a direct trace to his previous work:

> If I have been able . . . to penetrate into the sewers, to handle putrid matter, to spend a part of my time in the refuse dumps, in a sense to live in the midst of the most abject and disgusting products of large groups of people, why would I blush to enter a sewer of another type (a sewer more impure, I swear, than all the others) in the hope of doing some good.[24]

This rhetoric and image of the sewer frames the "scientific" study in which he depicts the prostitute body as *not* inherently different from the body of other women.

Parent-Duchatelet produced the prostitute and the virtuous married woman as somatically the same. What he focused on in this regard was the women's genitals and reproductive capacity. He found that prostitutes did not differ from other women in fertility. The reason it had been assumed that they did was that prostitutes often lost their babies due to miscarriages and abortions.[25] Parent-Duchatelet contradicted the "general opinion . . . that the genital parts in prostitutes . . . must alter, and assume a particular disposition, as the . . . consequence of their avocation."[26] He writes:

> The genitals of prostitutes present no special distortion particular to themselves. In this regard there is no difference between them and the most virtuous married women.[27]

He reports that he and the doctors at hospital and prison infirmaries had encountered "women who have been working in prostitution for twelve or fifteen years . . . and whose genitals, the vagina in particular, show no trace of distortion."[28] As an example of this Parent-Duchatelet cites a fifty-one-year-old woman who had prostituted herself since the age of fifteen "whose genitals might have been confused with those of a virgin just coming to puberty."[29] He also reports similarity of clitoral size in prostitute and non-prostitute women: "some have been of the opinion that the clitoris must more frequently undergo enlargement in the prostitute body than in other women, and must be the reason for their lustfulness and shameful vices."[30] Parent-

Duchatelet documents that the sizes of prostitute and non-prostitute clitorises are the same:

> At the time when I carried out this research, there were in Paris only three prostitutes who were known to have a significant enlargement of the clitoris.[31]

While Parent-Duchatelet disproves that the prostitute differs somatically from other women, he reports that the prostitute genitals are situationally prone to diseases and abscesses, thus making her body a socially diseased body and a body that can and must be kept clean of disease through social regulation. He territorialized the prostitute body as pathological in the social-environmental sense: "Prostitutes frequently display, in the thickness of their labia majora, tumors which . . . grow at each menstrual period";[32] "[n]othing is more frequent than . . . abscesses in the thickness of the labia majora."[33] Parent-Duchatelet's view that there is no physical difference between the prostitute and non-prostitute body is overridden by his assertion that the sexual organ is prone to labial tumors and abscesses. The resultant image is precisely what he is arguing against: prostitutes' genitals are different.

Parent-Duchatelet developed a stereotype of the prostitute as a somatic type: prostitutes were plump, filthy, and spoke in a harsh voice. He identified the *"embonpoint"* of the prostitute as an environmentally acquired sign of the prostitute body. Parent-Duchatelet attributed their "remarkable portliness" to "the great number of hot baths" they took, "their inactive life," and their "rich diet."[34] And the prostitute body is equated with filth:

> A distinctive character of prostitutes is a remarkable negligence regarding cleanliness, of the body and of clothing; exceptions to this regularity can be considered as rare; it is said that these women are happy in mire and filth; they only care about their dress and external cover, the rest is neglected entirely.[35]

Parent-Duchatelet identifies a distinctive prostitute voice: There are "prostitutes who are remarkable for their beauty and their freshness, for their exquisite attire, for their elegance of manners . . . who have . . . everything it takes to please and to seduce, but what a disenchantment when they speak" and one hears that "raucous," "harsh," "husky" prostitute voice.[36] He goes on to say that one doesn't hear this among all prostitutes, but among the lowest class who are drunk and stand in front of cabarets. Thus Parent-Duchatelet slides from the visual image of the elegant high-class prostitute—that is what she is like until she opens her mouth—to the acoustic image of the raucous voice of the low-class whore. It is as if, for Parent-Duchatelet, the multiplicity of prostitutes are condensed into a single visual-acoustic image in which "she" is elegant until "she" opens "her" mouth, even though it is a different "she."

Parent-Duchatelet composed a personality sketch of the prostitute which sets her even further apart from the virtuous woman, giving her an identifiable spirit and behavioral repertoire. Prostitutes, for Parent-Duchatelet, are women with "lightness and mobility of spirit," women who cannot be "held still, pinned down," women who have difficulty in following "a chain of reasoning; the smallest thing distracts and carries them away"; women who lack concern for the morrow and are indifferent to what is to become of them in the future.[37] He found anger to be frequent among these women, and his description of the distinctive qualities of this anger reminds one of the hysterical women of Freud's case studies. Parent-Duchatelet describes their anger as "an energy of body and spirit that is truly remarkable,"[38] setting them apart even from women of their class:

> [I]t is a flow of words which by its nature and by the originality of its expression gives rise to an eloquence which is peculiar only to this class and which differs from that of market women and the other classes of the common people.[39]

Parent-Duchatelet also suggests that the prostitute personality displays a greater tendency toward lesbianism; interestingly, this claim, which resurfaces time and time again in the subsequent literature, is based on the observation of a prison population and had more to do with the camaraderie of the women during meals than with any sexual practice.

Different though she may be, Parent-Duchatelet links the prostitute with the social realm of the ordinary citizen and the home. By emphasizing that prostitution was only a stage of life for most prostitutes, Parent-Duchatelet marked the fluidity of identity between the prostitute and other working-class women, an aspect of Victorian prostitution that is central in Walkowitz's study. Parent-Duchatelet writes:

> A good number of former prostitutes reenter the world, they surround us, they come into our homes, our households; we are constantly exposed to the chance of confiding our dearest interest to them, and consequently, we have major reasons to watch this population, and

not to abandon it as many people advise; to seek to diminish its vices and its faults and, in this manner, to alleviate, as much as possible, the evil they could do to those with whom they would later find themselves in contact.[40]

He bases the need for regulation at least partially on the permeability of the boundary between the prostitute and non-prostitute body and the reintegration of the prostitute into respectable society.

Another of the purposes of social regulation is to prevent the carnivalization of public space:

If when stationing themselves in the public way prostitutes remained isolated from one another, the difficulty caused by their presence could be tolerated to a certain point, but it is very difficult to get them to do that. . . . they have a remarkable tendency to form groups and to take over certain public areas: . . . very serious inconveniences result from this custom.[41]

It is to this visible concentration producing a spectacle in the cityscape, the intrusion of prostitution into the life of the city, that Parent-Duchatelet objects, rather than the exchange of money for sex per se. He thus recommended removing prostitutes from the streets to protect public morality.

The duplicity of the assumption underlying Parent-Duchatelet's research—that prostitutes are different from ordinary women and that prostitutes are the same as ordinary women—sets up a binary opposition of sameness and difference between prostitute and non-prostitute women which becomes the template for many subsequent studies. In the contemporary secondary literature some authors focus on sameness and others on difference. Walkowitz reads Parent-Duchatelet as marking the prostitute body as a working-class body, the same as the body of other working-class women. Corbin and Gilman, on the other hand, read Parent-Duchatelet as inscribing the prostitute body as a diseased, polluted body. As I see it, he does both.

Parent-Duchatelet's analysis of the causes of prostitution repeats this ambiguity. He strongly contended that lack of work and insufficient salaries were the primary causes: "Of all the causes of prostitution, particularly in Paris and probably in all large cities, none is more active than lack of work and the misery which is the inevitable result of insufficient wages."[42] Yet he also mentions laziness as "first among the causes determining prostitution."[43] He defines laziness as "the desire to procure happiness without work."[44] He ranks vanity and the desire for fine clothing as equal to laziness. He states: "vanity and the desire for the glitter of luxurious clothes is with idleness one of the most active causes of prostitution, particularly in Paris."[45] These multiple causes are then ranked and inscribed over and over again by William Acton, by the British Royal Commission, and by Havelock Ellis.

William Acton: A Moral Typology of the Bad Prostitute

William Acton, a "man of science" who specialized in the diseases of the urinary and generative organs, greatly influenced the prostitution debates centered around the Contagious Diseases Acts in Britain. His "stereotyped vision" of the prostitute "would dominate the debates over the C. D. Acts in the 1870's and 1880's."[46] Acton's study, *Prostitution Considered in Its Moral, Social, and Sanitary Aspects*, was central in crystallizing the discourse and conceptual framework embraced by both the regulationists and repealers in these debates. The second edition of *Prostitution* (1870) was published in support of the Acts. His work on prostitution is "a combination of scientific observation and analysis, social criticism and open propaganda."[47] Acton's study is derivative from Parent Duchatelet: "the categories of social analysis as well as the actual social details owed much to . . . Parent."[48] Like his mentor, Acton ambiguously characterizes the prostitute body as the same and different from normal women. Like Parent-Duchatelet, Acton in his early chapters makes a strong link between the prostitute and the "normal" woman: "Prostitution is a transitory state through which an untold number of British women are ever on their passage."[49] Acton directly writes the prostitute body as the mother body: "multitudes are mothers before they become prostitutes, and other multitudes become mothers during their evil career."[50] Yet later, with the same set of words with which he equates the prostitute and mother bodies, he sets the two apart: "prostitutes . . . become . . . with tarnished bodies and polluted minds, wives and mothers."[51]

In his preface to the second edition Acton contextualizes his study with a question:

Who are those fair creatures, . . . "those somebodies whom nobody knows," who elbow our wives and daughters in the parks and promenades and rendezvous of fashion? Who are those painted, dressy women, flaunting along the streets and boldly accosting the passer-by? Who are those miserable creatures, ill-fed, ill-clothed, uncared for, from whose misery the eye recoils, cowering under dark arches and among bye-lanes? The picture has many sides; with all of them society is more or less acquainted.[52]

Acton paints a multivalent picture of prostitutes as part of the urban cityscape. Walkowitz accuses him of reproducing simple social and sexual stereotypes, from the elegant Haymarket streetwalker to the pathetic miserable creature.[53] No doubt he does; the prostitute is created—by Victorian social science and Victorian legal process—as a discursive stereotype, not a flesh-and-blood entity.

In his narration of the haunts of prostitutes Acton slides between prostitutes and working-class women. He notes their amiable interaction at the dance hall: "it is not unusual for the mechanic's wife to have sisters who are frail."[54] "Frail" is an epithet for the prostitute body. The reference is undoubtedly to moral frailty as he later cites Parent-Duchatelet's assertion that "their health resists all attacks better than that of the ordinary run of women who have children and lead ordinary lives. . . . They have iron bodies."[55] Acton observes that "the wives" accord to their frail sisters "the greatest measure of kindness, and a sort of commiseration, which not unfrequently culminates in their having a 'drop o'gin' together."[56] Walkowitz cites this in her documentation of the fluidity of prostitutes' social identity as a part of working-class society.

Following Parent-Duchatelet, Acton critiques the strongly held belief that "the career of the woman who once quits the pinnacle of virtue involves the very swift decline and ultimate loss of health, modesty, and temporal prosperity."[57] Acton's text is credited with altering the British medical discourse on prostitution which reproduced the picture of the prostitute in progressive decline until an early death. He refutes the claims

1. That once a harlot, always a harlot.
2. That there is no possible advance, moral or physical, in the condition of the actual prostitute.
3. That the harlot's progress is short and rapid.[58]

Yet prostitute women did not suffer rapid decline; they were in better health than many other women, and they moved in and out of "respectable society." Acton sees the need to revise the conventional symbol of prostitution—"the dirty intoxicated slattern in tawdry finery and an inch thick in paint."[59] He does not deny the existence of some prostitutes who fit this description but discounts this as the symbol of prostitution for the modern world. The modern prostitute is

[A] woman who, whether sound or diseased, is generally pretty and elegant . . . whose predecessors cast away the custom of drunkenness when the gentlemen of England did the same—and on whose backs [sic] . . . the ministers of fashion exhibit the results of their most egregious experiments.[60]

Acton describes prostitution as a "microcosm" of society. Prostitution "exhibits, like its archetype . . . all the virtues and good qualities, as well as all the vices, weaknesses, and follies."[61] Acton constructed a typology of the good prostitute and the bad prostitute which was derivative of a larger typology of the good woman and the bad woman. "Arrogant and offensive conduct," "mercurial temperament," and "intense assumption of superiority"[62] mark a prostitute "bad." What is the nature of her "badness"? Basically, she is a spectacle loose in the public sphere: "she who inflicts the greatest scandal and damage upon society"; "the flaunting, extravagant queen."[63] In the tavern bar: "she is a sort of whitewashed sepulchre, fair to the eye, but full of inner rottenness—a mercenary human tigress."[64] Acton marks her as having an inner rottenness, a step toward constructing the prostitute as congenitally degenerate in the manner of Havelock Ellis. Whether a high-class prostitute in Haymarket or Soho or a low-class prostitute in Lambeth or Whitechapel, she will remain "a drunken, brawling reprobate,"[65] a grotesque woman who carnivalizes public space. The good woman is in the shadow in public space. The good prostitute, like the good woman, is a "softer-minded woman" who "feels . . . disgust at brazen impudence, and all the pomps and vanities" in whatever rank she may be. She is "sober, genteelly dressed, well-ordered, often elegant in person," "well-meaning," "no abettor of extravagance," and she is "honest."[66]

Acton defines prostitute women as adhering to the Victorian norm of asexuality: "uncontrollable sexual desires of her own play but a little part in inducing profligacy of the female."[67] He marks this as an interspecies biological phenomenon: "Strong passions, save in exceptional cases, at certain times, and in advanced stages of dissipation, as little disturb the economy of the human as they do that of the brute female."[68] In Acton's discourse only the male is sexual. His view was encoded in *The Royal Commission* and represented the stereotypical construction of female sexuality in the Victorian period.[69]

Acton stresses that the endings found in novels of the "guilty, solitary wreck, perishing, covered with sores, in some back garret, in a filthy court,"[70] Zola's Nana for example, are "the altogether rare exception."[71] Citing Parent-Duchatelet, Acton writes "notwithstanding all their excesses and exposure to so many causes of disease, their health resists all attacks better than that of the ordinary run of women who have children and lead orderly lives."[72] Acton goes substantially further than Parent-Duchatelet in marking the prostitute body a non-diseased body. We shall see that he later contradicted this marking. Using statistics supplied by the registrar-general, Acton showed that for the years 1864–1866 for the city of London only seventy-three women, prostitutes or not, and fifty-four men died of syphilis.[73] Using statistics from the 1868 report of St. Bartholomews's Hospital, Acton declares "not a single female died from Syphilis."[74] Acton claimed to have made inquiries among the medical attendants of hospitals, penitentiaries, private practitioners, and parish authorities, all of whom corroborated his impression that "no other class of females is so free from general disease."[75]

To the question "How then is the disparition of this class of women to be accounted for?" Acton replies that he has every reason to believe that "by far the large number of women who have resorted to prostitution for a livelihood, return sooner or later to a more or less regular course of life."[76] There is a fluidity, a sliding between wives and prostitutes: "the better inclined class of prostitutes become the wedded wives of men of every grade of society, from the peerage to the stable."[77] He adds that because they are frequently barren (a statement not supported by Parent-Duchatelet) they "often live in ease unknown to many women who have never strayed."[78] Like Parent-Duchatelet, Acton argues that because prostitutes are integrated back into society their bodies should be regulated to be kept free of disease.

Acton unpredictably moves from the healthy prostitute body to the prostitute as "spreader" of "a loathsome poison."[79] Disease has been rewritten to take on a moral as well as a physical meaning, and the two meanings are collapsed into one: "The moral injury inflicted on society by prostitution is incalculable; the physical injury is at least as great."[80] He calculated that one out of every four prostitutes of the 6,515 registered spread disease.

In chapter 4, "The Causes of Prostitution," Acton firmly marks the prostitute the diseased body. The sliding between the healthy and diseased body, the oscillation between the mother and the prostitute, is gone. The ambiguity is lost. It is this marking that has been appropriated as a dominant cultural image:

What is a prostitute? . . . She is a woman with half the woman gone, and that half containing all that elevates her nature, leaving her a mere instrument of impurity; degraded and fallen she extracts from the sin of others the means of living, corrupt . . . a social pest, carrying contamination and foulness to every quarter . . . who
"like a disease,
Creeps, no precaution used, among the crowd, . . .
and poisons half the young."[81]

Using economic metaphors Acton equates prostitutes with "articles of luxury."[82] He argues that the "supply" of prostitutes creates the demand for them: "the want of prostitutes increases with the use of them."[83] Prostitution is the cause of its own existence. Among the primary causes of prostitution Acton lists "the natural instinct," "the sinful nature," "idleness," "vanity," and "love of pleasure."[84] These are innate—"a part of human nature, independently of the accidents of birth, fortune and education."[85] Later he states that although vanity, idleness, love of dress, love of drink, and love of excitement are all factors, "by far the larger proportion are driven to evil courses by cruel biting poverty."[86] Acton reproduces Parent-Duchatelet's ambiguity between poverty as the noble cause of prostitution and the less noble causes, vanity and love of dress, etc. Underpinning his narrative is the argument that the primary causes of prostitution are "absolutely ineradicable";[87] therefore, "it is useless to shut our eyes to a fact; it is better to recognize it—to regulate the system, and ameliorate . . . the condition of its victims."[88]

The British Royal Commission on the Contagious Diseases Acts: The Encoding of the Prostitute Body

The prostitute body was encoded by the *British Royal Commission on the Contagious Diseases Acts* both as the polluter of the male body politic and as a necessary evil. The British Contagious Diseases Acts of 1864, 1866, and 1869 were introduced piecemeal over the five-year period: their scope and techniques of control were extended with each repeal and reenactment. The Acts identified sex as a public issue, differentiated male from female sexuality, marked certain types of sexual activity as dangerous, and produced the prostitute body as the site of disease and pollution. The Contagious Diseases Acts created prostitution as a distinct legal category; until the Acts prostitution had been regulated by the 1824 Vagrancy Act: prostitutes were considered one among other groups of social outcasts who disturbed the public order. Although the Acts were repealed in 1886, their influence extended well beyond the twenty-two-year period of their operation and the geographic boundaries of Britain. The Acts had inscribed a disciplinary regime on the body of the prostitute.

The Acts were "framed . . . for the purpose of guarding the men of the army and navy from contagion."[89] The 1864 Act, in the words of the Royal Commission of 1871, provided for "the separation from the community of women in a condition to spread contagious disease."[90] The 1864 Act covered eleven military stations, garrisons, and seaport towns in England and Ireland. It provided for the surgical examination of prostitutes deemed by the police inspector to be affected with a contagious disease; if the women were found diseased the Act provided for their detention in certified lock hospitals (a hospital containing venereal wards) for up to three months. The 1866 repeal of the 1864 Act and reenactment extended the Act in three ways: (1) spatially, to cover more military districts; (2) compulsory periodic examinations were introduced for every "common prostitute"; and (3) the detention time of every prostitute found to be infected was extended for up to six months. The determinants of prostitute status used by the police were "residence in a brothel; solicitation in the streets; frequenting places where prostitutes resort; being informed against by soldiers and sailors; and lastly the admission of the woman herself."[91] According to Superintendent Wakeford, "it is not the practice of the police to act upon one but upon several concurrent proofs."[92] The 1866 reenactment, according to the *Royal Commission Report*, "not only recognized prostitutes as agents in the propagation of the disease; but sought so far to control their conduct as to render the practice of prostitution, if not absolutely innocuous at least much less dangerous."[93] The *Report* thus marks unregulated prostitution dangerous. The changes from the 1864 to the 1866 Acts were brought about on the recommendation of the Medical Committee, formed under the jurisdiction of the War Office and the Admiralty, to determine the best way of diminishing the effects of venereal disease on the men in the army and navy and to examine the effectiveness of the 1864 Act. The Medical Committee recommended that "a periodical inspection or examination of all known prostitutes be made compulsory, under a well-organized system of medical police."[94] The term "medical police" signals a more overt and extensive system of police control over the prostitute body. The 1869 Act extended the Contagious Diseases Acts to five additional districts and the jurisdiction of the Acts to a ten-mile radius of the districts in which they operated; enforced fortnightly examinations upon all known prostitutes; increased the maximum period of detention in the hospital to nine months; required the detention of women who were unfit for examination (menstruating); and provided for the moral and religious instruction of the women confined. The latter included lessons in personal hygiene and domestic labor; the belief was that " 'fallen women' needed to re-learn their femininity through moralizing domestic labour."[95]

Of all the knowledge production around the Contagious Diseases Acts,[96] the *Royal Commission Minutes and Report* (1871) gives the best overview of the working of the technology of power (doctors, police, clergy, military officials, and social workers such as hospital and reformatory matrons) in the construction of the prostitute body. The Royal Commission examined eighty witnesses. Representatives of the two opposing societies formed for the respective purposes of extending and repealing the Acts were present; in fact, Josephine Butler and Mrs. Lewis (repeal leaders) both gave testimony. Competing discourses are found in the Royal Commission; the minutes read as a conversation of multiple voices. Yet what is produced is a single composite picture of the prostitute. The prostitute body is as much characterized by the questions of the commissioners as by the answers of those questioned. I will examine the testimony of eight witnesses; their spoken testimony is recorded in the *Minutes of Evidence Taken before the Royal Commission.* I have chosen to examine the testimony of one military hospital administrator—Dr. Graham Balfour; two surgeons—Dr. Sedley Wolferstan and Dr. John Coleman Barr; one hospital social worker—Lucy Bull; one minister—Reverend Alexander Lowry; one police officer responsible for the administration of the Acts—William Wakeford; and two female repealers—Josephine Butler and Mrs. Lewis.

Dr. Graham Balfour, as well as being the Deputy Inspector General of Hospitals for the army, was also head of the statistical branch of the medical department of the army. His testimony consisted, to a large extent, of statistical evidence of venereal sores and gonorrhea among enlisted men at the twenty-eight principal stations in the United Kingdom during the years 1864 to 1870. He used statistics to argue a progressive decrease in syphilis in those stations protected under the Acts from 120 (per 1,000) in 1865 (the first year of the Acts) to 54.5 in 1870.[97] In the unprotected group the diminution is not present.

Balfour's statistics were used in the *Royal Commission Report* recommending extension of the Acts. Balfour's objection to the examination of sailors and soldiers set the prostitute body apart as "dangerous": he claimed that "the women whom you examine are following a dangerous trade"[98] and warned that inspection "would be extremely unpopular to the well-conducted and steady men."[99] The *Report* substantiates Balfour's position by making a distinction between sex for gain, which is the sex of prostitutes, and the "irregular indulgence of a natural impulse," which is the sex of men who have intercourse with prostitutes.[100] The *Report* clearly sets male and female sexuality apart: "there is no comparison to be made between prostitutes and the men who consort with them."[101]

Dr. Sedley Wolferstan, the house surgeon to the Royal Albert Hospital, a lock hospital in Davenport, contradicts Balfour's statistical evidence: "I have no doubt that the women subjected to the Acts contract the disease more frequently now than they did when the Acts first came into operation."[102] He further states: "I think the Acts have had the effect of increasing disease among prostitutes."[103] Wolferstan argues that the examination itself spreads venereal disease due to lack of sanitation. When questioned about the health of the men, Wolferstan replied that the only means he had of judging the men were the tables published by the army and navy authorities;[104] the implication is that the officials enforcing the Acts, such as Balfour, provided untrustworthy records. Wolferstan argued against compulsory examination and for the voluntary system. He contends, against police reports and the official *Royal Commission Report*, that compulsory examination drove many women "to such a mode of following their calling that the police were unable to get hold of them."[105] Wolferstan documents that the police made mistakes, sending women who were not prostitutes to be examined by him. He cites the case of Harriet Hicks, who had an ulcer and was committed to the hospital as being diseased: she was discharged on the evidence of the man she had lived with for six years that he had not been diseased. This vignette tells the reader two things: that the line between prostitute and unmarried non-prostitute poor women who lived with men without being married to them was vague and that the medical profession was unable accurately to diagnose contagious disease. The latter being the case, confinement in the hospital was contingent on the label of prostitute. The *Report* notes that "The medical evidence which was submitted on the part of opponents of the Acts, dwelt chiefly on the admitted difficulty of distinguishing the contagious from the non-contagious discharges to which females, and especially prostitutes are liable."[106] If one were labeled a prostitute, then any ulceration and vaginal discharge would be considered unsafe and the woman would be sent to the lock ward. One reads in Dr. Thomas R. Pickthorn's testimony[107] that special rules of diagnosis applied to women labeled as prostitutes: "no man will dare to say that any ulceration in a prostitute is safe. . . . I want to separate prostitutes from other women."[108]

Supporters of the Acts, such as Dr. John Coleman Barr, surgeon to the lock hospital at Aldershot, a garrison camp where the majority of prostitutes were camp followers, stressed the physical and moral improvement of the prostitute brought about by the implementation of the Acts. The Acts were depicted by Barr as saving the prostitutes. He portrays the prostitute woman as degenerate prior to the Acts: "they were very dirty, in fact, filthy; they were covered with vermin, . . . some almost like idiots in their manner, and all of them very badly diseased."[109] They were bad-tempered and ill-behaved: "many were apt to show their temper very rapidly, breaking windows and using a good deal of bad language."[110] Barr is questioned by the Commission as to whether he had observed "improvement in the demeanor and persons of the women" who had come up for examination under the Acts. Barr replies that they "come decently dressed"; "their appearance . . . entirely changed, so far as external appearance goes . . . I do not believe any one would tell they were prostitutes, from their outside demeanor only."[111] Barr goes so far as to attribute the reformation of many women to the periodic examinations—specifically, "the conversation held with them and advice they receive."[112] Barr marks the prostitute a sick woman: "the mere fact of being a prostitute is being a sick woman"[113]—morally and physically sick. Barr argues that the Acts have "made the prostitute a more respectable person";[114] surveillance and regulation of the body make it respectable. The *Report* extends Barr's testimony:

> The Contagious Diseases Acts . . . have purged the towns and encampments to which they have been applied of miserable creatures who were mere masses of rottenness and vehicles of disease. . . . their better nature was probably for the first time touched by human sympathy.[115]

This is, as well, the argument of Lucy Bull, matron of the Royal Albert Hospital. According to Bull, when women first came to the hospital

they suffered "want of carefulness or cleanliness, and . . . insubordina-
tion."[116] The leading questions of commission members presuppose
the character profile of prostitutes, which Bull confirms: "Is it your
experience that these women are very thoughtless, and have no
thought but from day to day?" Bull responds: "Yes, I believe that is so
in point of fact."[117] She states that it is necessary for girls leaving
prostitution to stay in homes for two years "to redeem their character."[118] After attributing the cause of "this sin" prostitution to "extreme poverty," Bull is questioned as to whether she admits other
causes, such as "vanity and love of dress."[119] Bull confirms love of
dress. Marianne Valverde, in her article "The Love of Finery," decodes
the meaning of "love of dress." It was a code word for idleness and
moral impurity (decay, decrepitude). Valverde points out that many
who put forth love of dress as a cause of prostitution failed to distinguish between necessary dress—that is, adequate clothing—and surplus finery. Valverde states that this "should be kept in mind while
interpreting alleged confessions by prostitutes that they entered the
trade in order to buy clothes."[120] She also indicates that prostitutes
were copying the dress of their wealthier sisters; the evil associated
with dress and adornment, then, was class determined.[121] Imitation of
the "respectable" woman by the "low" woman was transcoded as a
marker of impurity.

In the testimony of Reverend Lowry, chaplain to the hospital at
Portsmouth, one finds an emphasis on "the love of dress"; Lowry
states "tawdry dress will make them think they are fine ladies."[122]
When questioned "Do you find the love of dress is often an impedi-
ment to a change of life?"[123] Lowry replies that he is able to determine
whether a "girl" is going to give up the life of prostitution by whether
she has given up decorative dress and adornment. Austere clothing
equals moral good for poor women; the articles of adornment that
Lowry is referring to are hair adornments and earrings. The questioning of Lowry and his responses show the transition in and out of prostitution by working-class women. He claims that the morals of the
lower orders are different and that many people are proud to have
daughters who are prostitutes and look on "the life as a respectable
thing."[124] He substantiates Acton's claim that a great many of the
young women get married: "the sailors do not object to marrying prostitutes . . . they actually . . . rather prefer it."[125]

The testimony of William Wakeford, supervisor of the police responsible for the implementation of the Contagious Diseases Acts in Devonport and Plymouth, provides insight into the administration of the Acts. Wakeford documented the decrease in the number of brothels in the district from 356 when the first Act came into operation in 1865 to 124 in December 1870; the number of "bad women" decreased from 1,770 to 579 during this same period. Wakeford denies the existence of clandestine prostitution.[126] His testimony reveals the extensiveness of the police surveillance: the register kept by the police in Devonport, he states, "contains the name of every known prostitute."[127] The reasons Wakeford cites for the removal of women from the register substantiates Parent-Duchatelet and Acton's findings: "a great number get married, and a great number become reformed."[128]

Feminist discourse within the Repeal Movement inverted the argument about female transmission of disease while retaining the same language and operating on the same terrain as the dominant discourse. The repeal campaign organized around three key objections to the Acts: (1) the double standard involved in punishing the women and not the men for engaging in the same sexual act; (2) the class bias of the Acts, which targeted and punished public prostitutes, i.e., streetwalkers; and (3) the interference of the state. Feminists wrote the prostitute body as the victim of male pollution, a female body "invaded by men's bodies [and] men's laws."[129] Female Repealers thus denied the prostitute any identity other than passive victim. Two "honest" women, Josephine Butler and Mrs. Lewis, depicted the prostitute as the fallen woman capable of being reclaimed and "brought back to womanly dignity and virtue";[130] as having the potential to be turned into a "married and honourable wife with little children."[131] Thus the prostitute is reclaimed as mother and wife.

Mrs. Lewis was a home missionary in Birmingham. In her testimony we find the ideology of rescuing prostitutes. She refers to the "girls" who have been sent to the Magdelen Institution—a home for women leaving prostitution—as "now living reformed and industrious lives,"[132] "now married and honourable wives with little children around them."[133] Lewis contends that the legislation is "dreadfully" irreligious and immoral.[134] She gives cases of "honourable," "prudent Christian women" being summoned for fortnightly examinations.[135] Lewis implies that what is immoral is that the police cannot tell the difference between prostitutes and honourable women, but then she testifies that she has advised prostitute women "to do the same as I would do in their position"[136]—resist the police. Dr. Pickthorn documented prostitutes' resistance and attributed it to the Ladies National Association (LNA) preventing and dissuading the prostitutes from attending examinations. The questioner tries to stress the difference between "a respectable lady like [Lewis] and [her] respectable daughters"[137] and prostitute women. Lewis denies difference, saying:

> Well, right is right, either to the rich or poor, the outcast, or whoever he may be. . . . the golden rule with all is, to do unto others as you would have them do unto you, and so I said I would rather go to prison. That is my idea of resistance.[138]

This statement introduces two pieces of information: the prostitute herself is admitted to the hearing of the Royal Commission only indirectly, through the honest woman or good girl; the prostitute resists the police on the advice of the honest woman. Prostitutes' opinions of the Acts are reported by Lewis. She reports conflicting views among prostitutes: "in some cases the women think that the Act . . . is a very bad Act, that it degrades them and debases them . . . and it stamps every bit of the woman out of them."[139] Others "hardened to the streets"[140] considered that the Act was a very good Act because "there is a hospital to go to when diseased, plenty of good food and wine, a doctor and a chaplain to attend to them."[141] She states that some of the women use the status conferred on them by the Acts to call themselves "Queen's women,"[142] and she reports the words of prostitute women of Portsmouth who considered the Act to be

> [T]he best thing that can be for them, because if they did not submit to the examination they should lose almost all their income, for married men would not come to them and the youths dare not for fear of infection, and after examination they are free to go anywhere.[143]

The testimony of Josephine Butler, the most well-known female repealer and the leader of the LNA, challenged all the presuppositions of the dominant discourse, except for the markings of the prostitute body as the "fallen," "impure," unvirtuous woman. Butler, who operated her house as a refuge for "fallen women," defines successful reclamation as occurring when women are "brought back to womanly dignity and virtue";[144] the prostitute, possessing neither, is marked out in opposition to the pure woman. Rescue and reclamation could restore the prostitute to her pre-fallen state of virtous morality and asexual purity. Much of Bulter's testimony consists of challenging the class and gender bias of the Acts. Butler informed the Commission that:

> This legislation is abhorred by the country as a tyranny of the upper classes against the lower classes, as an injustice practised by men on women and as an insult to the moral sense of the people.[145]

Yet her discourse retains the dominant depiction of prostitution as a condition of depravity and pollution; however, the blame or responsibility is shifted from the woman to the man, her customer. Butler's testimony is a revolutionary decoding of the Acts but it also is a repetition and reinscription of the image of the prostitute body embodied in the official discourse.

Butler, quoting from the original protest document of the LNA, stated their key objection to the Acts: "We protest against this legislation in as much as moral restraint is withdrawn the moment the State recognizes and provides convenience for a vice, which by providing this convenience it declares to be necessary and venial."[146] The use of prostitutes is marked a necessity by the Acts and as pardonable. In her criticism of the legislation Butler marks prostitution a "vice," a "sin," and inscribes the sexual activity of prostitutes as "impure and unlawful intercourse."[147] The LNA called for "chastity among men":[148] it represented what writers such as Parent-Duchatelet, Acton, and the majority of commissioners and witnesses of the Royal Commission considered to be natural male desire as a socially constructed and condoned desire. Unchastity is marked a sin in men as well as women: however, the conceptual dichotomy of chaste and unchaste is not questioned. Butler states that "nothing can be done until the vices of men are attacked and checked."[149] She reports that the legislation is considered by male and female repealers to be "an outrageous piece of sex legislation."[150] They insisted that legislation be directed against both sexes and against the rich as well as the poor. Butler pointed out that the Acts were upheld by the regulationist as serving two ends which are absolutely contradictory: the provision of clean harlots for the army and navy and the reclamation of women. The latter she claimed is only put forward to stave off the vast opposition to the Acts among the "working classes."[151]

Butler produced a distinction between the image of the prostitute on the street (the vamp) and the true image beneath the street image (the wretched soul); however, she bases this on her own imagined experience as a prostitute:

[I]f I was a woman of this class my life would be this, and it is the life of thousands: I should be weeping all day, sorrowful and wretched. When evening came I should dress, take drink, and go out, and I should say every witty and sharp thing I could to fascinate my patrons. . . . it is while acting their odious part that men meet them, and form their judgement of them.[152]

Butler argued that the Acts "professionalize"[153] women who are occasional prostitutes; once registered they have the label "prostitute." The identity sets them apart from their life as "milliners, dressmakers, seamstresses and domestic servants."[154] Walkowitz emphasizes that the Contagious Diseases Acts created prostitutes as a separate class of women and dislocated them from their working-class communities.

As much as they questioned the assumptions underlying the Acts, including the assumptions about male sexuality, the LNA, as represented in the testimonies of Lewis and Butler, failed to articulate alternative representations of female sexuality: they embraced the asexual image of the female body and wrote it as the image of respectability.

The Sexualized Prostitute Body: Pathology and Perversity

The years from 1890 to 1910 saw a major transformation in sexual theory. Sexology and psychoanalysis sexualized the female body. The stereotype of the asexual female body underpinning official Victorian social historical documents, such as the *British Royal Commission on the Contagious Diseases Acts*, was exchanged for a stereotype of the sexual female body. Sexology and psychoanalysis sexualized a particular "normal" female body and a particular "normal" sexuality, pathologizing other bodies and sexualities. I will look at the markings on the prostitute body by two theorists who were central figures in the emergence of the modern sexual female body—Havelock Ellis and Sigmund Freud.

Havelock Ellis published the seven volumes of his *Studies in the Psychology of Sex* between 1897 and 1928. Paul Robinson claims that *Studies in the Psychology of Sex* "established the basic moral categories for nearly all subsequent sexual theorizing."[155] It is in *Sex in Relation to Society* (1910), Volume VI of his study, that Ellis analyzes prostitution. His objective in this volume is "to place each subject . . . in relation to those fundamental principles of sexual psychology which

. . . have been set forth in the preceeding volumes."[156] He uses his findings in Volume I, *Sexual Inversion* (1897), Volume II, *The Evolution of Modesty, the Phenomena of Sexual Periodicity, Auto-Eroticism* (1899), and Volume III, *The Analysis of the Sexual Impulse, Love and Pain, the Sexual Impulse in Women* (1903) to aid in delimiting the prostitute body.

Ellis produces a radical change in the construction of the prostitute body in three ways: He links the act of prostitution with the ritual of orgy, that religious/sexual space of premodern times. He produces the so-called born prostitute as a criminal type. And he constructs an image of the prostitute/lesbian body. Because his text is a survey, often relying on a collage of others' work to support his own views, Ellis has produced a disjointed and conflicted portrait of the prostitute in which she is simultaneously a secularized remnant of the lost pagan sacred and a somatically degenerate criminal. This ambiguous tension between the sacred and the profane, the first pole of which was repressed in the medical-legal-moral discourse of the nineteenth century, determines the imaginary of modernity.

Ellis begins his writing on prostitution with "the orgy"—the "occasional outbursts of license,"[157] the carnivalesque transgression where the religious and the secular elide, that functioned to uphold the social system in premodern times. Contemporary civilization encourages prostitution as a fragment of orgy, "a moment of organic relief,"[158] he claims. The modern prostitute, for Ellis, as for Baudelaire, embodies a moment of contact with the sublime through the fleeting union of the profane and the sacred. The remainder of his text serves, however, as a documentation of the profane, interrupted at the end by the identification of the prostitute with the normal woman.

Ellis, citing a collage of prostitution studies which includes Parent-Duchatelet's, reaffirms the view that the root cause of prostitution is poverty. Reproducing Parent-Duchatelet's ambiguity, he proceeds to undercut this claim by using his discussion of the relationship between economic necessity and prostitution as a preamble to the production of the prostitute as a biologically constituted entity. He begins with the acknowledgment that economic considerations have "a highly important modificatory influence on prostitution."[159] This is Ellis's framing to get to the question: "To what extent are prostitutes predestined to this career by organic constitution . . . [and] by the possession of abnormal personal characteristics?"[160] Relying heavily on Cesare Lombroso and Guglielmo Ferrero, Italian criminologists who wrote *La donna deliquente: La Prostitute e la donna normale* (1893), to define prostitute sexuality as a biologically degenerate form of female sexuality, Ellis cites their equation of the prostitute with the criminal—"prostitution represents the specific form of feminine criminality"—and the criminal with the insane;[161]

> The psychological as well as anatomical identity of the criminal and the born prostitute could not be more complete: both are identical with the moral insane, and therefore, according to the axiom, equal to each other.[162]

The prostitute becomes "the born prostitute."[163] In *Sexual Inversion* Ellis states: "it is almost possible to look upon prostitutes as a special human variety analogous to instinctive criminals."[164] Parent-Duchatelet's taxonomy which produced the prostitute as congenitally the same as other women and as the social disfigurement of the female body, a construction central in Acton's discourse and in the *Royal Commission on the Contagious Diseases Acts*, is superseded by Ellis, who marks the prostitute as innately degenerate and criminal.

Ellis through collaging contradictory studies inscribes the prostitute both as having a strong sexual impulse and as being sexually frigid. "Frigidity," as indicated by Sheila Jeffreys, was used as a code word for non-heterosexual activity: masturbation and lesbian sexuality.[165] Based on two studies, one of 180 Italian prostitutes and the other of sixty German prostitutes, Ellis inscribes masturbation as "almost universal"[166] among prostitutes. In his work *Auto-Eroticism* Ellis had marked masturbation as common and normal among both sexes, with adult masturbation being more frequent in women than in men. Ellis went against the pervasive tenet in Victorian sexual ideology which held that masturbation led to illness and insanity. Ellis insisted that there was no evidence linking masturbation with any serious mental or physical disorder. He also marks prostitutes as being frequently homosexual—more homosexual than other women:

> Homosexuality, though not so common as masturbation, is very frequently found among prostitutes . . . and it may indeed be said that it occurs more often among prostitutes than among any other class of women.[167]

He suggests that prostitutes have "a congenital tendency to sexual inversion."[168] Ellis had legitimated male homosexuality as acceptable sexual behavior, in his *Sexual Inversion*, by arguing that homosexuality was congenital but not degenerate. He thus undermined the dominant opinion that homosexuality was a vice and a pathology. However, he uses "congenital inversion" among prostitutes as a stepping stone to list other anomalies of prostitutes, thus (re)marking female inversion as degenerate: "The occurrence of congenital inversion among prostitutes . . . suggests the question whether we are likely to find an unusually large number of physical and other anomalies among them."[169] In his one chapter on female homosexuality in *Sexual Inversion* Ellis questions why there has been found a greater frequency of lesbianism among prostitute women than non-prostitute women; he runs through some of the usual causes—the loss of feeling for men due to the commercialization of the prostitute's relation with men and disappointment in love—but ends with the prostitute's "neurotic heredity" and "physical and mental degeneration."[170] What are the reasons for the ambivalence in Ellis's construction of the lesbian as opposed to the male homosexual? Ellis did not question the popular image of lesbianism as he did the image of male homosexuality: whereas he challenged the stereotyped effeminacy of the male invert, he constructed the female invert as mannish. Ellis writes:

> The chief characteristic of the sexually inverted woman is a certain degree of masculinity. . . . There is . . . a very pronounced tendency among sexually inverted women to adopt male attire. . . . When they retain female garments, these usually show some traits of masculine simplicity . . . there are all sorts of instinctive gestures and habits. . . . The brusque, energetic movements, the attitude of arms, the direct speech, the inflexions of the voice, the masculine straightforwardness and sense of honor, and especially the attitude toward men, free from any suggestion either of shyness or audacity, will often suggest the underlying psychic abnormality to a keen observer.[171]

For Ellis lesbians and prostitutes (perhaps due to their overlapping) are degenerate.

Ellis's views on female sexuality were ambiguous. He argued for the physical necessity of sexual intercourse to both males and females; he states in his work on prostitution that "the emotional and physical results of ungratified excitement are not infrequently more serious in women than in men."[172] Thus he contradicts the pervasive Victorian dichotomy between the asexual respectable woman and the sexual unrespectable woman. Contextualized by his volume *The Analysis of the Sexual Impulse, Love and Pain, the Sexual Impulse in Women*, however, it is clear that correct female sexuality is heterosexual and subordinate to male sexuality: "the masculine tendency to delight in domination, the feminine tendency to delight in submission still maintain the ancient traditions when the male animal pursued the female."[173] Ellis asserted woman's right to sexual pleasure, but he also determined the correct form of pleasure: submission and passivity in "normal" heterosexual intercourse. Margaret Jackson criticizes Ellis and the sex reformers for depoliticizing sexuality by removing it from the sexual-political arena and consigning it to the sphere of the natural: "Ellis by arguing that male dominance and female submission were biologically determined and inherent in heterosexual relations—and . . . essential to female sexual pleasure—gave scientific legitimation to precisely that model of sexuality which feminists were challenging; he thereby helped to render it immune from feminist attack."[174]

Ellis points out that "for some authorities prostitutes are merely normal ordinary women of low social rank" while for others they are "among one or other of the abnormal classes."[175] He then furnishes much data to support the second proposition, in the form of a collage of physical abnormalities cited from Pauline Tarnowsky's comparative physical investigation of fifty Russian prostitutes and fifty peasant women and Fornasari's study of eighty-seven Italian prostitutes. Tarnowsky produced the prostitute as showing various signs of degeneration: irregular skull size, asymmetry of face, anomalies of hard palate, teeth, and ears. Fornasari's study revealed that "prostitutes were . . . of lower type than the normal individuals, having smaller heads and larger faces."[176] Although Ellis reproduces Fornasari's admission that his subjects were not numerous enough to justify far-reaching generalizations, Ellis chooses to appropriate some of Fornasari's results, producing the prostitute as the grotesque body: a body of greater weight, shorter stature, greater height of face, greater distance from chin to ears, larger jaw size, bigger hands, longer feet, and larger thighs.[177] Ellis summarizes a list of the anthropometrical characteristics possessed by prostitutes:

[P]rostitutes tend to be in weight over the average, though not in stature. . . . The estimated skull capacity and the skull circumference and diameters are somewhat below the normal, not only when compared with respectable women but also with thieves. . . . the eyes have been found to be decidedly darker than those of either respectable women or criminals.[178]

Mixing acquired and hereditary characteristics Ellis reproduces the prostitute as a congenital type, somatically different from normal heterosexual women and somatically closer to the criminal.

Ellis ends his chapter on prostitution by writing the prostitute as a woman: "For thousands of years prostitution has been defended on the ground that the prostitute is necessary to ensure the 'purity of women.' In a democratic age it begins to be realized that prostitutes are also women."[179] Ellis states that, from the modern moral standpoint (his standpoint), unacceptable cruelty is involved in the traditional dichotomous construction of the prostitute as dishonorable and the wife as honorable. He contends that the wife in the home may be in as much need of moral rescue as the prostitute in the street. Ellis quotes from British sex reformer J. A. Godfrey:

> If the public prostitute is a being who deserves to be treated as a pariah, it is hopelessly irrational to withhold every sort of moral opprobrium from the woman who leads a similar life under a different set of external circumstances. Either the prostitute wife must come under the moral ban, or there must be an end to the complete ostracism under which the prostitute labors.[180]

It appears that it is for Ellis not the sexuality per se of prostitutes and clients that is objectionable but rather the exchange of money. He assumed that the liberation of woman's *normal* heterosexuality would abolish prostitution: "there is a tendency towards the slow elimination of prostitution by the successful competition of higher and purer methods of sexual relationships freed from pecuniary considerations."[181] The sexual relations of the prostitute and the prostitute wife, with their basis in "pecuniary considerations," will give way to healthy sexual relations with their basis in "normal" desire, so Ellis contends.

One reads much ambiguity in Ellis's construction of the prostitute body. This is partly due to his use of different writers in a collage style; however, he uses these authors to substantiate his own assumptions which mark the prostitute as a congenital degenerate, a sexual deviant (even if he condones male sexual inversion), a criminal, and a woman the same as many wives.

Sigmund Freud, although he writes very little on prostitutes and prostitution, produces three unique inscriptions on the modern prostitute body. Freud marks the prostitute as a sexually desublimated childlike woman; he identifies an innate aptitude for prostitution in

all women; and he is the first to point out that the conscious mind of
the male creates the split between the asexual idealized woman and
the sexual prostitute as a defense against the unity of the sexual and
maternal in the unconscious. With Freud there is an official abandon-
ment of the congenital and moral degeneracy models of the prostitute
and a move toward viewing prostitutes and all other deviants as either
psychologically ill or immature, as suffering neurosis or arrested development. The older images continued to flourish alongside and un-
derneath the official Freudian view.

In his essay "Infantile Sexuality" (1905) Freud presents the prostitute as manifesting the "natural" extension of the child's innate
polymorphous perverse sexuality: "Prostitutes exploit the same polymorphous, that is, infantile disposition for the purposes of their profession."[182] The infantile disposition is one in which "the mental dams
against sexual excesses—shame, digust and morality"[183] have not been
constructed or are still in the process of being constructed. The infantile disposition is one in which the "civilized" attitude toward sexuality is absent. Freud can be read as giving the "polymorphously perverse disposition" not only a gender base but also a class base: it is in
"an average uncultivated woman"[184] that the polymorphously perverse
disposition can be found. However, in the next breath Freud implies
that in every woman the act of seduction may bring out this tendency
toward perversion. Freud marks prostitution as perversion but then
marks the "disposition to perversions of every kind . . . a general and
fundamental human characteristic."[185] Going against Ellis's construction of the prostitute as a congenital type, Freud extends it as a gender
characteristic; he produces all women as possessing as a potential the
disposition that prostitutes live out:

> [C]onsidering the immense number of women who are prostitutes or
> who must be supposed to have an aptitude for prostitution without
> becoming engaged in it, it becomes impossible not to recognize that
> this same disposition to perversions of every kind is a general and
> fundamental human characteristic.[186]

Freud, in "A Special Type of Object Choice Made by Men" (1910),[187]
identifies "love for a Harlot" as a neurotic "condition of love."[188] Although, in this essay, he marks the prostitute "a lower type of sexual
object"[189]—a woman who lacks "sexual integrity" and has "the character of a light woman"[190]— Freud unites the light woman and the
normal woman, the whore/mother, in the unconscious. The prostitute

is to a large extent a creature of the male imaginary, a construction of the male unconscious which is then read into woman. The sexual aspect of mother, in the male conscious mind, is displaced unto the prostitute:

> The grown man's conscious mind likes to regard the mother as a personification of impeccable moral purity. . . . This very relation . . . of sharpest possible contrast between the "mother" and the "harlot" would prompt us to study the developmental history of the two complexes and unconscious relation between them, since we long ago discovered that a thing which in consciousness makes its appearance as two contraries is often in the unconscious a united whole.[191]

For Freud the whore/mother split has its origin in the Oedipus Complex when the male child represses his desire for his mother and idealizes her. When the child realizes that his parents engage in the "ugly sexual behaviour of the rest of the world,"[192] the mother/whore difference is collapsed: "the difference between his mother and a whore is . . . not so very great, since at bottom they both do the same thing."[193] Freud constructs both an unconscious unity of the female body (the image of the mother and whore as one) and a conscious splitting of the unified image into a duality of female types: the maternal and the prostitute.

Like the other texts, Freud's marking of the prostitute body is ambiguous: she is simultaneously the mother body and a lower type of sexual object; the polymorphously uninhibited sexual woman and the woman lacking sexual integrity.

Conclusion

Taken together these texts of Parent-Duchatelet, Acton, the British Royal Commission, Ellis, and Freud provide us with the dominant stereotypical images through which we have come to construct our conscious and unconscious knowledge of "the prostitute." At conscious and unconscious levels we hold contradictory images of the prostitute body: the prostitute as the diseased physical and moral body; the prostitute as a suffering victim; the prostitute as a working-class body; the prostitute as the sexual deviant—the lesbian and the perverse woman; the prostitute as an urban blight signifying a diseased city; the prostitute as the mother body; the prostitute as the criminal; the prostitute as the physically abnormal body; and the prostitute as the desublimated sexual woman. Each of these images is formulated in contrast to the determining side of the female dichotomy: the respectable woman in her various manifestations. The prostitute contains traces of the respectable woman: she is a mother, her body is the same as the "normal" woman, she is redeemable and can be reabsorbed into the family as a wife. There is a sliding between both sides of the dichotomy in every derivative couple, but the dichotomy stays intact and functions to magnify an overarching cultural representation: that is, the prostitute as the other within the categorical other, the prostitute as the profane woman.

The modern prostitute body was produced as a negative identity by the bourgeois subject, an empty symbol filled from the outside with the debris of the modern body/body politic, a sign to women to sublimate their libidinal body in their reproductive body. Markings produced by phallocentric discourse have dominated our image of the prostitute; these are the markings that feminists address. The next chapter will examine four feminist constructions of the prostitute body: two modern texts which respond to but remain trapped within phallocentric discourse and two postmodern texts which open spaces for prostitutes to speak and to produce their own public discourse.

4

WRITING THE PROSTITUTE BODY
Feminist Reproductions

THE PROSTITUTION debate within feminism keeps recycling: prostitution is important to feminism because the prostitute body is a terrain on which feminists contest sexuality, desire, and the writing of the female body. During the 1970s feminism produced three ideological positions on prostitution: the liberal, the socialist, and the radical feminist.[1] The liberal and socialist feminist approaches were responses to and critiques of the classical "malestream" liberal and Marxist positions on prostitution. Radical feminism critiqued both the hegemonic phallic view and liberal and socialist feminist views. All three feminisms are modernist in the sense that the prostitute body is fit into a theorized totality of feminist space; there is no space for the prostitute herself as speaking subject, particularly if her speech might contradict the feminist construction of her body. With the entrance of postmodern feminism, the debate changed radically in the late 1980s.

Postmodern feminism's most significant accomplishment has been to open space for the others of liberal, socialist, and radical feminism to speak and theorize their own subject positions. Postmodern feminism has shown that the three dominant feminisms can oppress women of difference through the appropriation or occlusion of their spaces and the silencing of their voices. Postmodern feminism has also shown that it is impossible to keep the ideological positions of different feminisms clear-cut and separate: feminisms overlap and feminisms incorporate parts of the dominant discourse they critique. These lessons are important when one is reading a marginal and transgressive female body, such as the prostitute body, both written and contained within the context of larger discursive projects.

This chapter will examine the writing of the prostitute body in the texts of four very different contemporary feminist theorists who influence the current feminist critique of Western political and social theory. These four theorizations either represent, have evolved out of, or critique the original three ideological positions. The four texts are Carole Pateman's critique of liberal social contract theory; Catharine MacKinnon's critique of the phallic sociocultural-political reality; Luce Irigaray's critique of Western philosophy and psychoanalysis; and Gayle Rubin's critique of conventional and feminist "normalization" of sexuality. The trajectory is from a critique of liberalism to a discourse of "radical sexual pluralism" that recuperates some of the assumptions of liberalism for its own political project.

The theorists have been selected because of the place prostitution holds in their constructions of female sexuality. Catharine MacKinnon and Gayle Rubin were key players in the North American sex debates which dominated the feminist terrain of the 1980s and divided many feminist theorists and activists into antipornography and anticensorship camps. The sexuality of deviant female others, such as prostitutes and sadomasochists, quickly became one of the sites of struggle in the anticensorship/antipornography debate. Luce Irigaray, in her deconstructive reading of patriarchal texts, constructs a "feminine" female sexuality; she explicitly links the prostitute body to phallic, or male-defined, female sexuality. Carole Pateman, in her disclosure of the sexual contract as the silent companion of the social contract, presents the prostitution contract and the marriage contract as commensurable private and public manifestations of the "law of male sex right."

These four theorists have also been chosen so as to display the difference between modernist feminism, which Jacques Derrida terms "reactive,"[2] a feminism which merely inverts the masculine/feminine dichotomy of phallogocentrism, and postmodern feminism which opens to a multiplicity of differences. Carole Pateman's rereading of the social contract is the underside of the liberal-humanist and Marxist projects she critiques; Catharine MacKinnon puts a unitary feminist epistemology in place of the dominant male epistemology. If one agrees with Derrida that the aim of feminism is to produce a way of constituting sexual difference that is neither asexual, as it is in the work of Josephine Butler, or oppositional, as it is in the theories of Pateman and MacKinnon—that the aim is sexual difference as multiplicity—then Irigaray partially achieves this in her concept of non-phallic or "feminine" female sexuality, as does Rubin, who realizes a "multiplicity of sexually marked voices"[3] in her theory of radical sexual pluralism.

Prostitution: The Public Sexual Contract

Carole Pateman, in her book *The Sexual Contract*, reads the absence, the underside, of the social contract upon which the principles of liberalism are founded. In this context she provides a critique of the liberal, the liberal feminist, and the classical Marxist positions on prostitution. Liberal feminist discourse is an appropriate place to begin to examine feminist writing of the prostitute body because English-speaking feminism has been principally inscribed within the Enlightenment discourse of individual rights. The various strains of feminism have had to engage in one way or another with the terms of this inscription and prostitutes' rights activists reappropriate their inscription of their own body from liberal discourse.

The social contract, a seventeenth- and eighteenth-century device for the legitimation of civil society and political rights, is being used, according to Pateman, to uphold the inequality that exists in contemporary society. Pateman stresses the importance of the story of the original social contract: "in modern civil society crucially important institutions are constituted and maintained through contract."[4] Three such institutions are employment, marriage, and prostitution. A contractual relationship, theoretically, implies a voluntary commitment and an equal exchange between the parties involved. However, as has been commonly argued, the exchange of labor for a wage is neither equal nor voluntary if one party would die of starvation without entering into the contract.

It has been pointed out by a number of feminist theorists that the social contract is an agreement among free male individuals. What sets Pateman apart from numerous readers of the inherent inequalities of the social contract is her rereading of the social contract in a new context which she calls the "deep silence . . . about the sexual contract."[5] Her contention is that the original contract is simultaneously social and sexual; the sexual contract has been absorbed and rendered invisible in the social contract:

> The original pact is a sexual as well as a social contract; it is sexual in the sense of patriarchal—that is, the contract establishes men's political right over women—and also sexual in the sense of establishing orderly access by men to women's bodies. The original contract creates . . . "the law of male sex-right."[6]

The contract, as it creates society, creates "the law of male sex right" by establishing legitimate access to women's bodies. The original contract constitutes not only freedom but also domination: the liberation of the fraternal brotherhood from paternal authority and the domination of the fraternal brotherhood over women. Freedom and domination are contingent on sexual difference. There are two patriarchal rights: the paternal (father/son) and the masculine or phallic (husband/wife)—the right of the father and the right of the male. Contract theorists, such as John Locke, wrote paternal right—that is, the right of the father to rule over all succeeding generations—out of the social contract; every adult generation of men is equal. On the other hand, they underwrote the social contract with masculine right.[7] The original contract, among all the individuals in the natural state to unite into civil society, is constructed on sexual difference: "Only masculine beings are endowed with the attributes and capacities necessary to enter into contracts, the most important of which is ownership of property in the person; only men, that is to say, are 'individuals.' "[8] That ownership of property in the person is exclusively a male attribute is crucial to Pateman's critique of prostitution.[9]

For Pateman, civil society consists of two spheres: the public sphere of male equality and the private sphere of male domination over women and children. Social contract theorists and conventional readers of social contract theory focus exclusively on the public sphere, disregarding the private sphere as obviously irrelevant to civil society. The private sphere is structured by the marriage contract: Pateman contends that the original sexual contract is displaced onto the marriage contract and that this makes it very difficult to retrieve and recount the lost story of the sexual contract as both a private and a public contract. Pateman's purpose for retrieving the sexual contract is not merely to pinpoint a silence and absence in the history of political theory. Rather, her reclaiming has a contemporary purpose: "The story helps us understand the mechanisms through which men claim right of access to women's bodies and claim right of command over the use of women's bodies."[10]

The prostitution contract is an example of male sex right in the public sphere. Prostitution is "part of the exercise of the law of male sex-right, one of the ways in which men are ensured access to women's bodies."[11] Pateman contends that because prostitution is treated like other capitalist enterprises and understood as a private contract between prostitute and client, the public character of prostitution is obscured. Pateman reads prostitution as "the public recognition of men as sexual masters."[12]

In chapter 7 of *The Sexual Contract*, entitled "What's Wrong with Prostitution," Pateman provides a critique of the contractarian justification of prostitution. The contractarian argument, which has been adapted by liberal feminists, presents prostitution as a form of work and the prostitute as a free worker the same as any other wage laborer or petty entrepreneur. Contractarians assert that the prostitute is the possessor of property in her own person and is as such capable of selling her labor. The prostitute contracts out a certain form of labor power (the capacity for sexual activity) for a specific period of time in exchange for money. A free exchange exists between the prostitute and the client, according to contractarians. Like the worker, the prostitute contracts out the use of her body for a limited time; the prostitute does not sell herself or her body. She sells a sexual service. Contractarian Lars Ericsson (cited by Pateman in her article "Defending Prostitution: Charges against Ericsson") states: "a prostitute must necessarily sell 'not her body or vagina, but sexual services.' If she actually did sell herself she would no longer be a prostitute but a sexual slave."[13] Pateman argues that the prostitute is, in fact, a sexual slave. She bases this argument on her contingent argument that the worker is a wage slave. Pateman's central criticism of contract theory is premised on the absence of property in the person. She argues that the worker's property in the person is "a political fiction"[14] for proletarian men and for all women:

> The capitalist does not and cannot contract to use the proletarian's services or labour power. The employment contract gives the employer right of command over the use of the worker's labour, that is to say, over the self, person and body of the worker during the period set down in the employment contract.[15]

Individuals act as if they contract out only their labor power or services, but what they contract out is their "self, person, and body." Pateman's critique of the contractarian and liberal feminist positions, however, goes farther: it has at its foundation a not-so-silent moral postulate that there is something specially "wrong with prostitution." Pateman writes "if the prostitute is merely one worker among others, the appropriate conclusion must be that there is nothing wrong with prostitution . . . that is not also wrong with other forms of work."[16] And this just cannot be the case for Pateman. This moral postulate underpins her critique of the classical Marxist position on prostitution.

The classical Marxist understanding of prostitution follows from Marx's statement that "prostitution is only the specific expression of the universal prostitution of the worker."[17] The Marxian position is an inversion of the contractarian position: the employment contract, according to the Marxian position, is a contract of prostitution. Prostitution, for Marxists, is exploitative in the same way that the selling of all labor power is exploitative. Pateman equalizes the prostitute and worker on the grounds that neither own property in their persons. It is in this equation that the internal logic of Pateman's text subverts itself. Pateman claims that the similarity between the employment contract and the prostitution contract, between the wage slave and the sex slave, is that

> [T]he man who contracts to use the services of the prostitute, like the employer, gains command over the use of her person and body for the duration of the prostitute contract.[18]

The difference is the capitalist has no interest in the body and self of the worker beyond the production of commodities, whereas the prostitute's client is only interested in the body of the woman: "sexual access to that body is the subject of the contract."[19] The pivotal argument in her analysis of contracts—the original contract, the employment contract, the prostitution contract—is the disclosure that not all individuals effectively own property in their persons and the contract favors those who do: the capitalist, the husband, the client. Those who do not—the worker, the wife, the prostitute—are equalized. Pateman inadvertently supports the liberal (feminist and contractarian) characterization of prostitute as worker and the Marxist characterization of worker as prostitute.

At the center of Pateman's sexual contract is a silent value judgment on commercial sexuality and certain sexual activities. The nature of Pateman's sexual presuppositions is most obvious in an aside she places in a footnote: this is her equation of oral sex with the silencing of women. She observes that in the United States between 1930 and 1960 clients' request for oral sex had increased 80 percent, which, I would hasten to add, reflects a general change in sexual activity. Pateman, however, uses this increase to make the following inference:

> Could it be conjectured that men's current widespread demand to buy women's bodies to penetrate their mouths is connected to the revitalization of the feminist movement and women's demand to speak?[20]

Heterosexuality doesn't fare well in Pateman's rewriting of the story of contemporary inequalities; but conjugal heterosexuality fares differently and better than commercial heterosexuality. Crucial to Pateman's reading of the sexual contract is that the marriage contract has as its foundation male sex right: the subordination of women and the domination of men. Yet Pateman does state: "a form of marriage in which the husband gains legal right of sexual use of his wife's body is only one possible form. The conjugal relation is not necessarily one of domination and subjection, and in this it differs from prostitution."[21] Pateman inscribes only one form of prostitution: the form in which the client gains right of sexual use of the prostitute's body. If access to women's bodies is the defining feature of male sex right, how is it transformed into something else in marriage? If contemporary marriage can after all be founded on principles which do not subordinate women, what is it about prostitution that prevents this from occurring? In her essay "Should Feminists Oppose Prostitution?" Laurie Shrage, a contributor to the prostitution debate in the journal *Ethics*, for which Pateman wrote her response to Ericcson, suggests a form of prostitution in which the prostitute would not be subordinate: "the female prostitute would . . . assume the role not of a sexual subordinate but of a sexual equal or superior."[22] What marks the prostitute as a sexual equal is control of the sexual encounter: "hav[ing] the authority to determine what services the customer could get, under what conditions the customer could get them, and what they would cost."[23]

What is especially "wrong with prostitution" for Carole Pateman is not entirely that it is the public manifestation of male sex right—for then it would be merely the public version of the private marriage contract. Rather, she has a visceral disagreement with commercial sex. Pateman's rereading of the social contract and writing of the sexual contract turn out to be premised on the time-honored value judgment which perpetuates the division of the female body into the two traditional female bodies, the wife and the prostitute, neither of which is in control of her body, though one has more potential for ownership, due to the love, commitment, and mutual responsibility, which Pateman assumes is inherently present in the marriage contract and absent in the prostitution contract.[24]

Desire, Pleasure, and Prostitution

While Carole Pateman inscribes her theory in the margins of social contract theory, actually making it impossible for those who have read her text to neglect the sexual contract underpinning the social contract, Catharine MacKinnon superimposes her theory over Marx's primary concepts. MacKinnon exchanges Marx's central concept of the alienation of labor for the alienation of female sexuality. The pivotal concept in MacKinnon's theorization of feminism is sexuality: "Sexuality is to feminism what work is to marxism: that which is most one's own, yet most taken away."[25]

MacKinnon is "producing a feminist political theory centering upon sexuality."[26] The crucial question, then, concerns the content that MacKinnon writes into her pivotal concept: What is female sexuality for MacKinnon, and, for the purposes of my text, what is the relationship between female sexuality and prostitution? MacKinnon mentions prostitution only four times; yet it is at the core of her conception of female sexuality in the hegemonic (heterosexual masculinist) order. She writes: (1) "prostitution—the fundamental condition of women";[27] (2) "the stigma of prostitution is the stigma of sexuality is the stigma of the female gender";[28] (3) "feminism observes that men have the power to make prostitution women's definitive condition";[29] and (4) "feminism stresses the indistinguishability of prostitution, marriage and sexual harassment."[30] Prostitution is the central metaphor for female sexuality. Prostitution, for MacKinnon, signals that female sexuality is entirely constructed as an object of male desire. MacKinnon, needless to say, has no concept of the possibility that a prostitute could have sexual agency and exercise sexual control in her commercial sexual encounters.

Woman's sexuality is not her own property: "Women's sexuality is, socially, a thing to be stolen, sold, bought, bartered, or exchanged by others . . . women never own or possess it."[31] Female sexuality is an absence that is filled with the content of male desire:

[W]oman is . . . a being who identifies and is identified as one whose sexuality exists for someone else. . . . What is termed women's sexuality is the capacity to arouse desire in that someone.[32]

Male sexuality constructs male and female sexuality and then mis-attributes female sexuality to women. The dominant form of sexual-ity—heterosexuality—"institutionalizes male sexual dominance and female sexual submission."[33]

For MacKinnon, these are the features of heterosexuality: sexuality in which sexual harassment is indistinguishable from sexual initia-tion; where the distinction between intercourse and rape is a distinc-tion of quantity, not quality—that is, difference of experience; and in which violation (penetration and intercourse) defines the paradigmatic sexual encounter. Andrea Dworkin, a popularizer of MacKinnon's view, the rhetorician of MacKinnon's theory, marks the female condi-tion as that of occupation and collaboration. All intercourse, by the very action of penetration, is violation:

> There is never a real privacy of the body that can coexist with inter-course: with being entered. The vagina itself is a muscle and the muscles have to be pushed apart. The thrusting is persistent invasion. She is opened up, split down the center. She is occupied—physically, internally, in her privacy. . . . Violation is a synonym for intercourse.[34]

Laurie Shrage comments that "Dworkin invokes both images of phys-ical assault and imperialist domination in her characterization of het-erosexual copulation. Women are split, penetrated, entered, occupied, invaded, and colonized by men."[35] Women who not only engage in but enjoy heterosexual intercourse are assigned only one position—that of the collaborator. The male point of view constructs female sexuality and is in control of its representation: "men create the world from their own point of view, which then becomes the truth to be de-scribed."[36] Women consequently are deprived of both their own sexual experience and the terms in which to describe it.

Ironically, it is MacKinnon's grafting of feminism onto Marxism that undermines her theory. MacKinnon reproduces two, very phallic, aspects of Marxism: its powers of totalization and its systematicity. She claims that prior to her theorization feminism had no systematic analysis. Woman's situation was attributed to a number of factors—biology, gender construction, mothering, reproduction, family—but had no primary site of oppression. MacKinnon writes sexuality as the primary site of women's oppression. She conceives of all sites of wo-man's oppression and exploitation as "consequences of sexuality."[37] MacKinnon refers to her theory as "feminism without any modifiers" to indicate its self-sufficiency and totality as a theory. Feminism "fundamentally identifies sexuality as the primary social sphere of male power."[38] The understanding of the centrality of sexuality emerges, claims MacKinnon, from "consciouness raising on diverse issues."[39] These diverse issues are rape, incest, battery, sexual harassment, abortion, prostitution, and pornography, which then are marked as the sites of sexuality. Consciousness raising on diverse issues turns out to mean consciousness raising on sites of sexual exploitation, and these are then taken as the constituents of sexuality itself: there is no space for other manifestations of sexuality. MacKinnon has produced a circular system and created a tautology in theory.

MacKinnon's reason for equating Marxism and feminism is: "both marxism and feminism are theories of power. Both are total theories. That is, they are both theories of the totality, of the whole thing[.]"[40] What MacKinnon, in effect, does is replace the counter-hegemonic male critique of liberalism—Marxism—with a female counter-hegemonic critique rooted in Marxian presuppositions.

MacKinnon employs three central concepts of Marxism equating sexuality with labor, desire with value, and "women's point of view" with class consciousness, but one may note the absence of class action. By implication women and the proletariat are presented as occupying similar positions; this is not a new or an unusual equation. Both labor and sexuality are socially constructed and constructing and both are universal and historically specific. Marx theorizes both a general, universal aspect of labor as conscious, purposeful life activity and a specific historic aspect of labor as alienated labor. MacKinnon, on the other hand, has no space for non-alienated female sexuality:

> Marxism teaches that exploitation and degradation somehow produce resistance and revolution. . . . What I have learned from women's experience with sexuality is that exploitation and degradation produce grateful complicity in exchange for survival. . . . [41]

MacKinnon ends this observation by exclaiming: "The issue is not why women acquiesce but why we ever do anything but."[42] Here then MacKinnon may be opening a small space for other forms of sexuality beyond the exploitation and degradation which are, according to her, synonomous with heterosexuality.

In another place, MacKinnon draws an analogy between women's sexuality in a masculinist regime and black culture in racist society:

> [W]omen's sexuality . . . like Black culture . . . can be experienced as a source of strength, joy, expression, and as an affirmative badge of

pride. Both remain nonetheless stigmatic in the sense of a brand, a restriction, a definition as less. This is . . . because . . . the social reality is that their shape, qualities, texture, imperative, and very existence are a response to powerlessness. . . . They are created out of social conditions of oppression and exclusion. They may be part of a strategy for survival or even of change. But, as is, they are not the whole world, and it is the whole world that one is entitled to.[43]

Here is a larger break in MacKinnon's text which exposes a gap in her theory. Marx expected revolution to come from labor; the black power movement, black consciousness, and the African National Congress expect liberation to come from black culture; but MacKinnon in her construction of female sexuality as "nothing but" prostitution, entirely constructed for the benefit of males, is blind to the potential for anything but disempowered female sexuality. The blind spot in her theory is the possibility for female sexual agency in a sexist/racist/classist system. MacKinnon's female sexuality is so thoroughly shaped by male sexuality that we have no idea of what female sexuality is. It is a historical absence which elides into a biological given. For her, active male sexuality and contingent female sexuality are practically transhistorical. For MacKinnon, women's sexuality, regardless of the form it takes, is not an expression of agency and autonomy: "attempts to value sexuality as women's, possessive as if women possess it, will remain part of limiting women to it, to what women are now defined as being."[44] Anyone who claims the subject position of sexual agency suffers false consciousness:

> Women who are compromised, cajoled, pressured, tricked, black-mailed, or outright forced into sex . . . often respond to the unspeakable humiliation . . . by claiming that sexuality as their own. Faced with no alternative, the strategy to acquire self-respect and pride is: I chose it.[45]

MacKinnon leaves no room in the masculinist regime for multiple truths or dissenting truths: the truth and reality of female sexuality is the construct of male desire; female sexuality is defined by men and forced on women. Homosexuality is no less gendered than heterosexuality; all sexual subjects reproduce the dominant order.[46]

MacKinnon equates desire in her theorization to value in Marx's theorization:

> Desire . . . is parallel to value in marxist theory . . . it occupies an analogous theoretical location. It is taken for a natural essence or preso-

cial impetus but is actually created by the social relations, the hierarchical relations, in question.[47]

MacKinnon's aim in drawing the parallel between desire and value is
a Marxification of "desire." That is, her aim is to produce desire as
strictly a social construct that has its origin in a social relation. Mac-
Kinnon explicitly appropriates and reproduces only one aspect of the
Marxian concept and this is its qualitative aspect which establishes
that value is an expression of social relations; similarly, desire is an
expression of the gender (masculine/feminine) relations among people.
For MacKinnon all desire is socially constructed and is representable;
I would argue in contrast that desire is also that which is unrepresent-
able, the undefinable, that which exceeds systemic definitions and requirements. The systemic requirement of desire in a masculinist
system is that it construct and represent female sexuality for the pleasure of men. Yet desire is excess: it is both totalizing and detotalizing.
Value, on the other hand, is by definition a totalizing concept.

MacKinnon assumes the quantitative aspect of value: value is "the
equivalent form"[48] through which various types of labor are rendered
commensurable, equalized, and made exchangeable. Value's quantitative aspect makes everything commensurable. But desire cannot be
reduced to commensurability. Even heterosexual desire does not always manifest in the prescribed male-dominant form. Many different
forms of desire exist within the hegemonic system, both inside heterosexuality and outside of it: there are many heterosexual scripts and
many non-heterosexual scripts; there are many desires that do not
conform to the requirements of the masculinist system.[49] By contrast,
there can be no value that does not conform to the systemic requirements of capitalism. The concept of desire cannot do the work that
value does; that is, it cannot make different forms of desire commensurable.

Value is the amount of socially necessary labor time; what is excess
is the surplus value essential for the reproduction of the capitalist
system: surplus value is the excessiveness of capitalism within the
system itself. MacKinnon could have argued that desire simultaneously reproduces the masculinist system and exceeds (transgresses) it.
This would leave intact her critique of the hegemonic order, but it
would allow for the excess that MacKinnon is forced to ignore in order
to produce a totalizing theory; a theory which cannot account for resistance and multiple sexualities. In Marx's theory, as Jon Stratton has

observed, "[t]he working class, as a constructed Other, always had the possibility of exceeding their representation."[50] MacKinnon will not see a similar possibility for women. One finds the break for the admittance of excess into MacKinnon's text in her deployment of the concept of desire, her equation of women with the proletariat, and her comparison of women's sexuality with black culture; but it is written only to be negated and reabsorbed, not as a site of resistance.

MacKinnon reproduces the hegemonic discourse and system she is critiquing. Feminism, as constructed by MacKinnon, is the mirror image of the hegemonic order, and she knows it. She herself points out that she can be accused of doing exactly what she does, which is to reproduce the binary divisions of phallocentrism (masculinity, activity, dominance, sadism/femininity, passivity, submission, masochism) in her theorization of feminism:

> [T]o be realistic about sexuality is to see it from the male point of view. To be feminist is to do that with a critical awareness that that is what you are doing. This explains why feminist insights are often criticized for replicating male ideology. . . . Because male power has created in reality the world to which feminist insights . . . refer, many of our statements will capture that reality, simply exposing it as specifically male for the first time.[51]

Her feminism exposes the construction of reality as a male construction but is confined within this exposure. Her feminist epistemology is based on a critique of phallic knowledge from "the point of view of all women."[52] She assumes a unitary women's experience which is derived out of critiquing the unitary male point of view: "It takes as its point of departure the criticism that the male point of view on social life has constructed both social life and knowledge about it."[53] MacKinnon works inside the masculine/feminine dichotomy: "woman" becomes the dominant term. As Christie McDonald warns: "such a scheme of reversal . . . only repeat[s] the traditional scheme (in which the hierarchy of duality is always reconstituted)[.]"[54]

According to the sexual scripts approach to the construction of sexuality, sexual practices are learned at three levels of scripting: cultural scripts (the paradigmatic social norms that construct and determine sexual behavior), interpersonal scripts (meeting of social convention and personal desire), and intrapsychic scripts (the realm of the self-process).[55] It is in the interpersonal and intrapsychic domains that the cultural script can be and often is undermined and transgressed. According to the hegemonic heterosexual white cultural script,

> A "normal" man is active, aggressive, independent, exclusively het-
> erosexual, more or less restricting his heterosexuality to the active
> thrusting of his penis into the passive receptive vagina; a "normal"
> woman is passive, submissive, dependent, exclusively heterosexual,
> more or less restricting her heterosexuality to the passive reception of
> the actively thrusting penis.[56]

Therefore, "abnormal" scripts such as those scripts in which both
male and female bodies pursue active and passive libidinal aims, or in
which the female is more active than the male, undermine the dominant order. A serious flaw in MacKinnon's and Dworkin's reconstruction of female sexuality is that they reproduce the female sexual organ
as a passive muscle, a hole. If one takes the female sexual organ as an
active (w)hole capable of taking the penis or penis object in, expelling
it, or prohibiting entry, one leaves room for different constructions of
heterosexual encounters. MacKinnon follows the type of thinking crit-
icized by Gad Horowitz that takes "the image of active penis in passive vagina as a model . . . of the total sexuality and personality of men
and women."[57]

MacKinnon is a theorist of the center. She ignores the margins of
sexuality and difference and constructs woman exclusively as a hegemonic category. Woman is nothing but a prostitute, and the prostitute
is nothing but a hole, a passive object of the omnipotent phallus. Unlike MacKinnon and Pateman, Luce Irigaray theorizes both the masculinist regime's dominant moment(s) and its excessive moments.

Two Lips for Sale

Luce Irigaray, as a postmodern feminist, goes beyond the explana-
tion of how the feminine has been constituted as subordinate, inferior,
a lack, to explore also the limits of the discourses—that is, the excesses and ambiguities that take one beyond the discourse(s) under
scrutiny:

> Discourses, even hegemonic discourses, are not closed systems. The
> silences and ambiguities of the discourse provide the possibility of
> refashioning them, the discovery of other conceptualizations, the re-
> vision of accepted truths.[58]

Unlike Pateman and MacKinnon, Irigaray writes a sexual female subject, constructing a female imaginary that is not merely male-defined.
Irigaray's female subject is constituted by the hegemonic system but is

also capable of resistance to this constitution. According to the post-modern episteme "the gaps, silences and ambiguities of discourse provide the possibility for resistance, for a questioning of the dominant discourse, its revision and mutation. Within these silences and gaps new discourses can be formulated that challenge the dominant discourse."[59]

Irigaray uses Derrida's concept of *différance* to open the space for female self-inscription in terms other than those derived from a reaction to sameness, oneness, or identity with the masculine subject. Irigaray states her project and strategy:

> I am trying . . . to go back through the masculine imaginary, to interpret the way it has reduced us to silence, to muteness or mimicry, and I am attempting, from that starting-point and at the same time, to (re)discover a possible space for the feminine imaginary.[60]

Irigaray focuses on philosophical discourse—Plato, Descartes, Hegel, Marx, Nietzsche, Freud—because "this discourse sets forth the law for all others, inasmuch as it constitutes the discourse on discourse."[61] It is philosophy's power to "reduce all others to the economy of the same"[62]—in particular, to write woman as man's other, his negative, a mirror for reflecting his masculinity—that Irigaray is deconstructing. She focuses on the points of textual excess that undermine the text.

The feminine imaginary encompasses both sexuality and subjectivity: there is a parallelism between phallic male sexuality and phallocentric representational systems (dominant discourses). Irigaray uses the metaphor of "two lips" to provide an image (a representation and construction) of autonomous female sexuality that is based on a plurality of pleasure sites rather than the phallocentric polarity of the clitoral and vaginal division and the resultant binary Freudian division of woman into active immature sexual beings and passive mature sexual beings. She writes "two lips" in the following way:

> [W]oman . . . touches herself in and of herself without any need for mediation, and before there is any way to distinguish activity from passivity. Woman "touches herself" all the time . . . for her genitals are formed of two lips in continuous contact. Thus, within herself, she is already two—but not divisible into one(s)—that caress each other.[63]

Ironically, it is Irigaray's pivotal concept of "two lips" constructed to critique the essentialist phallocentric markings of vaginal passivity and clitoral activity that has generated charges of essentialism from some feminist critics. Elizabeth Grosz, in response to these criticisms, contextualizes Irigaray's use of "two lips":

> The "two lips" is not a truthful image of female anatomy but a new emblem by which female sexuality can be positively represented. The two lips is a manoeuvre to develop a different image or model of female sexuality, one which may inscribe female bodies according to interests outside or beyond phallocentrism, while at the same time contesting the representational terrain that phallocentrism has hitherto annexed. It accords women activity, satisfaction and a corporeal self-sufficiency usually denied them in heterosexist cultures.[64]

Sexuality is a means of self-discovery; this is sexuality that is excessive to heterosexuality: autoeroticism and lesbianism. Heterosexuality in Irigaray's theorization doesn't fare any better than in MacKinnon's and Dworkin's representations: Irigaray writes about how the autoeroticism of the two lips caressing each other is "disrupted by a violent break-in."[65] She constructs heterosexuality as "the brutal separation of the two lips by a violating penis."[66]

"Two-lips," needless to say, is also, and primarily, a referent for woman-as-speaking-subject. The female imaginary is polyvocal and polysexual; that is, the female subject has no unitary voice or sexuality: she contains a multiplicity of female voices and sexualities.

The prostitute is produced in three ways in Irigaray's text: the first is in keeping with MacKinnon's and radical feminism's construction of prostitution as the condition of all women in a patriarchal social structure. Irigaray writes that the pleasure woman gets in Freud's construction of heterosexuality, which is woman as an "obliging prop for the enactment of man's fantasies,"[67] is a "masoschistic prostitution of her body to a desire that is not her own and . . . leaves her in a familiar state of dependency upon men."[68] Prostitution here means sex which is not one's own and is constructed according to the desire of the other. The second is economic: Irigaray admonishes women "to earn their living in order to escape from the condition of prostitute."[69] The presupposition is that prostitutes do not earn their own living. Here again Irigaray's production/representation of the prostitute is identical with other feminist discourses, such as Marxism and radical feminism, which perceive prostitution as a state of dependency upon men.

It is in her rereading of Marx and his analysis of the commodity, "Women on the Market," that Irigaray produces the prostitute in a unique way. It is here that she inadvertently undermines her construction of the prostitute body and subverts her own text, for here she marks the prostitute body as a female body not divided by binary oppositions, leaving a space for the prostitute as a speaking subject who actively intervenes in the male exchange economy. Perhaps Irigaray's intent was to produce the prostitute as occupying a mimetic position who by taking herself to market and naming her price mimes male discourse and in so doing disrupts the male exchange economy, exposing the exchange of women at its foundation; except that Irigaray seems to only conceive of the prostitute as "a vehicle for relations among men."[70] Thus I want to propose that the prostitute becomes a site of textual excess: she escapes the mastery of Irigaray's constructions, undermines Irigaray's presentation of women as commodity-objects, and by so doing alters the author's meaning.

Irigaray, following Lévi-Strauss and Lacan, writes that "the circulation of women among men is what establishes the operation of society."[71] The use, consumption, and circulation of women's bodies are the foundation for society. She employs Marx's concept of value to describe the social status of women. "Women-as-commodities" have a use value and an exchange value, that is, women are "two things at once: utilitarian objects and bearers of value."[72] Quoting Marx, Irigaray writes: "They manifest themselves therefore as commodities, or have the form of commodities, only insofar as they have two forms, a physical or natural form, and a value form."[73] Women-as-commodities are divided into two categories: natural usefulness and exchange value, matter-body and a cultural envelope, private use and social use. Women-as-commodities do not have their value in and for themselves; even their use value (reproduction of children and of the labor force) is "a mirror of value of and for man."[74] Irigaray concentrates on the qualitative aspect of value; that is, that women posit a social relationship between men:

> The exchange value of two signs, two commodities, two women, is a representation of the needs/desires of consumer-exchanger subjects: in no way is it the property of the signs/articles/women themselves. . . . [T]he commodities—or rather the relationships among them—are the material alibi for the desire for relations among men.[75]

Thus the exchange of women supports what she calls "the reign of masculine hom(m)osexuality." "[H]om(m)osexuality is played out through the bodies of women . . . heterosexuality has been up to now just an alibi for the smooth workings of man's relations with himself, of relations among men."[76]

Women have three positions in Irigaray's symbolic order: mother, virgin, and prostitute. The mother is pure use value; the virgin pure exchange value; the prostitute is both. The mother is both a natural value (matter-body), man's link with nature, and a reproductive instrument (her use value is the reproduction of the species). Mothers do not circulate as commodities, for this would threaten the social order: "[M]others, reproductive instruments marked with the name of the father and enclosed in his house, must be private property excluded from exchange."[77] The virgin "is . . . the place, the sign of relations between men . . . she is a simple envelope veiling"[78] the social exchange between men. Once the envelope is violated woman becomes a use value, the private property of one man and thus removed from exchange among men. The prostitute does not fall into the binary opposition of use and exchange value: "the break between usage and exchange is, in her case, less clearcut";[79] she is one, the other, and both simultaneously:

> In her case, the qualities of woman's body are "useful." However, these qualities have "value" only because they serve as a locus of relations—hidden ones—between men. Prostitution amounts to usage that is exchanged.[80]

The characteristics of female sexuality are derived from these three social roles. Irigaray lists the attributes of female sexuality as "the valorization of reproduction and nursing; faithfulness; modesty, ignorance of and even lack of interest in sexual pleasure; a passive acceptance of men's 'activity'; seductiveness, in order to arouse the consumers' desire while offering herself as its material support without getting pleasure herself."[81] It is clear that there is no ownership of pleasure in any of these positions. The pleasure found in the exchange economy is that of the masculine subject; it is the pleasure of appropriation, ownership, and exchange. "Heterosexuality is nothing but the assignment of economic roles: there are producer subjects and agents of exchange (male) on the one hand, productive earth and commodities (female) on the other."[82] The sociocultural endogamy of masculine hom(m)osexuality precludes the participation in the exchange economy of the other: woman. "Men make commerce of them, but they do not enter into exchanges with them."[83] In an earlier interview, "The Power of Discourse," Irigaray states:

> In our social order, women are "products" used and exchanged by men. Their status is that of merchandise, "commodities." How can such objects of use and transaction claim the right to speak and to participate in exchange in general? Commodities, as we all know, do not take themselves to market on their own. . . . The use, consumption, and circulation of their sexualized bodies underwrite the organization and the reproduction of the social order, in which they have never taken part as "subjects". . . . [W]hat would become of the symbolic process that governs society . . . if women, who have been only objects of consumption or exchange, necessarily aphasic, were to become "speaking subjects" as well?[84]

Here Irigaray leaves a space for the prostitute as an active, speaking exchange partner, and thus for a positive construction of the prostitute to counterbalance her overtly negative production. It is this positive construction of the prostitute body that Janet Feindel, a Toronto sex worker activist, playwright, and performance artist, derives from Irigaray's text. In the words of Feindel:

> ['I']he prostitute is paid money for her body currency; moreover, she has gained access into the symbolic order of the economy. . . . She is also not silent. By bartering and naming her price she is breaking the "silent" exchange of women. By naming it and defining it and consciously bringing into light what has traditionally been repressed she is no longer a passive participant in the exchange.[85]

It is the ambiguous unity in the prostitute body of use and exchange value that positions her as a speaking subject. Commodity society simultaneously produces and constrains the prostitute as an autonomous subject: it produces her as an active agent of exchange while constraining her sexual (inter)subjectivity. The prostitute negotiates sexuality only as a commercial exchange inside the male exchange economy; but she does negotiate it. Irigaray's intention is to construct the prostitute as at least as exploited as the mother and the virgin, for she mistakenly sees the prostitute only as an object of exchange between two men, the pimp and the client: "The economy of exchange—of desire—is man's business."[86] She has no conception of the prostitute as exchanging her own use-value, as being the object of exchange and the seller. Inadvertently, however, she produced a space in which the prostitute can write herself as an agent of exchange, an active participant who exchanges her own use value. As a subject capable of speech the prostitute owns her own two lips and enters with her two lips into the hom(m)osexual endogamy of male subjects.

Irigaray perceives the female imaginary—that is, autonomous female sexuality and subjectivity—as coming from outside of male hom-(m)osexuality and heterosexual pleasure: female autoeroticism and lesbianism. Even though one can read the prostitute, in Irigaray's text, as an active exchange partner in the male exchange economy and as a speaking subject, she cannot be read as sexually autonomous in the way that the lesbian and female masturbator who avoid contact with males are. One can read Irigaray as leaving a space for the prostitute as speaking subject; this space, however, is delimited by the contours of the masculine discourse it occupies. It is Gayle Rubin's construction of prostitution as a sexuality and prostitute as a sexual identity that provides the theoretical basis for extending this space beyond male discourse into prostitute space.

The polyvocal subjectivities and polysexualities of Irigaray's feminism of difference are really limited to those women who construct their sexuality outside the male exchange economy. Irigaray's multiple voices and sexualities fall inside of what Rubin, whom I have dubbed a "radical sexual pluralist postmodern feminist," marks as the (lesbian) "charmed circle" of sexuality.

Radical Sexual Pluralism: Pervert (Prostitute) Space

Gayle Rubin, one of the best-known contributors to "the sex debates" which have since the mid-1980s redefined the terrain of North American feminism, is a theorist of marginality; she theorizes a space for minority sexual subjects such as prostitutes. Her article "Thinking Sex: Notes for a Radical Theory of the Politics of Sexuality" is a central theoretical text in *Pleasure and Danger: Exploring Female Sexuality*. *Pleasure and Danger* consists of conference papers from the 1982 Barnard "Scholar and Feminist" conference at which feminisms of difference, by providing alternative mappings of female sexuality, contested the radical feminist terrain of Catharine MacKinnon and Andrea Dworkin. Since this conference, prostitutes have theorized their sexual space speaking as feminists and as sex workers.

In "Thinking Sex" Rubin borrows from the discourses of sexology, gay liberation, and social construction theory to develop a radical pluralist theory of sexuality; she articulates these discourses with a critique of radical feminism. I read Rubin as a postmodern feminist theorist: she opens theoretical space for a multiplicity of sexual voices; she appropriates various elements of opposing ideologies and incorporates them into a new theory. Through a pluralism of theory, with no one privileged site, she constructs a space for difference(s). What makes Rubin's theory pluralist is the articulation of a number of contradictory discourses; what distinguishes it as "radical pluralist" is that she writes from the subject position of those sexually marginalized: those marked by hegemonic and counter-hegemonic discourses as sexual deviants—"perverts." It is in this context that Rubin writes the prostitute body.

Central to Rubin's theorization is the development of a pluralist sexual ethics which holds that no noncoercive sexual act, sexual identity, sexual community, or sexual object choice is morally or medically privileged over others as closer to some sexual ideal. Theoretical systems that have defined and delimited sexuality, such as religion, psychology, and feminism, have all privileged a single sexual standard: "For religion, the ideal is procreative marriage. For psychology, it is mature heterosexuality."[87] For radical feminism it is "monogamous lesbianism that occurs within long-term intimate relationships."[88] Rubin appropriates "a positive concept of sexual variation" from sexological discourse as a foundation for a pluralist sexual ethics: "sexology and sex research . . . treat sexual variety as something that exists rather than something to be exterminated."[89] She integrates this concept of sexual variation with social construction theory which rejects transhistorical and transcultural definitions of sexuality premised on some idea of sexuality as a "natural force." According to constructionist theory, physically identical sexual acts have a different social significance and subjective meaning depending upon their cultural and historical context. Rubin cites Michel Foucault's *The History of Sexuality*, Jeffrey Week's work on gay history, and Judith Walkowitz's research on nineteenth-century prostitution as examples of constructionist scholarship on sex.

Rubin uses two metaphorical representations, the erotic pyramid and the charmed circle, to depict the stratification of sexual populations and sexual practices according to a hierarchical system of sexual value that structures modern Western society:

Marital, reproductive heterosexuals are alone at the top of the erotic pyramid . . . below are unmarried monogamous heterosexuals in couples, followed by most other heterosexuals. Solitary sex floats ambiguously. . . . Stable, long-term lesbian and gay male couples are verging

on respectability, but bar dykes and promiscuous gay men are hover-
ing just above the groups at the very bottom of the pyramid. The most
despised sexual castes currently include transsexuals, tranvestites, fe-
tishists, sadomasochists, sex workers . . . and the lowest of all, those
whose eroticism transgresses generational boundaries.[90]

The sexual value system dichotomizes sex into good and bad, normal
and abnormal, natural and unnatural. "Good," "normal," "natural"
sexuality falls inside the charmed circle; other sexuality is at the outer
limits of this circle:

> According to this system, sexuality that is "good," "normal" and
> "natural" should really be heterosexual, marital, monogamous, repro-
> ductive, and non-commercial. It should be coupled, relational, within
> the same generation, and occur at home. . . . Any sex that violates
> these rules is "bad," "abnormal," or "unnatural." Bad sex may be
> homosexual, unmarried, promiscuous, non-procreative, or commer-
> cial.[91]

Rubin compares the dominant sexual morality, the heterophallic
morality, to ethnocentrism: "This kind of sexual morality has more
in common with ideologies of racism than with true ethics. It grants
virtue to the dominant groups, and relegates vice to the underprivi-
leged."[92] A pluralist sexual ethics based on a democratic morality, pro-
poses Rubin, should assess particular sexual acts by

> the way partners treat one another, the level of mutual consideration,
> the presence or absence of coercion, and the quantity and quality of
> the pleasure they provide.[93]

Rubin is attempting to set forth a democratic morality that doesn't
privilege one site of sexuality. She could be read as privileging the
sexualities disprivileged in the hegemonic construct, except that hers
is not a prescriptive theory: Rubin is opening social space for those
who have been relegated to the outer limits of the charmed circle of
sex. What is crucial about Rubin is that she does not privilege one
form of sexuality over another:

> It is just as objectionable to insist that everyone should be lesbian,
> non-monogamous, or kinky, as to believe that everyone should be
> heterosexual, married, or vanilla—though the latter set of opinions
> are backed by considerably more coercive power than the former.[94]

For Rubin, a prostitute and client, engaging in commercial sex, who
treat one another with respect and dignity, are just as ethical as a
monogamous lesbian couple, engaging in noncommercial sex, who

treat one another with respect and dignity. Two factors have made the latter appear as a more ethical sexual exchange than the former. One is the deep-seated belief which I pinpointed in relation to Pateman's privileging of the marriage contract over the prostitution contract that sexual exchange which takes place in the context of love, commitment, and some form of responsibility through time is necessarily more ethical than sexual exchange that is anonymous and perhaps limited to a single encounter. Once one steps over what Rubin diagrams as a (shifting) "imaginary line between good and bad sex,"[95] this moral judgment is exposed as one among other possible moral judgments. The second factor is that the sexual exchange between a prostitute and client is, in the majority of cases, a heterosexual exchange. Heterosexual exchanges have more potential to reflect and reproduce the gender inequalities of the social structure. Rubin stresses that the sex industry reflects the sexism of the society as a whole. She stresses the need to "analyze and oppose the manifestations of gender inequality specific to the sex industry without attempting to wipe out commercial sex."[96] A radical pluralist theory of sexuality does not preclude critiques of gender oppression in both dominant and marginal forms of heterosexuality or analyses of the relationship among consent, desire, and power in a sexist, racist, and classist society. Radical pluralist is not the same as a liberal pluralist position that posits all individuals as equal regardless of socio-structural inequalities.

What is especially interesting in Rubin's theorization of prostitution is her production of the prostitute as a sexual/political identity. Rubin writes the prostitute as a sexual minority like the homosexual and prostitution as a dissident sexuality like homosexuality. Drawing upon Judith Walkowitz's study *Prostitution and Victorian Society*, Rubin documents the transformation of prostitution from a temporary job to a permanent occupation through legal reform and police persecution. It is from this constructed position as an outcast group that prostitutes began to construct their own identity. Rubin points out that this is the same process of identity formation that produced the modern homosexual, and that bisexuals, sadomasochists, transsexuals, et al. are attempting to imitate. In modernity, the state and the medical profession have codified what were previously merely sexual behaviors as identifiable and persecutable sexual minorities. Stigmatized sexual populations develop their identity through collective resistance to the dominant constructions.

Rubin distinguishes between prostitutes and other sexual minorities: "Sex work is an occupation, while sexual deviation is an erotic preference."[97] Prostitutes, as sexual minorities, however, share many common features with homosexuals: (1) "Like homosexuals, prostitutes are a criminal sexual population stigmatized on the basis of sexual activity"; (2) "prostitutes and male homosexuals are the primary prey of vice police"; (3) "like gay men, prostitutes occupy well-demarcated urban territories and battle with police to defend and maintain those territories"; and (4) "the legal persecution of both populations is justified by an elaborate ideology which classifies them as dangerous and inferior undesirables."[98] Rubin, beyond identifying prostitution as an occupation, doesn't further theorize prostitution as work. However, she does provide a critique of what society does to sex work and the sex worker through criminalization and stigmatization:

> The underlying criminality of sex-oriented business keeps it marginal, underdeveloped, and distorted. . . . It . . . renders sex workers . . . vulnerable to exploitation and bad working conditions. If sex commerce were legal, sex workers would be more able to organize and agitate for higher pay, better conditions, greater control, and less stigma.[99]

The system of sexual hierarchy and what Rubin calls the "ideologies of erotic inferiority"[100] produce the sex worker as "powerless" and make her work "dangerous."

Rubin challenges feminism as the privileged site of a theory of sexuality. This challenge, directed specifically at MacKinnonite radical feminism, has two main points. First, sexual dissidents have historically fared poorly in feminist theory and continue to be targeted as sources of oppression to women:

> A good deal of current feminist literature attributes the oppression of women to graphic representations of sex, prostitution . . . sadomasochism, male homosexuality and transsexualism.[101]

Rubin counterposes dominant sites of oppression which hold much more weight than these targeted sexualities: She queries "[w]hatever happened to the family, religion, education, childrearing practices, the media, the state, psychiatry, job discrimination, and unequal pay?"[102] Second, feminism conflates sex and gender into a unitary theory of oppression. Retracting her own 1975 construction of the "sex-gender" system which fits closely with MacKinnon's theorization of sexuality as producing gender, Rubin argues that gender and sexuality are socially distinct. She writes: "In contrast to my perspective in 'The Traffic in Women,' I am now arguing that it is essential to separate gender and sexuality analytically to more accurately reflect their separate social existence."[103]

Rubin is calling for a theory of sexuality which can incorporate feminism's critique of gender hierarchy into a theorization of sexual hierarchy. The reason she is doing so is that feminist critiques of gender relations often distort and obscure much of the sexual difference among women. The concept of radical sexual pluralism opens a space for those sexual others, those at the bottom of the erotic pyramid, those outside the charmed circle of "good" sex, to write their own bodies and produce their own discourses.

Conclusion

Feminists as diverse as Carole Pateman, Catharine MacKinnon, and Luce Irigaray reproduce the prostitute body in the inverse terms of the hegemonic discourses they are criticizing. Pateman, accepting the dichotomization of women into wives and prostitutes, sets out to prove that both are manifestations of male sex right while presupposing the absolute inferiority of the prostitute's position vis-à-vis that of the wife. What Pateman, in effect, does in reading the sexual contract as the underside of the social contract is to disadvantage the prostitution contract and privilege the marriage contract. MacKinnon makes the negative side of the female couple madonna/whore a pivotal concept in her analysis of woman's condition; she then reproduces the whore as woman's fundamental position in masculinist societies. Irigaray opens a space in her deconstruction of Western philosophy for the prostitute to speak, but only in the context of prostitution as work: she can name her price, she can take herself to market. This opening is a noticeable paradox in a theorization which claims that women are commodities used and exchanged by men. Rubin, with her concept of radical sexual pluralism, opens a space for prostitutes not only to speak within other discourses, such as the masculine exchange economy entered by Irigaray's prostitute and mainstream feminist discourse, but to fashion their own discourse. It is precisely Rubin's view, developed by way of social construction theory, of prostitution as not just sex work but also as a sexual/political identity that distinguishes the radical sexual pluralist position from liberalism and Marxism.

Prostitute discourse itself is a contested terrain, as the following chapter will convey. The division between prostitutes' rights advocates and WHISPER advocates is a reproduction of the division in the sex debates between radical sexual pluralism and radical feminism, this time from the position of those othered in feminist discourse. Prostitutes' rights discourse borrows from the liberal and Marxist constructions of the prostitute body redefined in the context of radical sexual pluralism. WHISPER is closely affiliated with radical feminism. A third discourse, that of Prostitutes Anonymous, which can be articulated with either of these dominant groups, is a reappropriation and empowerment of the "diseased" prostitute body from the prostitute subject position.

5

REWRITING THE PROSTITUTE BODY
Prostitute Perspectives

In postmodernity, the prostitute has emerged simultaneously as a new political subject and as a plural, rather than a unitary, subject. The prostitute subject position, like any other, is inevitably nuanced. Specific experiences in prostitution have given rise to different and contested constructions of the prostitute body: a site of work, a site of abuse, power, sex, addiction, and even pleasure. The prostitute struggle is a pluralistic struggle with overlappings, antagonisms, distinctions, and ruptures among its three constituting discourses: those of prostitutes' rights, WHISPER (Women Hurt in Systems of Prostitution Engaged in Revolt), and Prostitutes Anonymous.

At the heart of prostitute discourse is a dichotomization of the prostitute body in terms of empowerment/victimization. Incompatible though these two alternative understandings of prostitution might seem to be, all three constituting discourses concur that prostitution as it exists is problematic. What fundamentally distinguishes prostitutes' rights groups from WHISPER and Prostitutes Anonymous is that the rights groups focus on the project of constituting the prostitute as a new political subject on the boundary between sex and work and on transforming the identity of the prostitute inherited from modernity. The rights groups are especially interested in the enactment of changes in the judicial-political order. WHISPER and Prostitutes Anonymous identify prostitution with the negative aspects of its construction in modernity. WHISPER calls for the abolition of prostitution; Prostitutes Anonymous, framing prostitution as an "addiction," encourages its members to leave the life. Prostitutes' rights groups are concerned about the empowerment of the prostitute in the context of a patriarchal and capitalist society; WHISPER contends that the prostitute can never be empowered until she ceases to be a prostitute. Prostitutes Anonymous is concerned about prostitution only insofar as it has become an addiction-type problem for the individual prostitute. Each of the constituting discourses has divergent places of origin. Prostitutes' rights have their roots in the tradition of liberalism recontextualized within the new radical pluralism. WHISPER's discourse can be traced through the formulations of Josephine Butler and the Ladies National Association to MacKinnon/Dworkin and antipornography radical feminism. Prostitutes Anonymous is a response to the psychiatrization of "the prostitute" which constructed prostitution as sickness and "sexual addiction."

That prostitutes, hitherto marginalized and stigmatized and/or excluded in hegemonic and feminist discourses, are now producing their own discourse is a manifestation of postmodernity. Only prostitutes' rights, however, approximate a postmodern discourse; WHISPER presents a modernist discourse which claims to possess the "true" way of viewing prostitution; Prostitutes Anonymous lays claim to an ideologically neutral or positionless discourse.

This chapter is constructed around the following argument: All three prostitute discourses are reverse discourses; that is, they counter the hegemonic discourse on prostitution. Prostitutes' rights discourse, however, goes beyond that to displace the hegemonic inscriptions on the prostitute body through the production of new meanings; the prostitute is constructed as healer rather than disease producer, as educator rather than degenerate, as sex expert rather than deviant, as business woman rather than commercial object. Prostitutes' rights discourse, by appropriating the rights discourse of hegemonic and feminist liberalism and articulating these rights demands in the context of collective identity politics, transgresses the liberal framework while adhering to it. Identity politics is based on "the active affirmation of the experiences, dignity, and rights of historically marginalized or excluded people,"[1] going beyond the conventional liberal construction of all human beings as essentially "the same" and therefore entitled to the same (abstract) rights.

Michel Foucault came close to contending that the adoption of rights language by those whose identities were first constructed as the others of bourgeois rights discourse, such as prisoners and homosexuals, is "a reinscription of the 'same' term toward a new possibility."[2] It is a radical rewriting of the concept of rights and an undoing of the original discourse from a position of difference. Foucault questions: "When today one wants to object in some way to the disciplines and all the effects of power and knowledge that are linked to them, what is it that one does, concretely, in real life, . . . if not precisely appeal to this canon of right[?]"[3] This demand for rights from the position of the subjugated other constitutes a "turn . . . towards the possibility of a new form of right."[4] These are not classical rights—the right of the sovereign, the right of the universal selfsame bourgeois individual; they are the rights of difference which function to undermine the judicial-political order rather than sustain it.

When prostitutes call for the extension of individual and human rights to themselves, they are calling for the extension of rights to an other that the original and subsequent rights discourses were constructed to exclude. Prostitutes' rights activists use the philo/legal instrument of domination: rights; they negotiate in the language of the dominant discourse; yet the language of rights takes on a strange kind of rhetoricity when it is spoken not only from the position of other but from the position of the other of the other.

"Woman" is the primary signifier of the other in liberal rights theory. As I contend in my introduction, those who have been produced as other become sites of presence further down the historical road. As suggested in the preceding two chapters, feminist discourse since the eighteenth century has consistently reproduced prostitutes in the position of female other. Mary Wollstonecraft, in *A Vindication of the Rights of Women* (1792), argued for the extension of human rights to (middle-class) women; in so doing, she produced an other within the universal category "woman": "unfortunate females"—prostitutes— whom she refers to as "poor wretch[es]."[5] The proceedings from the Second World Whores' Congress are published under the title *A Vindication of the Rights of Whores*. In her essay "Not Repeating History," editor Gail Pheterson writes: "two hundred years later. . . whores are standing publicly with their sisters and demanding inclusion in the Vindication of the Rights of Women."[6] Prostitutes, "the other of the other," are now present as new political subjects.

Prostitutes' collective public demand for the legal right to be recognized as citizens just like all others is not a demand for equality in spite of difference but a demand for equality based on the distinct difference of being a prostitute. What lies just beneath the surface of the demand for legal rights and equality is a doubly transgressive ethical gesture: an affirmation of a "negative" identity and a revaluation of values through the recognition of commercial sex as being just as valid and worthy as noncommercial sex.

WHISPER situates itself in the position of countering prostitutes' rights discourse from the position of radical feminism. It reproduces the meanings that radical feminism inscribes on the prostitute body: as such, it is a simple reversal of the hegemonic discourse. WHISPER counters the meanings produced in the dominant discourse, but, like radical feminism, it cannot transgress and displace the dominant discourse; it reproduces the prostitute as victim but seeks to empower her by liberating her from her prostitute identity.

Resistance is inherent in any constituting discourse. Counter-discourses are formed when those identified as other begin to speak on their own behalf, to represent themselves, and thus to provide alternative mappings of their subject position and their specific territory in the social field. The shape of the other is determined, in large degree, by the shape of the dominant discourse. The dominant form of resistance is usually manifest as counter-identification whereby the other rejects and inverts in some way the identity constructed by the dominant discourse; yet it never goes beyond that to transgression, displacement, and dis-identification. I will attempt to show that, whereas WHISPER discourse manifests counter-identification, prostitutes' rights discourse involves dis-identification.

After briefly sketching the postmodern understanding of the subject, outlining Ernesto Laclau and Chantal Mouffe's theorization of new political struggles and new political subjects, and applying Laclau and Mouffe's theory to tracing the emergence of the new prostitute subject and prostitutes' struggle, this chapter will examine prostitutes' rights discourse followed by WHISPER as its counter-discourse. Prostitutes Anonymous will be discussed last as it is a nonideological discourse that can be articulated with either rights groups or WHISPER, as is concretely indicated by the divergent ideological positions of its two founders.

The Prostitute as a New Political Subject

Much postmodern theory presents the subject as an entity that is constituted by discourses, in direct refutation of the Enlightenment conception of the subject as a constituting entity. But at a secondary level, one level removed from the (de)totalized "grand" (non-)scheme of postmodern epistemology, there is space for new social agency; the agency of a multiplicity of subjects. Postmodernism is based on a theoretical pluralism that facilitates the expansion of social ontology to include the "redefinition and redescription of experience from the perspective of those who are more often simply objects of theory."[7] Postmodern pluralism indicates both a pluralism of subjectivities within each individual subject and a pluralism of different subjects within any collective subject position. Postmodernist pluralism is a pluralism of difference in contradistinction to the modernist liberal pluralism of sameness or similarity whose explicit aim has been to reduce or unify the difference of "the many" into "the one." For example, a modernist discourse such as Marxism constructed the prostitute as a worker, the same as any other worker, and also the worker as a prostitute: reducing both the prostitute and the worker to a singular position determined by the capitalist market, the position of the human commodity. A postmodern discourse, prostitutes' rights, present the prostitute as worker, healer, sexual surrogate, teacher, therapist, educator, sexual minority, and political activist.[8] Inside the constructions of worker and sexual minority operates the tension between empowerment and victimization; constructions such as healer, sexual surrogate, teacher, and therapist are employed as empowering characterizations to destabilize the traditional negative representations of the prostitute.

Ernesto Laclau and Chantal Mouffe's theorization of new democratic struggles and new political subjects provides the framework for understanding the emergence of the prostitutes' movement in the late 1970s/early 1980s. Laclau and Mouffe coin the term "new democratic struggles" for what many other social and political theorists refer to as new social movements. They do so for an important theoretical reason: what is occurring is the extension of the democratic revolution to previously occluded forms of subordination and subjugation. The political is expanded to include new subjectivities. The democratic revolution began with the nineteenth-century demand for equality by the propertyless white male. Democratic discourse has extended its field of influence from the political equality of citizens into other social fields and social relations: the sexual, the racial, the cultural. Laclau and Mouffe call this the "extension of egalitarian equivalences":[9] chains of equivalences extend from a particular struggle with specific demands to other struggles with other demands. Prostitutes' demand for rights is part of the radical democratic struggle for the extension of equality to more and more areas of the social terrain. Chantal Mouffe argues that

The new rights that are being claimed today are the expression of differences ... they are no longer rights that can be universalized. Radical democracy demands that we acknowledge difference— ... the particular, the multiple, the heterogeneous—everything that has been excluded by the concept of Man in the abstract.[10]

Prostitutes began to engage in what Laclau and Mouffe term "democratic struggle" in the 1970s when prostitutes in various localities organized against police harassment and for the decriminalization of prostitution. The French prostitutes' strike in 1975 (International Women's Year) was the local event which generated international energy for the prostitutes' rights struggle. Rights activist Tracy Quan refers to the French prostitutes' strike as "our Stonewall"[11]—the event which, like the gay struggle at Stonewall, sparked off protest and political demands that previously had been unspeakable: the right of prostitutes to exercise control over their bodies and the right of prostitutes to set their conditions of work. Local groups coalesced into an international movement in the 1980s with the formation of the International Committee for Prostitute Rights (ICPR) in 1985; two World Whores' Congresses, the second of which united first and third world women, have been held. A World Whores' Summit took place in San Francisco in 1989. The prostitute rights struggle is a First World and Third World coalition forging links "from Bangkok to the Netherlands to Brazil to New York and points beyond."[12]

The prostitute struggle emerged at the intersection of the women's struggle and the lesbian/gay struggle; both these had their inception in the new left and civil rights struggles. Once the principle of equality is admitted in one domain and encompasses one group of people, the eventual questioning of other and related forms of inequality tends to ensue, according to Mouffe and Laclau.

First-wave feminism demanded political equality first and foremost; second-wave feminism, of the late sixties and early seventies, at first focused on economic equality; soon this was extended to equality in the domain of sexuality. For the past twenty years much of feminist discourse has been articulated around the right to control one's own body, through critique of sexual harassment, abuse, rape, incest, and the criminalization of abortion. At the heart of this critique has been a problematization of compulsory heterosexuality. The lesbian/gay struggle has brought to the forefront the equal right of sexual minorities to sexual pleasure and to the same level of social recognition and benefits enjoyed by the dominant groups.

The hegemonic discourse—heterophallic liberal capitalism—continues to construct prostitutes in subordination as it has done since its inception in the eighteenth and nineteenth centuries. Only in the latter part of the twentieth century, due to the women's movement's discourse which combines "control of one's body" with economic demands such as equal pay for equal work, could prostitutes interpellate themselves as women concerned about the right to control their bodies and women who have work demands. The feminist demand for reproductive rights is extended by the prostitutes' rights struggle to encompass "all of the things a woman might choose to do with her genitals, including . . . lesbianism and commercial sex."[13] The lesbian and gay movement demanded equal rights for sexual minorities: prostitutes' rights advocates started to view themselves as a sexual minority who engage in a form of sexuality as work; they also redefined "the prostitute" as a sexual identity. At the same time as prostitutes were interpellated as equals by feminist and gay/lesbian discourses, the state stepped up its harassment and arrest of women working as prostitutes. The transcripts of the Second World Whores' Congress confirm that "personal experience of state abuse is usually the catalyst for political action among prostitutes."[14] For instance, both Peggy Miller, who founded the Canadian Organization for Prostitutes' Rights (CORP), and Margo St. James, who founded the American rights organization Call Off Your Old Tired Ethics (COYOTE), did so after being arrested on prostitution charges. Gloria Lockett, former co-director of COYOTE, came to COYOTE when she was charged with "pimping," "pandering," soliciting, "running a house of prostitution," and "being in a house of prostitution."[15] These two historical processes, the first of which involves the extension of democratic equivalence to prostitute women, and the second of which arbitrarily refused women's right to work as prostitutes, mobilized prostitutes as political subjects. It is the contradiction between the extension of democratic equivalence and the state's campaign against prostitutes that produced the prostitute as a new political subject.

A third contradiction which arose in the early 1980s within the women's movement—the antipornography struggle—contributed to the interpellation and crystallization of prostitute subjects into two distinct prostitute subject positions: prostitute rights activists, who view prostitution as sexual activity and as work and produce the prostitute as an identity, and WHISPER activists, who view prostitution as sexual abuse, an institution of male dominance and power, and construct the prostitute as a non-identity. Both positions evolve out of the right of women to control their own bodies.

The prostitute struggle is part of the radical pluralist democratic struggle that has as its basis the equality of difference. There is a chain of equivalence connecting the prostitutes' struggle for control over their bodies to all women's struggle for the right to control their bodies. PONY (Prostitutes of New York) states as part of its mandate:

> In response to the current attack on a woman's right to safe, legal abortion, PONY seeks to defend and extend every woman's sexual freedom. Whether we have sex for reproduction, recreation or remuneration is our personal business, not the government's.[16]

Both the prostitutes' rights movement and WHISPER engage in coalition politics, forming alliances with different segments of the women's movement. The prostitutes' rights movement has formed a strong alliance with the lesbian and gay struggle on the issue of AIDS prevention, since prostitutes and gay men are the two most scapegoated categories for AIDS. WHISPER, as part of the feminist struggle against sexual abuse, is a member of the National Coalition against Sexual Assault in the United States.

The Prostitutes' Rights Struggle

The prostitutes' rights movement, international in structure and membership, is by far the largest of the three prostitute organizations. ICPR describes itself and the prostitutes' rights struggle as an "international grass roots movement."[17] Membership in the prostitutes' rights struggle is open to all, but leadership is in the hands of sex workers. Gail Pheterson, the editor of *A Vindication of the Rights of Whores*, says that it is "unprecedented for prostitutes to speak on their own behalf and on the behalf of other oppressed people."[18] The prostitutes' struggle is linked to the struggle of all oppressed people. Pheterson stresses that "there are no models for a prostitution politics from the perspective of prostitutes."[19] Josephine Butler's struggle against the Contagious Diseases Acts was on behalf of prostitutes; the Ladies National Association encouraged prostitutes to resist arrest and examination, but never included prostitutes as political spokespersons who spoke from the subject position of prostitute. Pheterson continues: "The movement for prostitutes' rights is forging a new politics of prostitution."[20] What is unique about this "new politics" is the "self-representation of whores and alliances between women."[21]

In discussing the prostitutes' rights struggle I will use documents from the following organizations: ICPR; the National Task Force on Prostitution (NTFP), the United States umbrella organization for prostitutes' rights groups; COYOTE; PONY; and CORP.[22] The texts on prostitutes' rights include transcripts from the Second World Whores' Congress, published as *A Vindication of the Rights of Whores*; transcripts from a conference entitled "Challenging Our Images: The Politics of Prostitution and Pornography" (published as *Good Girls/Bad Girls: Feminists and Sex Trade Workers Face to Face*); films by prostitute activist and filmmaker Scarlot Harlot; and interviews with prostitutes' rights activists in San Francisco (COYOTE), New York (PONY), and Toronto (CORP). Because the movement is both an international and a grass-roots struggle, I use the local texts to intercut the international text.

The North American rights activists evince a wide spectrum of characteristics: all of those I interviewed were women (there are male activist prostitutes whom I did not interview); the women were white and black, from working class and middle class backgrounds, both university and non-university educated, lesbian, bisexual, and heterosexual in their noncommercial sexual orientation. They were between the ages of twenty-nine and forty-five and have worked as street prostitutes, call girls, brothel prostitutes, S/M fantasy facilitators, porn stars, phone sex workers, strippers, and sex writers. Often one person has engaged in a number of these types of prostitution over time or is engaging in a number of these activities at present.

The format for this section will be to outline how the prostitutes' rights movement constructs the prostitute as an identity, its location of prostitution as situated on a sliding boundary between work and sex, the movement's appropriation of liberal rights discourse, its relationship to feminism and its role in the feminist struggle, and the role prostitutes' rights activists play as sexual-health teachers.

Prostitute as a Sexual Identity: Prostitution as Sex and Work

Rather than disassociate from the label "whore," which, through nineteenth-century sexual categorization and definition, came to mean "unchaste," "defiled," and "diseased," prostitutes' rights advocates reclaim the word, giving it a positive meaning and demanding rights as whores.

How do prostitutes define "whore" and the whore identity? COY-
OTE founder and co-director of ICPR Margo St. James said in a talk
she gave at the 1985 Toronto conference, "Challenging Our Images:
The Politics of Prostitution and Pornography": "I prefer the word 'whore'
[rather than 'prostitute']. . . . I want to reclaim it like lesbians have
reclaimed the word 'dyke' over the last decade."[23] In her introduction
to *A Vindication of the Rights of Whores* Gail Pheterson, co-director
of ICPR, provides this definition of "whore":

> The whore label is attached to anyone who works or has worked in
> the sex industry as . . . a provider of sexual service or entertainment.
> The whore as prostitute or sex worker is the prototype of the stigma-
> tized woman or feminized man. But not only prostitutes are labelled
> whores. Any woman may be designated "whore" within a particular
> cultural setting, especially if she is a migrant, target of racist dis-
> crimination, independent worker or victim of abuse.[24]

Thus the prostitutes' rights struggle links itself along a chain of equivalences with all stigmatized women and men. An important reason
that "prostitute" was chosen over "sex worker" as the signifier of
identity is that "[w]ithin the sex industry, the prostitute is the most
explicitly oppressed by legal and social controls";[25] others, such as
pornography models, strippers, and call girls, often disassociate from
the label "prostitute" to raise their status. The ICPR identifies all
women who sell sexual services of any kind as prostitutes, as well as
non-prostitute women who have been marked as "whore" due to their
sexual assertiveness. ICPR states: "In general, a whore-madonna division is imposed upon women wherein those who are sexually assertive
are considered whores and those who are sexually passive are considered madonnas."[26]

PONY, as part of its statement of purpose, defines sex workers as
"sexual professionals," sex as "an essential, nourishing part of life,"
and commercial sex as "of benefit to humanity."[27] PONY spokesperson Veronica Vera, in an interview with me, elaborated PONY philosophy on sex and prostitution:

> [S]ex is a nourishing, life-giving force and as a consequence sex work
> is of benefit to humanity. . . . [S]ex workers are providing a very valu-
> able service to be honored. Sex work . . . is a good service, it is the best
> service that one individual can do for another individual.[28]

Linking sex, knowledge, and power, Vera categorizes sex workers as
"the new sex experts."[29] The strategic positioning of sex workers as

"sex experts" moves prostitutes from being the objects of scientific discourse to being the owners and producers of sexual knowledge. PONY, drawing upon its ancient sacred lineage, redefines sex work as "a sacred craft" and sex workers as engaging in "an empowering act." Vera says:

> By affirming sex as a nourishing, healing tool, by being tolerant of one another's sexual needs, by affirming sex workers as practitioners of a sacred craft, we accept and affirm our own humanity, an empowering act.[30]

CORP activists publicly politicize the positive identity of whore, producing buttons, pamplets, posters, and banners which read "whorepower," "whores are safe sex pros," "proud to be a whore," and "I'm a safe sex pro."

Tracy Quan, PONY activist, said in an interview in *Vox* magazine: "To embrace the identity of prostitute is to embrace a multitude of contradictions."[31] For Quan being a prostitute means:

> [L]ooking honestly at others and maintaining a sense of humor, remaining sexy and human in the face of other people's prejudices, wanting to be the best at what I do for a living.[32]

PONY activist Annie Sprinkle cautions against giving any one meaning to prostitution or any "true" definition to being a prostitute:

> [A]s a prostitute I did feel used and really treated like shit, really taken advantage of. There were times when I was in total power. There were times when I received a lot. There were times when it was wonderful. I got in it for the money. But I also got in because I needed to be touched. I wanted the attention. I wanted the status. There are so many reasons. The problem is that everyone is always trying to simplify it.[33]

Sprinkle continues: "There are a lot of different ways prostitutes feel about their work."[34] For her it was both painful and pleasurable:

> Dealing with people's anger, greed, fear, judgements, prejudices and neediness could be painful. . . . There were guys who managed to manipulate me into doing things they knew I really didn't want to do. . . . There were guys that ripped me off for the money I had earned. . . . Many were disrespectful and unappreciative.[35]

> Prostitution can also be a wonderful, satisfying job. I got pleasure in making people feel better. . . . I was really giving to people and nurturing and teaching. . . . I got off sexually. . . . I had orgasms when I worked, not with all the guys. . . . Sometimes I would do it to have

sex, like with Samuel. . . . I like having sex with him. He has been my client for sixteen years. It is my longest relationship.[36]

Rights activists are careful to hold the tension between the positive and negative aspects of prostitution so that prostitution never completely becomes one or the other. They are also careful to situate the negative aspects of prostitution in the context of the broader sex-negative society. Veronica Vera makes a distinction between sex work and the negativity that has come to be associated with it:

> Sex work . . . is a great service that is couched in all sorts of negative stuff. The "bad" part is the negative stuff that we put on it: from the client's feeling of sexual guilt to bad laws and cops harassing women on the street.[37]

Rights activists in a strategic political move define prostitution as an activity midway between sex and work: perhaps the best example of this is Annie's public claim that although she really likes her long-term client of sixteen years, and she enjoys having sex with him, she would not do it if he was not paying her.[38] Valerie Scott, spokesperson for CORP, makes a distinction between sex for work and sex for fun: "both are sexual activities. The main difference is that in the context of sex for fun you are usually having sex with someone you really desire; in the context of sex as work you may desire the client but most times you don't, especially if your sexual orientation isn't white middle-aged heterosexual guys. If it is and you are working as a whore then there can be a lot of pleasure in the work."[39]

While holding that prostitution is a sexual activity, rights groups center on the work side of the sex work construction in order to undermine the negativity associated with prostitution. This is a strategic emphasis: as a political movement rights organizations are more likely to have an impact on government policies and social attitudes if they focus on the work aspect of prostitution, rather than try to legitimate it as sexual activity (although their discourse shifts into the latter legitimation). In its *Statement on Prostitution and Feminism* at the Second World Whores' Congress, ICPR identifies the sale of sex as an act of "sexual self determination"[40] and links "the right to offer sex for money" to a chain of rights equivalences which include "the right to refuse sex and to initiate sex, . . . the right to use birth control (including abortion), the right to have lesbian sex, the right to have sex across lines of color and class, the right to engage in sado-masochistic sex."[41]

Much feminist and, particularly, WHISPER criticism of the prostitutes' rights discourse is premised on the belief that prostitution cannot be voluntary in a racist, sexist, capitalist, patriarchal social field. The ICPR takes this criticism strongly into account in its validation of prostitution as work whether it is voluntary or necessary. Prostitutes' rights groups do not claim that prostitution is a free choice; they claim that it is as free a choice as other choices made in a capitalist, patriarchal, and racist system. They recognize the differences among types of prostitution and the interconnections among racism, capitalism, and patriarchy in which, of the 10 to 20 percent of prostitutes who are street workers, 40 percent are women of color; 55 percent of women arrested are women of color; and 85 percent of prostitutes in jail are women of color.[42] Prostitutes' rights discourse does not deny that economic and sexual inequalities are causes of prostitution:

> Prostitution exists, at least in part, because of the subordination of women in most societies. This subordination is reflected in the double standard of sexual behavior for men and women, and is carried out in the discrepancy between women's and men's earning power, which results in women in the United States earning sixty-seven cents for every dollar men earn, and even less in most other countries.[43]

CORP leaders Valerie Scott, Ryan Hotchkiss, and Peggy Miller say in a collective interview, "Realistic Feminists," that

> No one should have to do anything they don't want for a living, but that's not a reality in life. Most of us end up taking jobs where there are certain compromises made. . . . We don't think any woman should have to make the choice to work as a prostitute any more than any woman should be forced to work in a factory or forced to be a lawyer or a doctor, for that matter.[44]

Although rights discourse contextualizes prostitution as being symptomatic of women's oppression in society, it does not offer any critique and/or analysis of the structural basis which produces gender, class, and race inequalities. Nor can it. A discourse premised on the extension of basic human and civil rights, as radical as the demand may be, as far as it may go in changing the identity and status of the claimant group and even in undoing the traditional concept of rights, can only act as an intervention. It is an act of micropolitics concerned with its specific struggle, with forming alliances with other related struggles, and not with a change in any totality.

Drawing upon the liberal contractarian depiction of prostitution as labor, prostitutes' rights discourse depicts prostitutes either as self-employed or working for a third party and prostitution as a small business. Prostitutes' rights groups demand that prostitution be subject to the same laws as other small businesses and prostitutes to the same laws as other entrepreneurs and workers. This equation of prostitution with business and prostitutes with entrepreneurs or independent workers underlies the demands of the *World Charter for Prostitutes' Rights*.

Prostitutes' Rights: An Appropriation of Rights Discourse

The *World Charter for Prostitutes' Rights*, drafted at the First World Whores' Congress in 1985, encodes the same rights for prostitutes as for any other citizen. Rights can be divided into three types: moral, legal, and human. A moral right is the right to have something done or not done by another; a legal right is a right recognized by law; human rights are rights an individual has because she or he is a human being. These three types are not exclusionary. A human right "is a moral right in the sense that it expresses a moral requirement which may or may not be embodied in law. . . . [H]uman rights have legal pretensions: they address moral issues of political significance and their advocates seek the recognition of human rights in the laws of society."[45] Human rights are publicly declared and have a semiofficial status without being legally enforceable; for example, the rights set out by the *United Nations Charter* and the *European Convention on Human Rights* are not legally enforceable.

Prostitutes' demands for legal and human rights are based on the moral claim that prostitutes deserve to have the same rights as all other human beings. Their *Charter* calls for the extension to prostitutes of

> all human rights and collective civil liberties, including the freedom of speech, travel, immigration, work, marriage and motherhood and the right to employment insurance, health insurance and housing.[46]

Their *Statement on Prostitution and Human Rights* demands that "prostitutes be redefined as legitimate citizens" and that "prostitution be redefined as legitimate work."[47] *The Statement on Prostitution and Human Rights* drafted and endorsed at the Second World Whores' Congress demands the same human rights for prostitutes as those set out in the *European Convention on Human Rights*. It seems as if ICPR chose to mimic the *European Convention* over the *United Nations Charter* because their meeting was convened at the official conference hall of the European Parliament in Brussels. In an interview at the World Whores' Summit in San Francisco, Gail Pheterson stated:

> Basic denial of citizenship status to prostitutes cuts across all other rights. Whore-identified women are not considered citizens. And any woman can be called a whore at any time for somehow stepping over the line. We are not considered citizens. That's clear from the Human Rights Convention of the European Community, for instance, wherein a whole list of human rights concludes with the sentence: "That none of these rights hold if one is considered a moral offense to society." And obviously, prostitutes are always included in that clause.[48]

Pheterson continued:

> The laws that forbid prostitutes to travel, to raise their own children, to have homes, to have any associates, lovers, or even to live with their families without the families being called pimps, are laws which affect all women and which restrict us, control us, justify violence against us.[49]

The *Statement on Prostitution and Human Rights* demands thirteen rights and freedoms that would redefine prostitutes as "ordinary" and "legitimate" citizens. It calls for "the right to life," "liberty," and "security of person."[50] The *Statement* calls for the right to fair administration of justice, indicating that the application of laws and regulations against prostitutes is usually arbitrary, discriminatory, corrupt, and hypocritical. The *Statement* demands the right of the prostitute to marry and have a family; the right to keep one's possessions and not have them confiscated on the ground that they were obtained with "illegal" money; and the right to leave a country—known prostitutes are denied the right to travel across international borders. It demands freedom of expression and freedom of peaceful assembly and association—prostitutes are prevented from forming partnerships and cooperatives by procuring laws and/or bawdy house laws. The right to join a trade union is included under freedom of association: "Until prostitutes are recognized as legitimate workers, rather than as outlaws or vagrants or bad girls, they cannot officially form trade unions."[51]

The *Statement* calls for the "prohibition of discrimination in the enjoyment of rights and freedoms guaranteed by the Convention";[52] that is, it calls for the extension of the citizenship rights guaranteed in the *European Convention on Human Rights* to prostitutes and, consequently, the end of their pseudo-criminalization. "Pseudo-criminalization" refers to the fact that in many countries, including Canada and the United States, it is not illegal to be a prostitute but aspects of prostitution such as solicitation are illegal. The *Statement* documents that some prostitutes—prostitutes of color, foreign prostitutes, street prostitutes, drug-addicted prostitutes, and juvenile prostitutes—suffer more discrimination than others. Finally, the *Statement* calls for prohibiting the expulsion of foreign women who have entered a country under conditions of third-party deceit or force.[53]

The *World Charter for Prostitutes' Rights* makes a distinction between forced and voluntary prostitution which further clarifies the distinction made by NTFP. NTFP makes this distinction between voluntary and forced prostitution:

> Voluntary prostitution is the mutually voluntary exchange of sexual services for money or other consideration; it is a form of work, and like most work in our capitalist society, it is often alienated, that is, the worker/prostitute has too little control over her/his working conditions and the way the work is organized. Forced prostitution is a form of aggravated sexual assault.[54]

Instead of "voluntary prostitution" the *World Charter for Prostitutes' Rights* demands the decriminalization of "all aspects of adult prostitution resulting from individual decision."[55] In her report of the discussion leading up to the drafting of the *Charter*, Pheterson indicates that the change from "voluntary" to "individual decision" occurred because "truly voluntary choices for women were uncommon at best . . . especially [for] poor women in poor countries."[56] The choice to work as a prostitute is voluntary but it often has socioeconomic determinants. ICPR cites as these determinants "the lack of educational and employment opportunities for women throughout the world."[57] All prostitute representatives at the First World Whores' Congress "insisted unanimously on the recognition of prostitution as a legitimate work decision for adults, be it a decision based on choice or necessity."[58]

ICPR extends its condemnation of forced prostitution to "cases of voluntary prostitution under forced conditions."[59] Here it explicitly condemns the state-regulated brothel system: "State-regulated brothels such as those found in Hamburg, Germany, and Nevada, United States, allow no choice in clientele, no right of refusal, no right to a fair share of the earnings, forced isolation and forced overwork."[60] The ICPR *Statement* calls this "servitude" and demands its prohibition. The *Charter* calls for the regulation of prostitution and third parties (prostitute businesses which employ prostitutes as workers) "accord-

ing to standard business codes."[61] Prostitutes and prostitute businesses should pay taxes "on the same basis as other independent contrac-
tors and employers, and should receive the same benefits."[62] The
Charter states: "Prostitutes must have the same social benefits as all
other citizens according to the different regulations in different countries."[63]

The *Charter* very concisely makes a distinction between prostitution as work and prostitution as violence. The argument underpinning
the *Charter* is that the depiction of all prostitution as "violence against
women," found in WHISPER's discourse, for example, prevents distinguishing between prostitution in which one person is being harmed
by another (that is, prostitution which is exploitative) and prostitution
which is work. The *Charter* simultaneously calls for the decriminalization of commercial sex and the enforcement of existing laws against
"fraud, coercion, violence, sexual abuse, child labor, rape and racism"
inside and outside the context of prostitution.[64] The *Charter* disasso-
ciates these occurrences of exploitation and abuse from a necessary
connection with prostitution. When exploitation and abuse do occur
in the context of prostitution, they can be dealt with the same way as
in the context of a noncommercial sexual relationship or a nonsexual
business. CORP spokesperson Valerie Scott, at the "Challenging Our
Images" conference, explained that until prostitution is decriminalized, prostitutes cannot report prostitution-related abuse because they
fear being charged as prostitutes. She says:

> If prostitution was decriminalized and a pimp did show up at my door,
> I would be able to pick up the phone and call the police, and they
> would be able to charge him with extortion or coercion. I can't do that
> now, or I'll be charged with prostitution.[65]

The *Charter* also makes a distinction between adult and child prostitution and calls for services to prevent children from going into prostitution: "Employment, counseling, legal and housing services for run-
away children should be funded in order to prevent child prostitution
and to promote child well-being and opportunity."[66] The *Statement on
Prostitution and Feminism* states: "Pressures upon children, either
with kindness or force, to work for money or to have sex for adult
satisfaction, is a violation of rights to childhood development."[67] The
Statement on Prostitution and Human Rights classifies juvenile prostitution as "forced labor."

Child prostitution is often brought up in public forums when prostitutes are discussing their rights, usually to discredit their claims. Delores French, in *Working: My Life as a Prostitute*, states that the question she is most often confronted with is "What about children who work as prostitutes?"[68] She says:

> I answer the question briefly—"We are completely against coercive prostitution. I personally don't think anyone should begin working as a prostitute until their mid-twenties, until their attitudes about themselves and their own sexuality are fully formed."[69]

The asking of the question immediately equates prostitution and the sexual exploitation of children; the question reduces all prostitution to the worst possible type within the minute it takes to ask it. According to Margo St. James, the age issue was discussed at the early American Hookers' conventions and prostitutes agreed that twenty-five is the ideal age for entering prostitution: "we feel that a young person should find their own sexuality before they're subjected to a lot of commercial leering and lusting."[70] The *Charter* demands services and retraining programs for women wanting to leave prostitution, thus recognizing that "the right not to be a prostitute is as important as the right to be one."[71]

ICPR is careful to call for the decriminalization of prostitution and not its legalization, because the latter invites state control. Legalization is a system whereby the state regulates, taxes, and licenses whatever form of prostitution is legalized and criminalizes nonlegal forms and persons. For example, in Amsterdam there are two systems of prostitution, the legal form, located in the infamous red-light district, and the illegal form, which functions outside this designated area. Women with criminal records cannot work in the red-light area. The ICPR refers to the state control that exists in Austria, West Germany, Amsterdam, and Nevada as "state pimping."

Prostitutes' rights organizations are careful not to accept "law's terms in order to challenge law,"[72] an accusation Carol Smart levies against feminist adoption of the legal discourse of rights. The core of Smart's argument is that "the growth of legal rights which can be claimed from the state has induced the concomitant growth of . . . regulation."[73] Prostitute rights' activists demand decriminalization: they demand the dissolution of the prostitute's special status in law, freedom from state regulation as prostitutes, and subjection to the same state regulation as workers and business owners. Prostitutes are demanding equal legal rights as citizens; they are not demanding any special rights as prostitutes. Smart is correct: the legalization of prostitution often involves the establishment of special government agencies to deal with prostitution and the enactment of new laws which put the control of prostitution in the hands of the police or the state. Prostitutes' rights activists are very conscious of the openings for state interference if prostitution is legalized and consider legalization as the obverse of criminalization.

Decriminalization as a strategy, according to COYOTE spokesperson Norma Jean Almodovar,

> . . . involves no new legislation to deal with prostitution per se, there are already plenty of laws which cover problems of fraud, force, theft, negligence, collusion, etc. Those laws could be enforced against anyone who violated them, just as they are now, when force or fraud is used in any other profession.[74]

The call for decriminalization moves the struggle onto a different terrain where prostitutes have to be recognized in law not as "prostitutes" but as workers and business owners. The negative stigma that society attaches to the prostitute is detached if prostitution is treated as work. Legalization, on the other hand, reinforces stigmatization; prostitutes can be segregated into districts and excluded from the rest of society. As workers and business persons prostitutes can work where they want subject to the same kinds of zoning laws as other businesses. Norma Jean Almodovar contends:

> The police department (or the criminal justice system) has no business running or regulating prostitution any more than it should run restaurants or grocery stores or the movie industry. These are all businesses subject to business regulations and under civil authority. Prostitution is a business, a service industry. It should be run as a business, subject only to the same kinds of business laws and regulations as other businesses.[75]

Prostitutes' rights discourse has been constituted mainly as a response to the official and unofficial criminalization of prostitution. Canadian and American prostitute rights activists lobby federal, provincial or state, and municipal governments for decriminalization. Prostitute discourse deconstructs the dominant legal discourse by juxtaposing what the laws mean in reality with the letter of the law. Four laws criminalize prostitution in Canada: the anti-soliciting law, the bawdy house law, the procuring law, and the pimping law. In the United States the act of prostitution itself is generally prohibited as well as soliciting, pimping, pandering, and running a bawdy house. In a pamphlet put out by WHORE*CORP*, Canadian prostitutes name these laws "whorebashing." The pamphlet decodes the laws as forcing women onto the street and then punishing them for being there.

> While selling sex itself isn't a crime, if we solicit in public, we're busted for communicating for the purpose of prostitution. If we bring tricks to our own home or to any place continually, we're busted for keeping a common body house. If we arrange a meeting between a trick and another whore, we can be busted for procuring. Our lovers and friends can be charged with pimping if they take money from us, live with us or are "habitually in our company". . . . The law forces us into the gutter and then punishes us for being there.[76]

CORP often couches its critique of the legal system in sexual wordplay. For instance, CORP produced a "Good Bawdy-housekeeping Certificate" which assures that the premises are "certified to be a location where only the finest acts of prostitution are committed" and guarantees that the premises will never be reduced to a mere "common body house." CORP has produced signs and buttons that read "Keep Your Fucking Laws off My Body." A flyer produced during the free-trade debate in Canada shows a woman talking to a person in a car: overwritten are the words "FREE TRADE."

Prostitute as a Feminist Identity: The Prostitute Struggle as a Feminist Struggle

Prostitute rights activists deconstructed feminism as an identity at the Second World Whores' Congress. This was a twofold deconstruction: challenging the appropriation of this identity by non-prostitute women and calling for an alliance among prostitute and non-prostitute women in a joint struggle, thus extending the democratic equivalence across the arbitrarily rigid distinctions of sex for love and pleasure, sex for reproduction, and sex for money. In its *Statement on Prostitution and Feminism*, ICPR states:

> [U]p until now the women's movement in most countries has not, or has only marginally, included prostitutes as spokeswomen and theorists. . . . Due to feminist hesitation or refusal to accept prostitution as legitimate work and to accept prostitutes as working women, the majority of prostitutes have not been identified as feminists; nonetheless, many prostitutes identify with feminist values such as independence, financial autonomy, sexual self-determination, personal strength and female bonding.[77]

ICPR considers itself a feminist organization: "it is committed to giving voice and respect to all women."[78] The ICPR cites as an important goal "the development of prostitution analyses and strategies within women's movements which link the condition of prostitutes to the condition of women in general."[79] Prostitution analyses and strategies are to come from prostitutes themselves and not to be imposed from the outside. Margo St. James, at the "Challenging Our Images" conference, stressed that "[a]ny theory that comes out about prostitution should come from the inside out, not from the outside in."[80] The ICPR is calling for a feminist alliance where prostitutes' analyses of prostitution are respected, prostitutes are on an equal footing with other women on issues not specifically related to prostitution, and whore-identified women are leaders in the feminist struggle as well the prostitute struggle. Gail Pheterson says: "The strength of the prostitutes' rights movement rests on the strength of alliances between women."[81]

In its *Statement on Prostitution and Feminism* the ICPR points out that "[w]omen have been divided into social categories on the basis of their sexual labor and/or identity";[82] this is why the affirmation of solidarity among women and the alliance of the prostitute, feminist, and gay/lesbian struggles is important to break down stigmatic barriers that divide and weaken oppressed people. At the Congress, Margo St. James said: "I see all prostitutes as feminists. . . . Prostitutes need to identify politically as feminist women just as feminists need to identify personally as working girls."[83] English representative Helen Buckingham suggests that what prevents feminists from identifying with prostitutes is "feminists cannot seem to accept women providing sex for men."[84] A member of Women's Organization for Equality (WOE), an international organization of feminists who supported the Congress, confirms Buckingham's claim: "One of the questions that arises with me is that I see [prostitution] as a service that is being provided solely by women for men, and even if it's provided by men, it is usually provided for men."[85]

Interestingly, it is lesbian feminists who have forged the closest alliances with prostitutes, perhaps because both groups of women have had an overlapping negative identity imposed on them by heterophallic society. Havelock Ellis equated lesbians and prostitutes and marked them as deviants; the Nazis marked prostitutes and lesbians with black triangles in concentration camps to signify that they were "asocial" women.[86] Gloria Lockett, in an interview given when she was co-director of COYOTE, said:

> I find lesbians to be a lot more supportive. . . . Most of the women
> who support us are lesbians. It is the lesbians who are sure about
> themselves, they know who they are. One of the lesbians we have on
> our board is a woman who marched with Martin Luther King, Jr. . . . She
> understands that equal rights are equal all over.[87]

Joan Nestle, in the article "Lesbians and Prostitutes: A Historical Sisterhood," versions of which are published in both *Sex Work* and *Good
Girls/Bad Girls*, uses a collage method to trace the historical interconnections between lesbian and prostitute women. Nestle, reading between the lines of such standard and canonical texts as Sanger's
History of Prostitution, "pr[ies] women loose from the judgemental
language in which they are embedded."[88] Nestle reads the Greek *auletrides*—the prostitute flute players—as lesbians; she situates their
women-only banquets as lesbian festivals. The connection between
prostitutes and lesbians comes from having a history of persecution
for their sexual activity: "prostitutes and lesbians have shared a history of struggle with the law, religion and medicine."[89] Nestle talks
about how whores were actively involved in the lesbian bar scene of
the late fifties and early sixties and how the lesbian feminism of the
seventies and early eighties excluded the prostitute: "the prostitute
was once again the other, much as she was earlier, in the feminist
purity movements of the late nineteenth century."[90]

ICPR calls for "an alliance between all women within and outside
the sex industry" and "affirms solidarity with prostitutes who are homosexual men, transvestites and transsexuals."[91] ICPR recognizes the
differences in status among prostitutes and women and gives special
affirmation to those having lower social status. It "especially affirms
the dignity of street prostitutes and of women stigmatized for their
color, class, ethnic difference, history of abuse, marital or motherhood
status, sexual preference, disability or fat."[92]

Prostitutes as Sexual Educators and Health Teachers

Prostitutes' rights discourse not only counters the current dominant
medical-moral discourse which inscribes the prostitute body as a diseased body in terms of STD's (sexually transmitted diseases) and
AIDS but also reverses the image of the prostitute as "pollutor of the
body politic" to the prostitute as "safe-sex educator." Rights discourse
counters the scapegoating of prostitutes as disease carriers with knowledge and information. Priscilla Alexander, who at the time of the Second Whores' Congress was the co-director of both COYOTE and NTFP
and who is currently working as a consultant with WHO (World

Health Organization) on a five-year cross-cultural study of AIDS that includes prostitutes and their clients and lovers as well as non-prostitutes, reported:

> [P]ublic health figures indicate that only five percent of sexually transmitted diseases are related to prostitution in the United States. Still, prostitutes are blamed. In the case of AIDS there is enormous scapegoating of prostitutes in the United States based on absolutely no evidence. The studies that have been done indicate that the only prostitutes who have been found to carry AIDS antibodies are some IV-users. The one study that compares prostitute and non-prostitute women, which is in San Francisco, shows no difference between groups; in both cases those who tested positively for AIDS antibodies are either IV-users or in regular sexual relationships with IV-users or bisexual men.[93]

Alexander names this connection of AIDS with prostitution "Blame the Prostitute."[94]

The Congress's *Statement on Prostitution and Health* demands an end to forced testing of prostitutes for any kind of sexually transmitted diseases in combination with the easy accessibility of free, anonymous testing for sexually transmitted diseases (including AIDS) for all people. The *Statement* stresses that prostitutes are the same as other sexually active people and should be treated the same; it calls for "widespread education and regular screening for sexually transmitted diseases among all sexually active people."[95] Gloria Lockett, who administers Project Aware, which is a women's AIDS research group that runs AIDS tests on prostitute and non-prostitute women, reports: "four percent of the 400 women . . . so far tested are positive and they are either IV-users or sexual partners of IV-users or bi-sexual men."[96] Lockett stresses that "[m]ost prostitutes . . . take care of themselves. Our bodies are our tools and we know how to take care of our bodies."[97] The discussion at the session "Prostitution and Health" revealed that when prostitutes do not take care of themselves and their clients by using condoms, it is due to club management rules that disallow the use of condoms. When it was pointed out by West German representatives that "[c]ondoms are out in Germany"[98] and mandatory testing was in, the ICPR sent a telegram to the West German government—the chancellor and the Ministry of Health—condemning this practice and calling for a change. The telegram read:

> We are astonished to learn in this conference from the working women of all cities of the Federal Republic of Germany that your public health is relying on tests and not the prophylactic use of condoms to

prevent sexually transmitted diseases, including AIDS. Regular check-ups should be voluntary. . . . Regular check-ups do not prevent sexually transmitted diseases and condoms do. We urge massive education of the general public on the use of condoms . . . in order to prevent the spread of all sexually transmitted diseases.[99]

Prostitutes' rights groups have organized and administer safe-sex projects: with the AIDS panic prostitutes were again caricatured as the pollutors of the body politic, but, unlike their nineteenth-century predecessor, they have been able to represent themselves as "safe-sex educators" and "safe-sex pros," teachers who are able to disseminate knowledge to other prostitutes and to the public about safer sex. Toronto prostitutes run the Prostitutes' Safe Sex Project; they do street outreach work handing out condoms, bleach (for needle users), and information on safer sex techniques, providing information about the hours and addresses of health clinics for STD examinations. CAL-PEP (California Prostitutes Education Project) runs a similar street outreach program in San Francisco, as does PONY in New York. The CORP and CAL-PEP projects receive government funding. Priscilla Alexander suggests that "government funding for projects like CAL-PEP's AIDS-prevention project has added legitimacy to prostitution as an occupation."[100] Safe Sex Corp names the inscription of prostitutes as "disease carriers" as "hate propaganda."[101] PONY, in a strategic disassociation of AIDS from prostitution, uses the slogan: "money is free of AIDS."[102]

To conclude, there is a tension in prostitutes' rights discourse; the ability to hold this tension without privileging either side marks prostitutes' rights as a paradoxical and postmodern discourse. One can draw contradictory conclusions from rights discourse. On the one hand, it can be argued that the demand for rights from the position of marginalized collectivities destabilizes and undoes the meaning attached to the liberal concept of individual rights; that the enfranchisement of prostitutes as new political subjects holds "the promise and the affirmation of the future . . . as other . . . that which might no longer be what is."[103] On the other hand, it can equally be argued that prostitutes' rights discourse is premised on capitalist assumptions with the aim of producing the prostitute as a small-business woman and/or legitimate worker, in a manner which just serves to reproduce the system. The paradox is that prostitutes' rights discourse does both simultaneously and consequently does neither. It is precisely the production of the prostitute identity on the boundary between work and sex that facilitates holding these seemingly contradictory tenets. If prostitutes' rights activists just wanted prostitutes to "take themselves to market and name their price," as the whore in Irigaray's text does, then they would be constructing the prostitute as a petty bourgeois entrepreneur and not a radical political subject. But prostitutes' rights advocates situate this commercial exchange in the context of collective identity politics, which has as its goal both the affirmation of the prostitute as a positive identity and the realization of feminist goals such as the right to control one's body and to have economic control over one's life. Prostitutes' rights discourse reconciles the two contradictory strands in its discourse by presenting the market as the means for prostitutes to be in control of their sexuality and to have economic determination. Rights prostitutes want to use the market as means of controlling their own sexuality and of having economic determination.

WHISPER presents rights discourse as a colluding discourse which reproduces the oppression of prostitutes and of all women. The next section will present WHISPER's construction of the prostitute and prostitution; when WHISPER statements are direct refutations of the rights groups' position, their response will be provided. There is no point of reconciliation between WHISPER and the rights groups' discourses. There are only two things these oppositional discourses have in common: they are both produced from the prostitute subject position and they demand the decriminalization of the prostitute.

WHISPER

WHISPER, formed in 1985, is a Minneapolis-based national organization whose main focus is helping women get out of "the life." Its name was chosen to indicate that

> . . . women in systems of prostitution . . . whisper among themselves about the coercion, degradation, sexual abuse and battery that the sex industry is founded on, while myths about prostitution are shouted out in pornography, the mainstream media, and by self-appointed "experts."[104]

Like the prostitutes' rights organizations, WHISPER is a grass-roots movement that is both local and national; but it is not yet international. Like the prostitutes' rights movement, WHISPER is a first-person movement based on women's experience in prostitution.

WHISPER discourse, unlike prostitutes' rights discourse, however, does not allow for a number of equally valid prostitute subject positions. Rather, it produces the prostitute solely as victim.

Founder Sarah Wynter, aka Evelina Giobbe, claims that prostitutes' rights groups are not telling "the truth about what it is like to have to sell sex."[105] This claim to "the truth" marks WHISPER a modernist discourse. There have been and are a plurality of truths about prostitution. What is unique is that this is the first historical conjuncture in which prostitutes produce these truths. By claiming to be the one true voice of prostitution, WHISPER, at least philosophically, aims at silencing the different voices of prostitutes' rights activists and leaving no space for difference. WHISPER sets itself up as a counter-discourse to prostitutes' rights discourse and as an ex-prostitutes' struggle against both the hegemonic system and prostitutes' rights groups, which WHISPER constructs as being complicit with the dominant system.

The main difference between WHISPER and ICPR theorizations of prostitution is that ICPR theorizes prostitution as sexual activity and work, which may or may not be exploitative to varying degrees, and WHISPER theorizes prostitution as sexual exploitation. WHISPER focuses exclusively on the facts of prostitutes' exploitation and oppression. Certainly, any discussion of prostitution would be obscene if these aspects were ignored; analogous to this would be writing about the dignity of labor without mentioning exploitation. Yet, in WHISPER's inscription prostitution can be only exploitative.

WHISPER develops its critique of prostitution from radical feminist discourse: "prostitution is sexual abuse" and "prostitution is the paradigm for women's social and economic inequality."[106] As its basis, WHISPER has the radical feminist position theorized by Catharine MacKinnon that "[p]rostitution is the model for women's condition."[107] WHISPER's construction of prostitution and marriage closely resembles that of Carole Pateman in *The Sexual Contract.* Pateman constructs marriage and prostitution as the private and public manifestations of male sex right. WHISPER claims that "prostitution functions to extend to all men the same right of unconditional sexual access to women and girls hereto reserved for husbands and fathers within the institution of marriage."[108] WHISPER states:

> [T]raditional marriage is premised on the long-term private ownership of a woman by an individual man whereas prostitution is built upon the short-term public ownership of women by many men. Women are

kept socially, sexually, economically subordinate to individual men in marriage and to men as a class in prostitution. These systems allow males to exercise their prerogative to own and control women in both the private and public spheres.[109]

WHISPER's analysis is not new: it is a reformulation of the abolitionist position that goes back to Josephine Butler and the Ladies' National Association. What is new about the WHISPER analysis is the subject position from which it is done: WHISPER is a self-representative organization of ex-prostitutes. Evelina Giobbe speaks from first-person experience of abuse: "I was sold into prostitution and control of my life was taken away from me."[110] Wynter/Giobbe was a New York City call girl. She says that her experience in prostitution puts "the lie to the common belief about the hierarchy of prostitution, the streets being the worst-case scenario and call service being the best."[111] She states, "I was a young teenage girl . . . I wasn't an independent agent but controlled by a brutal pimp who had a stable of women."[112] In its theorization WHISPER draws "on the experiences of women used in systems of prostitution."[113] The key word is "used." WHISPER refuses to make any distinction between prostitution that is entered voluntary and prostitution that is forced. Women can only be used in prostitution. WHISPER supporter Kathleen Barry explains that "by refusing to make a distinction between forced and voluntary prostitution . . . we refuse to recognize prostitution as a profession."[114] Instead WHISPER "recognizes all commodification of women's bodies for sexual exchange as violations of human dignity and therefore of human rights."[115]

WHISPER completely rejects prostitutes' rights construction of prostitution as a profession. Prostitution is "a system of violence against women."[116] All prostitutes are battered women: Giobbe equates those who don't admit it and claim to like their work with assaulted women who say "Johnny didn't mean to hit me. He hit me because he loves me."[117] The prostitute has no autonomy, according to WHISPER; at most she can be "in charge of her exploitation" and the "manager of her own victimage."[118] Women who leave "the life" refer to themselves as "survivors." Giobbe writes "[s]urvivors describe the act of prostitution as 'disgusting,' 'abusive,' and 'like rape.' "[119] According to WHISPER, "prostitution is sexual abuse because prostitutes are subjected to a multitude of sexual acts that in any other context, would be perceived to be unwanted and coerced."[120] It is only the "exchange of money" that prevents prostitution from being classified as assault. Giobbe, in an attempt to deconstruct (the term she uses)[121] prostitution as a consensual act, makes the following analogy:

> If this construction [prostitution as choice] were applied to other victims of assault then one would have to logically assume that battered women or victims of incest . . . also choose abusive relationships because they accept monetary considerations from their assailants in the form of food, lodging and sometimes actual cash.[122]

WHISPER sets itself up as a counter-discourse to "challenge the authority of prostitutes' rights groups."[123] What WHISPER specifically counters is that prostitution is work; that it is freely choosen; that it takes place between fully consenting adults; that "prostitute" is a valid identity; and "that prostitution is a paradigm for women's sexual freedom and liberation."[124] This last is a claim that Giobbe imputes to prostitutes' rights discourse, citing Priscilla Alexander's depiction of power and sex. Alexander states: "Prostitution . . . involves an equation of sex with power: for the man/customer, the power consists of his ability to 'buy' access to any number of women; for the woman/prostitute, the power consists of her ability to set the terms of her sexuality, and demand substantial payment for her time and skills."[125] Giobbe refers to these above points, which WHISPER counters, as constituting "the sexual liberal analysis."[126] In her production of WHISPER as the "true" voice of prostitutes, Giobbe misrepresents prostitutes' rights discourse in a number of crucial respects. First, she accuses prostitutes' rights discourse of "decontextualiz[ing prostitution] from the patriarchal society we live in";[127] here Giobbe ignores the distinction between the possibility of prostitution-founded rights discourse and the negative way it is constructed in an international judicial-political system in which prostitutes do not have human rights. ICPR and its local groups situate prostitution within a capitalist patriarchal system: they, as I previously indicated, accept the capitalist market and want to make judicial-political changes which would give them control over their bodies and economic self-determination. WHISPER sees it as being impossible not only for women in prostitution but for all women to have control over their own bodies as long as prostitution exists. ICPR contends that women will not have control over their bodies until prostitutes have control over theirs. There is no in-between in these two discourses.

As I have indicated above, Giobbe claims that prostitutes' rights discourse marks "prostitution as women's work."[128] Prostitutes' rights discourse presents prostitution as work; ICPR as well as PONY and CORP include the gay male prostitute voice. Giobbe uses personal testimony from a woman who worked in the Nevada brothel system as evidence that prostitutes have no control over their work and can be used by the client in any way he chooses, citing the house rules in a Nevada brothel as reported by Jayme Ryan, "a woman who was used in the legal brothel system of Nevada":

> When you got a customer in your room you had to perform any sex act that he wanted. . . . We were strictly forbidden to use condoms unless the customer asked for one. . . . Once you were alone in your room with a customer you had no protection from him. There were many different occasions where a woman was brutally beaten or raped by a john but as long as he paid the house it was kept quiet.[129]

The implication is that the ICPR's construction of prostitution as work implicitly supports these working conditions; yet ICPR condemns legalized prostitution and state-run brothel systems for the violence they impose on women. ICPR makes a distinction between prostitution per se and violence against women in the context of prostitution, condemning the latter and demanding that the perpetrator be charged under criminal laws against rape, coercion, violence, and abuse. WHISPER, in accordance with the National Coalition against Sexual Assault's 1990 "Resolution on Prostitution," contextualizes all prostitution as forced sexual violence:

> [T]he conditions which create and perpetuate pros_itution, including male supremacy, poverty, racism, classism, lesbophobia, sex discrimination, sexual abuse, bigotry and despair, preclude prostitution from being a freely made choice. . . . [130]

Giobbe, in the article "Empowering Women to Escape Prostitution," cites three case histories where the women were repeatedly beaten by their partners who were also their pimps. Giobbe focuses on the pimp factor. As I wrote in my review of Lyn Madden's book Lyn: A Story of Prostitution,[131] the fundamental problem is that these men are abusers—"awful, disgusting, sadistic and often psychotic";[132] they need to be charged as abusers and for forcing the women into prostitution. WHISPER's analysis of prostitution is a very valuable critique; the problem with it is its self-construction as a critique of prostitutes' rights discourse as if prostitutes' rights discourse condones the abuse of women by not characterizing all prostitution as abuse.

Giobbe rejects "prostitute" as an identity. She reverses prostitutes' rights construction of prostitute as an identity:

> The process of "becoming" a prostitute entails the systematic de-struction of an individual woman's beliefs, feelings, desires and val-ues. Upon entering prostitution a woman typically acquires a new name, changes her appearance, and creates a fictitious past. . . . To be a prostitute is to be an object in the marketplace: a three-dimensional blank screen upon which men project and act out their sexual domi-nance. Thus the word "prostitute" does not imply a "deeper iden-tity"; it is the absence of identity: the theft and subsequent abandon-ment of self. What remains is essential to the "job": the mouth, the genitals, anus, breasts . . . and the label.[133]

Giobbe depicts "prostitute" as a "name men give to our oppres-sion."[134] WHISPER strategy is the reverse of prostitutes' rights: rather than deconstructing the meaning attributed to the word "whore" or "prostitute," WHISPER shows how, from the prostitute's point of view, the word is a label. "The role of prostitute is socially constructed by men for their benefit and then cast upon women irrevocably."[135] Giobbe's definition of a prostitute is "to be unconditionally sexually available to any male who buys the right to use your body in any way he chooses."[136]

Giobbe characterizes prostitutes' rights activists' conjoinment of "feminist" and "prostitute" as a contradiction:

> Feminism is a collective movement whose expressed goals are to dis-mantle systematic patriarchal control of women and as such stands in direct conflict with the objectives of the sex industry. Does this mean that a woman used in prostitution cannot hold to and aspire to femi-nist ideals? No. It simply means that she cannot truly actualize them within a closed system designed to keep her in a subordinate social position.[137]

A prostitute can "actualize" her feminist identity only after she leaves prostitution; she can become a feminist as an ex-prostitute.

Where WHISPER joins with the rights struggle is in its opposition to "misogynist laws." Giobbe states: "The legal system is abusive and constructed to uphold male interests."[138] WHISPER supports the re-peal of all laws that contain punitive provisions for women in prosti-tution: "all laws which penalize the prostitute (victim) must be de-criminalized."[139] WHISPER, however, strongly opposes the abolition of pimping laws (living off the avails of prostitution) and procuring

laws (setting up prostitute-client exchanges for another person): it considers the abolition of these laws as equivalent to promoting sexual
assault. WHISPER calls for patronizing laws which "criminally penalize clients or customers of prostitutes . . . for participating in the commodity exchange of women's bodies[.]"[140] WHISPER demands that
pimping be redefined

> from the crime of "living off the earnings of women in prostitution"
> to being a coercive system which not only puts women in prostitu-
> tion, but prevents them from leaving it meanwhile requiring that
> their bodies be rendered into commodities for sexual-economic ex-
> change[.][141]

Rights advocates argue that the pimping law prohibits them from having companions or working with a third party who manages their
business, if they choose. Rights advocates also contend that if prostitution were decriminalized, anyone trying to control them or force
them to hand over payment could be reported to the police and
charged under other laws. The procuring laws, according to rights advocates, isolate the women and prevent them from overtly working
together. Rights activists support what they describe as the sexual
rights of their patron clients. Women in WHISPER have experienced
abusive pimps and johns; women in rights groups have experienced
the persecution of lovers, friends, and customers under pimping and
procuring laws and patronizing laws.

WHISPER has two explicitly stated purposes: to educate the public
about prostitution as a system of exploitation and abuse, and to advocate the expansion of services to women and girls attempting to escape
the sex industry. It has formed a coalition with those in the struggle
against violence against women because of "the parallels between the
lives of women used in prostitution and women battered by their partners."[142] WHISPER membership includes survivors of prostitution and
other feminist supporters. WHISPER has developed three unique programs: the oral history project, which is a first-person documentation
of the lives of "women used in prostitution" (WHISPER has produced
and distributed a documentary video—*Prostitution: A Matter of Violence against Women*—which juxtaposes interviews with survivors to
mainstream media images of prostitution); the radical education
groups, which meet weekly to discuss prostitution on a personal, in-
stitutional, and cultural level; and the action group, which is a vehicle

for "collective struggle" by women who were "victimized" in prostitution to do outreach work with women "trapped" in the sex industry.[143]

WHISPER has produced a very effective poster: the poster is of two women sitting on a couch; the black woman is drinking a take-out pop; the white woman is filing her nails. A sign facing outside, so that the reader sees its mirror image, reads "Sauna Open 24 hours." Inside on the wall is a price list which reads: "15 mins.—$40, 30 mins.—$60, 45 mins.—$80, 60 mins.—$100, Two Girls—$150, Share a Shower—$5, Movies—$5." In front of the very bored women is a white, overweight male wearing a sports jacket and with his hands in his pockets, who looks at the two women (they do not return his gaze). The caption below tells the viewer how to read the picture. It says: "When you can't stand turning one more trick, turn to us."

WHISPER is doing crucial work for women abused in prostitution. The problem with WHISPER is its totalizing ideology—"all prostitutes are abused women," "prostitution—commercial sex—is sexual abuse." It does not allow for different constructions of prostitution. WHISPER produces the prostitute solely as a victim; it marks her victimage from the subject position of the feminist and the ex-prostitute; yet it is important to keep in mind that discourses and agents of oppression—the Contagious Diseases Acts of the nineteenth century and their enforcers and today's laws and law enforcers—justify their persecution of prostitutes on the ground that prostitutes are victims:

> When pressed for a reason why these laws are enforced, law enforcement officials state that prostitutes are victims and that prostitution is worse on the "victim" than rape or robbery. . . . [T]he solution to a voluntarily made choice to prostitute one's self is . . . incarceration to prevent further victimization."[144]

The problem with WHISPER is certainly not in its practical work with battered-women's shelters to include prostitutes in shelter services, nor is it the support WHISPER provides for women to get out of prostitution; the problem is its devaluation and negation of the possibility for a plurality of experiences in prostitution.

In conclusion, the ongoing explicit theoretical project of WHISPER is "to deconstruct the cultural mythology which situates [the] discourse about prostitution within the framework of 'women and work' and . . . place it in the framework of violence against women, a part of women's oppression under patriarchy[.]"[145] Rights groups and WHIS-

PER present two competing discourses produced from the experiential body of the prostitute. Because their points of departure—empowerment and victimization—are diametrically opposed, there is little common ground for the discourses. Yet both are produced from real-life experiences in prostitution. The prostitutes' rights movement recognizes the dual presence of positive and negative experiences in prostitution and includes as a *Charter* demand the funding of "[s]helters and services for working prostitutes and re-training programs for prostitutes wishing to leave the life."[146] WHISPER sees no positive aspects. Many of WHISPER's practical programs, however, could be integrated into prostitutes' rights discourse. Rights groups recognize that abuse occurs in prostitution. WHISPER is a closed discourse which, like its discourse of origin, radical feminism, leaves no space for conflicting perspectives.

Prostitutes Anonymous provides a neutral space where the rights groups' and WHISPER's ideological frameworks can overlap and come together in their differences.

Prostitutes Anonymous

Prostitutes Anonymous (PA), formed in 1987, is distinct from both prostitutes' rights groups and WHISPER; it is not political in the broad sense as are these organizations. Yet, if one accepts the feminist movements' reformulation of the political to include the personal, Prostitutes Anonymous is part of the prostitutes' struggle. Prostitutes Anonymous genealogy goes back to the anonymous fellowships that started with Alcoholics Anonymous and branched out to include other "12-step groups" focused on a number of other behaviors that have a high possibility of getting out of control, such as gambling, drugs, and overeating. It was formed by a Los Angeles ex-prostitute and ex-madame René LeBlanc out of her experience in Narcotics Anonymous. A group similar to Prostitutes Anonymous, which she called "Hookers Anonymous," was formed in New York around the same time by a New York ex-prostitute.[147] It too was formed out of the founder's personal experience in Narcotics Anonymous and in Alcoholics Anonymous. Hookers Anonymous affiliated with Prostitutes Anonymous, although the two founders' philosophies on prostitution differ.

Prostitutes Anonymous claims to be worldwide in membership; this reflects its potential more than the actuality; PA is primarily a North American–based organization. Prostitutes Anonymous is a twelve-step program for women and men who are either currently engaged in sex work or who have left the sex industry. Its goal is to "teach recovery using the 12-Steps as a tool."[148] The 12-Steps have been adapted from the program originally developed by alcoholics to recover from alcoholism. Steps one and twelve are modified to suit the particular fellowhip. The specific Prostitutes Anonymous 12-Steps read:

1. We admitted that we were powerless over prostitution—that our lives had become unmanageable.

2. Came to believe that a Power greater than ourselves could restore us to sanity.

3. Made a decision to turn our will and our lives over to the care of God as we understood Him.

4. Made a searching and fearless moral inventory of ourselves.

5. Admitted to God, to ourselves, and to another human being the exact nature of our wrongs.

6. Were entirely ready to have God remove all these defects of character.

7. Humbly asked Him to remove our shortcomings.

8. Made a list of all persons we had harmed, and became willing to make amends to them all.

9. Made direct amends to such people whenever possible, except when to do so would injure them or others.

10. Continued to take personal inventory and when we were wrong promptly admitted it.

11. Sought through prayer and meditation to improve our conscious contact with God as we understood Him, praying only for knowledge of his will for us and the power to carry that out.

12. Having had a spiritual awakening as a result of these steps, we try to carry this message to the prostitute who still suffers, and to practice these principles in all our affairs.[149]

Prostitutes Anonymous distinguishes between the prostitute who suffers and prostitution in general in much the same way Alcoholics Anonymous makes a distinction between the alcoholic and alcohol. PA doesn't judge prostitution; its "Opening Statement," one of the seven key pieces of PA literature read at every meeting, states:

> We do not say that there is anything wrong or right with the sex industry in itself. . . . Our group stance is that we are only here to deal with our problem with the sex industry, our addiction and recovery.[150]

In fact, "Why We Are Here" says: "After we came to Prostitutes Anonymous, we realized that the sex industry, the problems connected with it and the people were only a symptom of the real problem."[151] The "real problem" is addiction; PA then, unlike the medical-moral discourse, does not treat prostitution as a disease or the prostitute as diseased; PA views a person's addiction to prostitution as a disease. Prostitution becomes a disease only when the prostitute's life is unmanageable for her or him and the person feels trapped in prostitution and powerless. Prostitutes Anonymous redefines addiction from being a physical dependence, as it is in drug and alcohol addictions, to "the combination of obsession and compulsion."[152] PA explains the interrelationship between compulsion and addiction: "compulsion makes us do things against our wills and the obsession leads us back to compulsion."[153]

What is it that prostitutes become addicted to? According to Charlotte Davis Kasl, the author of *Women, Sex, and Addiction,*

> The addictive part is the ritual of getting dressed, putting on makeup, fantasizing about the hunt, and the moment of capture. "To know that you could go out there and they would come running. What power! Men would actually pay for sex". . . . For women in prostitution . . . that feeling of power, along with the excitement of living on the edge, is one of the hardest things to give up.[154]

The spokesperson for New York Prostitutes Anonymous, in an interview I conducted, confirmed Kasl's depiction of addiction in prostitution:

> There is an adrenaline rush that you get when a man gives you $200, $600, or if you spend the night with someone and you have $1,200 more than you did before you got there. . . . There is a high from it and the way we look at it, in PA, is that one is addicted to this high. I knew I was addicted to it before I went to PA. There was an actual euphoria that I got, and a number of women I talked to got also, after turning a trick. It was like getting high. . . . I really miss the excitement of the whole lifestyle.[155]

René LeBlanc, the Los Angeles founder of Prostitutes Anonymous, says, "Telling me to give up my prostitution is telling me to give up my power."[156] LeBlanc repeatedly suggests that "prostitution is the hardest addiction to break."[157] She gives two reasons for this difficulty: the prostitute's connection of prostitution with empowerment and because, in her words, "the more addicted I was, the more money I made; every other addiction you lose money."[158]

The Prostitutes Anonymous program consists of five elements: regular meetings in which the members participate in reading from PA literature, giving testimony, and recognizing members "time"—the length of time they have refrained from sex-related earnings; the 12-Steps; a one-to-one sponsor; phone therapy; and being of service to others wishing to leave the sex industry. The objective is to break the individual's addictive cycle.

PA stresses "principles over personalities" in recognition that the differences in types of prostitution can create divisions in the group and impede recovery. LeBlanc explains how the operating doctrine of "principles over personalities" came about:

> In the beginning we had the room divided up in half. The $20 streetwalkers were on one side and the $1,000 callgirls were on the other. They'd spit at each other. Every time a man came in the meeting they would chase him off. . . . The pimp that came in hated gay guys. I said "Hey, they let you in . . . not everybody will tolerate a rapist and a maimer." That tended to keep him in his place.
> Finally we wrote a format about how it doesn't matter who your clients were, how much you charged, what you did, men and women are allowed here. . . . [W]e are all equal in here.[159]

Prostitutes Anonymous's "Opening Statement" establishes: "We have all done different things, had different prices and limits, but please remember—we ALL share two things—addiction and recovery."[160]

PA defines "prostitute" as "a man or a woman who accepts money or goods in exchange for sex or a sex related activity."[161] The sex-related activities include prostitution, nude dancing, phone sex, pornography, and any other form of commercial relationships. PA doesn't recuperate the word "prostitute" as a positive term; rather, it is used to conjure the negative aspects of "the life" and to remind the members why they wanted to leave.[162] Each person who speaks at meetings introduces herself or himself by name followed by the statement "I am a prostitute." Although PA doesn't pass judgment on people in prostitution, it urges all members of PA to quit prostitution. PA literature explicitly says:

> You can still be in the sex industry when you join, but we suggest you try to come back out of the sex industry. There is only one requirement for membership, the desire to leave the industry and find recovery.[163]

A New York PA spokesperson does not agree that a person has to be out of the sex industry in order to benefit from PA. She says:

I think you can come to meetings if you are still a practicing prostitute. I know a lot of people who are not addicts that deserve to recover through the 12-Steps. The 12-Steps is just really getting to know yourself.[164]

PA is a practical program for prostitutes who have found their lives unmanageable. Its *Twelve Traditions* prohibit members as a PA group from being involved in any purpose other than recovery and carrying the message to others. Tradition ten states: "PA has no opinion on outside issues, hence the PA name ought never be drawn into public controversy."[165] PA, unlike both prostitutes' rights groups and WHISPER, does not have a political position. Its intentional position of neutrality can be articulated with both the prostitutes' rights movement's and WHISPER's philosophies of prostitution, or with any philosophy of prostitution. René LeBlanc's view of prostitution is close to WHISPER philosophy, but with her own twist. She says: "I see prostitutes as victims who have decided to become victimizers."[166] LeBlanc, having experienced sexual abuse, claims to initially have "enjoyed degrading the tricks . . . wreaking havoc . . . taking their money, doing terrible things to them."[167] The New York PA representative made it clear that she "believe[s] in all prostitute groups." Her own philosophy, however, is closer to rights groups. She continues: "I could be an absolute supporter of COYOTE or PONY."[168]

Conclusion

What I have attempted to do in this chapter is to present prostitute discourse as a contested terrain that reproduces the dichotomization of the prostitute as powerful sexual being and disempowered sexual victim. This tension is present in prostitutes' rights discourse and there is an untheorized space for it in the discourse of Prostitutes Anonymous.

The prostitutes' rights movement is attempting to construct a new prostitute identity which has traces to the ancient sacred prostitute: it presents sex workers as "practitioners of a sacred craft," sexual service as "a nourishing, life-giving force," and prostitution as an active expression of women's sexuality. Yet this new identity is formulated in the margins of the institution of prostitution in actually existing late capitalism. Prostitution is marked in the present social context by power imbalances: gender, class, and racial inequalities that structure society are played out in prostitution. Rights groups attempt to redress these unequal differences in the judicial-political realm. WHISPER argues that these inequalities can never be redressed so long as prostitution—the commodification of women's bodies—continues. Rights groups contend that if prostitutes were enfranchised and prostitution decriminalized then the means for actualizing the new prostitute identity on a collective basis would be in place. What prostitutes' rights discourse has accomplished is a destabilization of the "old" hegemonic identification of prostitute as stigmatized, vilified victim.

What becomes apparent is that "prostitute" is an ambiguous identity containing partially actualized positive possibilities in a negative reality. Rights discourse slides back and forth in this ambiguity. It is in prostitute performance art, a postmodern application of theory, that this ambiguity is most fully developed and held. The next chapter will present and examine the works of six North American prostitute performance artists who use artspace to reclaim and redefine the prostitute body.

PROSTITUTE PERFORMANCES
Sacred Carnival Theorists of the Female Body

Postmodernity revalues the aesthetic as a site for the intervention of little narratives; it is in little "ephemeral stories" that the assumptions of the great, institutionalized narratives(s) are questioned, (re)presented, challenged, and undermined.[1] Performance art is an excellent medium for the presentation of small, individualized life stories. In fact, women's performance art is mostly about personal experience: "real-life" presence of the artist, actor, author.

In chapter 5, I examined the ambiguity in prostitutes' discourse primarily between two oppositional constructions of the prostitute as a site of politicized resistance and as a site of oppression: empowerment/exploitation. Although there is room for holding both sides of this dichotomization of the prostitute body in rights discourse, this discourse tends to privilege empowerment. Some of the individual spokespeople, however, hold both sides of the dichotomy in their own body. It is in the little narratives of individual performance artists that the dichotomization of the prostitute body into an abused body and an empowered body is resisted and in so doing the broader binary division of women into feminist/mother/good girl and slut/male-identified/bad girl is destabilized, if not broken.

This chapter will examine the texts of six North American prostitute performance artists. The aim is to present their work as little narratives that function to intervene in the larger hegemonic, feminist, and even prostitute discourses. The overriding theme in these artists' works is the reunification of the sacred and the obscene in the same female body. What is operating is a genealogy of "the prostitute," narrated by prostitutes, that links the contemporary prostitute activist to the ancient sacred prostitute, while at the same time working over the modernist construction of the prostitute as a debased and defiled body.

The six performance artists are Candida Royalle, Annie Sprinkle, Veronica Vera, Gwendolyn, Janet Feindel, and Scarlot Harlot. Royalle,

Sprinkle, and Vera are New York artists; Gwendolyn and Feindel are Toronto artists; Scarlot Harlot is a San Francisco artist. Candida Royalle, as director and as actor, was instrumental in the first New York prostitute performance text: *Deep Inside Porn Stars*. This performance piece marked the inception of New York prostitute performance theater. Annie Sprinkle's work has evolved from *Deep Inside Porn Stars* into a number of performance pieces which she has collected into her work: *Post Porn Modernist*. Veronica Vera has produced *Bare Witness* in three media—writing, film, and performance. *Bare Witness* also had its beginning in *Deep Inside Porn Stars*. Gwendolyn and Scarlot Harlot are the most broadly political of these performance artists: Gwendolyn critiques (feminist) therapy in *Merchants of Love* and the antiporn movement in *Hardcore*; Scarlot is a guerrilla life artist whose multimedia protests cross over artspace and cityspace. Janet Feindel developed her character performances of eight strip women into a complete work and a published play: *A Particular Class of Women*.

Following the direction of the artists themselves, I have included texts that focus on strip women (Feindel) and women in the porno business (Club 90) as prostitute performance art. There is a very close linkage among porn actresses, strippers, and prostitutes, aside from the fact that one person often engages in two or all three occupations. Candida Royalle explains the connection between porn actresses and prostitutes:

> Pornography [is] like looking at prostitutes. It [is] just another version of prostitution. Instead of being with a prostitute . . . you look at a prostitute.[2]

Performance is one of the most effective means for those who have been constructed by others as objects of desire and undesirable objects to enter into discourse and create an immediate subject position from which to address the social. Those, such as prostitutes, previously coded as merely "obscene" and contained as carnivalesque transgression can reconstitute themselves in the performance medium as living embodiments of resistance, remapping, redefining, and reclaiming the deviant body, the body of the sexual outsider and social outcast.

The format of this chapter will be first to situate prostitute performance art in the context of the performance genre and its feminist subgenre, then to present the texts of the six prostitute performance artists, informed by my contention that a reunified female body emerges to varying degrees and in various manifestations in these texts.

Performance Art as a Postmodern Aesthetic

Performance art/theater is such an effective medium for the other precisely because it exemplifies postmodern aesthetics. Performance exists in the space between life and theater. There is a dissolution of the distinctions between the real and the representation of the real. Political possibilities abound in this "disruption or complication of strict boundaries and the coherent distinctions they maintain."[3] Performance art is a fragmented politics, a visual politics of the moment. It is "schizophrenically" ahistorical: presence and writing are simultaneous; present and past are immediately one in the situational moment. Performance is cross-disciplinary, combining live theater, video, film, dance, singing, and music.

Performance art works as a deconstructive strategy: it interrogates and destabilizes the dominant representational image and it disrupts and complicates the strict boundaries of texts. The performance text is a work-in-process. If there is a written script it often changes with each production; the stasis of the script gives over to spontaneity and interaction with the audience. Spectatorship is a part of the work: audiences are drawn into embarrassingly intense interaction with the performer(s). The voyeuristic narrative of traditional live theater is deconstructed, leaving the audience "exposed to the fearful proximity of the performer and the . . . consequences of [its] own desires":[4]

> Traditional live entertainment . . . is heavily dependent on narrative and on the woman "acting" the roles she has demonstrably escaped. With the odd variation an entertainment scenario will always be resolved in the same way. The stripper ends up naked, the heroine sinks into the hero's arms, the lustful or murderous woman comes to a stickly end, the singer pines for her lost love and the mother-in-law is perenially hateful. Performance art abandons these narratives.[5]

Postmodern performance theater "refuses to deliver itself as a commodity, refuses to satisfy the viewer who seeks to abstract or translate the performance."[6] Postmodern theater rejects the form of "fine" theater—"narrative impetus and coherence,"[7] opting for flexibility, discontinuity, and slippage.

Feminist Performance Art

A critique of modernism is inherent in performance art; feminism adds to this critique a critique of gender/patriarchy.[8] Jeanie Forte states:

> All women's performances are derived from the relationship of women to the dominant system of representation. . . . [Women's] disruption of the dominant system constitutes a subversive and radical strategy of intervention vis-a-vis patriarchal culture.[9]

Performance art is a deconstructive strategy in that it disrupts and complicates strict boundaries among texts and the coherent exclusionary distinctions they make. Women's performance art is deconstructive in an additional way: It is "the discourse of the objectified other."[10] It is the space of absence within the dominant discourse which becomes presence. Dominant discourse depends upon the construction of woman as other: " 'Woman' as object, as a culturally constructed category, is . . . the basis of the Western system of representation."[11] Women's performance art is doubly disruptive: it challenges the dominant representational system and it posits woman as speaking subject. Forte writes:

> Women's performance art has a particular disruptive potential because it poses an actual woman as speaking subject, throwing that position into process, into doubt, opposing the traditional conception of the single, unified (male) subject. The female body as subject clashes in dissonance with its patriarchal text, challenging the very fabric of representation by refusing that text and posing new, multiple texts grounded in real women's experience and sexuality.[12]

Catherine Elwes summarizes the importance of performance art as a feminist vehicle of critique:

> Performance art offers women a unique medium for making a direct unmediated address. Performance is about the "real-life" presence of the artist. She takes on no roles but her own. She is author, subject, activator, director, designer. When a woman speaks within the performance tradition, she is understood to be conveying her own perceptions, her own fantasies and her own analyses. She is both signifier and that which is signified. Nothing stands between spectator and performer. There is no man-made script to give the male spectator an easy escape via author-identification—nothing can protect him from

direct confrontation with the woman who returns his gaze and demands freedom of speech and equality of communication.[13]

Much women's performance art involves the presentation of female sexuality, for "the personal and autobiographical for women is inextricably linked with female sexuality."[14]

Elinor Fuchs notes a shift in feminist performance art from its inception in the 1970s, when the emphasis seemed to be on presenting the sacred female body, to the replacement in the 1980s of the sacred body by the obscene female body.[15] To exemplify the latter Fuchs cites, among others, Karen Finley and her infamous "shoving of yams up her ass" and "shitting in a bucket" as part of two performance pieces in which Finley critiqued the "classical" female body by juxtaposing its carnivalesque possibilities. The classical body is a "closed," "finished," "sleek," statuesque, "static" body; the carnivalesque, by contrast, is an "open, protruding, extended, secreting body, the body of becoming, process and change":[16] "an image of impure corporeal bulk with its orifices (mouth, flared nostrils, anus) yawning wide and its lower regions (belly, legs, feet, buttocks and genitals) given priority over its upper regions (head, 'spirit,' reason)."[17] The prostitute body traditionally was relegated to the "lower" realm. The carnivalesque female body is what Mary Russo, in "Female Grotesques: Carnival and Theory," depicts as "the figure of the female transgressor as public spectacle."[18] Russo points out that "a woman, making a spectacle out of herself, had to do with . . . a loss of boundaries. . . . [A]ny woman could make a spectacle out of herself if she was not careful."[19] Performers, like Finley, "make a spectacle out of themselves" in order to transcode, displace, and overwrite the male meaning attached to the female body.

Prostitute Performance Art

Prostitutes are "spectacles" in patriarchal discourse and much of feminist discourse; their performance work moves toward deconstructing female sexual spectacle. From their position as the carnival other in the dominant representation of the female body, from their position as a pornographic body, prostitute performance artists displace, transcode, and overwrite this representation. The effect of bringing the pornographic genre into artspace is a displacement of both pornography and art through their intertext.

In prostitute performance art there is a conscious crossing and re-crossing of the line between the sacred and profane until one slides and dissolves into the other. Prostitute performance discourse starts from the point of the pornographic; the transcoding comes from this position; often there is an elision of critique and burlesque; elements of burlesque remain as the parody of burlesque. Prostitute performance art transgresses in three ways. Like feminist performance it transgresses the performance genre itself. In addition, it transgresses the feminist subgenre from the position of the "low" other—those often excluded from the category "feminist." Prostitute performance art also transgresses in a third way, a way that is most philosophical and spiritual, the way of a "true" transgressor. There is in these texts not only a sliding of the profane and the sacred, so that "god is a whore,"[20] but a self-referential disclosure and critique of this transgression:

> [I]n a world which no longer recognizes any positive meaning in the sacred . . . transgression prescribes not only [a][21] manner of discovering the sacred in its unmediated substance, but also a way of recomposing its empty form, its absence, through which it becomes all the more scintillating.[22]

Prostitute performance presents a particular female body, the body that dominant discourse and feminist discourse have marked as the obscene, the other, from the position of this body—speaking. Yet the artist is not only this body, or even primarily this body; she is many things at once: an artist/actress, erotic/sexual being, intellectual/critic, political/social commentator. Catherine Elwes writes:

> An artist operating within a cross-disciplinary performance tradition can refuse easy categorisation and begin to put together what patriarchy has pulled apart. A performer may be sexual, but she is not a stripper, she may act but she is not an actress, she may be intellectual but she is not an academic, she may employ political analysis, but she is not a politician. . . . By being both intellectual and erotic, she escapes categorisation into existing disciplines with their attendant pigeon-holing for women.[23]

Partly, prostitute performance art is about the refusal to fit into predetermined categorizations; prostitute artists use their bodies as sites of resistance to reunify "what patriarchy has pulled apart."[24]

Deep Inside Porn Stars: Club 90

Deep Inside Porn Stars was a partially improvised and partially scripted performance of a bimonthly consciousness-raising session among seven of New York's top porn stars: Candida Royalle, Annie Sprinkle, Veronica Vera, Gloria Leonard, Sue Nero, Veronica Hart, and Kelly Nichols. Club 90 formed in 1983; five of the members still meet. My reconstruction of the performance event is from the script (first and second drafts) and interviews about the performance with Candida Royalle, Annie Sprinkle, and Veronica Vera. Annie Sprinkle and Veronica Vera used this first piece as a beginning for more detailed performance pieces which I will be discussing. The four others are not performance artists. The title *Deep Inside Porn Stars* is a trace to a porn film *Deep Inside Annie Sprinkle* (1982), of which Annie was writer, director, and star.

Director (and one of the actors) Candida Royalle describes *Deep Inside Porn Stars* as "a turning point." She explains:

> The media suddenly took a tremendous interest in us from a whole new angle. We were not just to be written off as bimbettes or victims. . . . We were women who really could think. . . . It was controversial because people would rather think of women who choose to be sex workers as stupid or victims. The idea in this kind of culture that women would choose in their right mind to do this work was very threatening.[25]

It was a turning point in three ways. The first of which Royalle discloses: the documentation by prostitute/porn stars that they are capable of thinking, talking, and communicating their feelings, that they are neither stupid nor victims, and that they made a choice to work in pornography. It was a turning point in the porn debate because a new feminist viewpoint was introduced, that of the female porn actor. And it was a turning point in terms of introducing a new genre of feminist performance art: prostitute performance. Annie Sprinkle and Veronica Vera's performance pieces evolved out of *Deep Inside Porn Stars*; Candida Royalle's woman-centered couple films, which she directs and produces under the label Femme Productions, were conceived in her autobiographical portion of *Deep Inside Porn Stars*.

Deep Inside Porn Stars was performed in January 1984 at Franklin Furnace (a New York performance space) as part of Carnival Knowledge's (a feminist artists' collective) month-long art exhibition and eight-piece performance series entitled "The Second Coming." The explicitly stated aim of this series was "to explore a new definition of pornography, one that is not demeaning to women, men and children."[26] From the *Deep Inside Porn Stars* program the reader learns that the inclusion of porn stars "speaking" about pornography is a unique experience in the feminist performance community. The program states:

> CARNIVAL KNOWLEDGE affords us a unique opportunity to be aligned with other feminist artists usually considered arch-adversaries of the adult entertainment movement. We welcome this moment when women, regardless of calling, can respectfully stand together.

Deep Inside Porn Stars evolved out of real-life consciousness-raising meetings among the seven women staging the performance. Club 90, named after Sprinkle's street address which later became home of the "Sprinkle Salon," had its beginning at a baby shower for Veronica Hart. Royalle narrates how Club 90 was started:

> At the baby shower all of Veronica's friends from outside the industry eventually left and there was nothing but women from the industry all together. We had such a wonderful time together. We were hanging out, not really having a political discussion. We were just playing together. We said "gee, we should do this more often on a regular basis." There was such a feeling of camaraderie. This was the spring of 1983 and we started meeting in the summer of 1983.[27]

Deep Inside Porn Stars is a presentation of Club 90's early meetings where the women discuss "the porn business" and political issues, such as how the industry did not classify lesbian sex scenes as sex and therefore didn't pay for them. Using the feminist consciousness-raising group as a performance structure in which to combine the media of dramatic monologue and dialogue, slide show, dance, and singing, in part improvisation and in part script, *Deep Inside Porn Stars* deconstructs the division between pornographic and non-pornographic women. The piece is set up to be voyeuristic, but voyeuristic of the persons behind the personas. The program tells the viewer that she or he is "about to experience a rare and intimate slice of [seven celebrated sex stars'] lives." Further playing on voyeurism, the program states: "The only ground rule which was established to insure the privacy of their inner circle, was that anything discussed during such meetings was not to leave those premises." What *Deep Inside Porn Stars* does is to bring the premises, in a dual sense, to the art world. The performance takes place in a replication of Annie Sprinkle's premises, her living room. The philosophical premise is that the pornography business is both damaging and liberatory for the women working in it. What the audience is to be voyeur to, as the program establishes, is the women's "innermost feelings about themselves and how performing sexually on the camera has affected their lives." The space that *Deep Inside Porn Stars* presents is the space between life and theater: the performance is based on real meetings.

During the first part of the performance the women inconspicuously remove their porn clothes: this is the physical manifestation of the women opening themselves up to each other and the audience. The stripping, subtle as it is, connects the audience visually to burlesque theater, reminding the spectators that most of the women worked and work stripping in these theaters. The women re-dress in ordinary, almost dowdy, day clothes, showing that the imaginal line between pornographic women and non-pornographic women is a fine line and easily transgressed. The women engage in actions which serve to disrupt the dominant system of representation of the pornographic. Annie, because the meeting is taking place in her home, is making tea and serves tea and cookies to each new arrival, inviting each to "warm yourself by the fire." Candida arrives in a party dress and bearing fruit—a banana later becomes a pacifier or penis substitute. Candida almost immediately asks, "So girls, how are your little pussies doing?" She is referring to the recent neutering of three of the women's cats but obviously this play on pussy has the not-so-subtle intent of bringing to the fore in the spectators' mind how the women made/make their money. Veronica Vera brings this reference to the forefront when she teases the others with a story about her "pussy" which she refuses to tell until all are assembled. Kelly Nichols enters with Veronica Hart and a doll representing her baby Christopher. Kelly gives an account of having just rescued Veronica and Christopher as they got off the bus. A doll serving as Christopher is present throughout the piece and is passed from woman's knee to woman's knee. Christopher's presence links the reproductive and maternal aspects of the female body that are written out of pornographic representations. The reference to rescuing Veronica and Christopher as they got off the bus serves to connect the life of a porn star to the small, tedious real-life troubles that are always absent from pornography.

The background chitchat is interrupted by each woman as she narrates her own story while slides documenting different life points are shown. Collectively, the women discuss their childhood sexual experiences, including a discussion about when they "lost their cherries." Almost all the women were either eighteen or nineteen, the same age as most women of their generation. The disclosure of this fact dispels the cultural myth that sex workers begin having sex at an earlier age than most women. Other childhood sexual experiences were also typical: Veronica Vera talks about the Catholic church and getting in trouble with the nuns for kicking a boy; the other women tease Vera about this being the first sign of her later status as a dominatrix. Annie discloses her shyness as a child and young woman; Kelly speaks about growing up with five brothers and being a tomboy. These typical female childhood experiences undercut the commonly held assumption that somehow porn stars and other sex workers have childhoods that are different from other women. Veronica Hart parodies this belief with a joke about having had twenty-seven marines when she was ten years old in defiance of her mother who had warned her not to let boys touch her.

Candida begins her biography by telling her real (non-stage) name: Candice. Like all the women she traces her childhood, showing slides of herself in a Girl Scout uniform, tap dancing, high school pictures, college shots of her at a peace rally, pictures from various theatrical productions as well as slides of herself singing in San Francisco jazz clubs. Candida begins by establishing that her childhood was like most other little girls:

> I was in the Girl Scouts, I had a lot of friends, I had a wonderful imagination to keep me entertained. . . . I was always a ham! I began posing for the camera and dancing very early. . . . As you can see . . . I was pretty popular in high school, though terribly insecure underneath it all . . . and in college I became a strong peace activist and a feminist, a fact that surprises most people.

Candida sings and dances as part of her solo presentation. Candida brings out the ambiguity of being in porn:

> People ask me why I went into porn . . . money was my superficial reason. But there are lots of other more complex reasons: attention, a need to express my sexuality under the guise of another being: Candida; and fear of success. . . . I've had lots of time since my last film three years ago to try and understand my choices. With the help of an incredible shrink I've grown to appreciate what porn did for me. As well as how much it hurt me. I've only recently, after all this time, begun to experience the pain and humiliation I hid from myself so

that I could do these films and make my money. And I can tell you, its been very painful at times. . . . But nothing is black or white. . . . Sometimes I feel very bitter, like I gave up a lot of my dreams to do porn. . . . But other times . . . I see myself as somewhat of a revolutionary, making women's porn films one day to replace the male-oriented films that still exploit women and promote archaic sexuality.[28]

As Candida ends her piece the women continue to talk about "the business of porn." Their discussion is unscripted: They criticize it for dividing women into good girls and bad girls and perpetuating this division and discuss the fine line between being a celebrity and a slut, male manipulation in the industry and the need for a revolutionary feminization of the industry (which Royalle later went on to initiate through her company Femme Productions). They talk about the loss of privacy and about how producers are always trying to "rip off" the actors and have them do scenes not in the contract.

The piece ends with a deconstruction of itself; it is a performance that never happened. Gloria Leonard says: "Wouldn't people just love to know what we discuss here?" Candida responds with, "Why don't we do a show about it." They all think about this idea, at first excitedly; then the spectators' anticipation of voyeuristic pleasure is punctured: they all respond with "NAAHH!!" This device duplicitously denies that the performance was a performance and makes the act of viewing more voyeuristic than if they had agreed to do a show, as the first draft of the script indicates.

Deep Inside Porn Stars is a consciousness-raising performance piece that allows the viewers to see behind the images of porn star, prostitute, bad girl. The viewer is bombarded with conflicting images: women stripping, typical little girls, women who are singers and dancers, women with babies, women who have been represented by the hegemonic pornographic genre as only sexual critiquing the industry; articulate, intelligent pornographic women.

Post Porn Modernist: Annie Sprinkle

Annie Sprinkle's show *Post Porn Modernist* is a combination of a number of shorter performance pieces that she has performed around New York since 1984.[29] Annie's *Post Porn Moderist* show is easily taken apart, rearranged, and presented in whole or part; each piece stands on its own and fits together in a totality that traces Annie's sexual evolution from a shy girl to a porn star to a sacred prostitute/goddess.

Post Porn Modernist[30] is used as a title to indicate the intermixing of sexual and art genres. As Annie defines it:

> "Post porn" implies something after porn, "postmodernist" implies something artistic, "post porn modernist" is a term we use to describe a genre of sexually explicit material: more experimental, more political, less exclusively erotic.[31]

Annie has added a second *"post"* in her show title: she now calls it *Post Post Porn Modernist*. The additional "post" is placed to enhance what she calls her "New Ancient" philosophy of the unification of the sexual and the spiritual. In a recent interview for her Toronto visit, in *Eye* magazine, Annie explains:

> Post post porn modernists celebrate sex as the nourishing life-giving force. We embrace the genitals as part, not separate, from our spirits. We utilize sexually explicit words, pictures and performances to communicate our ideas and emotions. . . . We empower ourselves by this attitude of sex positivism. And with this love of our sexual selves we have fun, heal the world and endure.[32]

This theme of the unification of the sexual and the spiritual informs and weaves through Annie's work.

Post Porn Modernist takes apart pornographic images through postmodernist techniques of parody, play, displacement, tracing, and overwriting. I will examine eight of the twelve vignettes composing *Post Porn Modernist*. Annie begins with a version of her biographical piece form *Deep Inside Porn Stars*; showing slides of Ellen and Annie she juxtaposes and unites these two identities. She says:

> I was born Ellen Steinberg, but I didn't like Ellen
> very much, so I invented Annie Sprinkle.
> Ellen was excruciatingly shy. Annie is an
> exhibitionist.
> Ellen was fat and ugly, and nobody seemed to want her.
> Annie is voluptuous and sexy, and lots of people want
> her.
> Ellen desperately needs attention. Annie gets it.
> Ellen wore orthopaedic shoes and flannel nightgowns.
> Annie wears six-inch spiked high heels and sexy
> lingerie.
> Ellen was afraid of men and sex. Annie is fearless.
> Ellen was a nobody. Annie gets asked for autographs.
> Ellen wants to get married and have children. Annie

wants fame and fortune.
I suppose Ellen Steinberg really is Annie Sprinkle,
and Annie Sprinkle is really Ellen Steinberg.[33]

This piece, accompanied by a current photo of Ellen/Annie as over-weight and out of shape, and a current photo of Annie/Ellen in porn gear looking voluptuous and toned, deconstructs the myth of the pornographic, showing that "sex goddess"—a category used to separate women and make those who do not live up to the image feel insecure—is mostly a matter of clothing and posing.

This sliding between the good girl and bad girl personas and the fact that both are culturally produced is brought out even more in "The Transformation Salon" vignette. Annie has presented a number of Transformation Salons; she is currently doing a "Slut and Goddess Salon"[34] and a "Drag King for a Day Salon."[35] The "Transformation Salon," which is part of her show, is made up of "before" and "after" slides of women as "regular people" and then transformed into "sex stars." Annie explains to the audience the rationale for these transformations:

> Feminists are always arguing that sex magazines should not glamorize women and make them look "perfect," because very few women can live up to that *Playboy* centerfold image. Thus, women are unsatisfied and insecure about their own bodies, and men are wondering why their lovers don't look like pin-ups. But as you can clearly see here, even pin-ups don't really look like pin-ups. So as a feminist myself, I say let's NOT STOP glamorizing women. Let's make them ALL look glamorous. . . . I do not judge whether the "before" or the "after" photo makes her look better. I think they are equally beautiful and sexy in both.[36]

Annie's speech positions her as a feminist; she occupies the space denied to the pornographic woman by feminism. Her speech further undercuts (if the pictures are not sufficient in and of themselves) the belief that there is such a woman as a porn star. Visually the photos break down the male-created binary division between good girl and bad girl. The one slips into the other and is exposed as cultural artifice. Writing about a presentation of the "Transformation Salon" as part of the Kitchen's 1988 "Carnival of Sleaze," Elinor Fuchs claims: "the sequence was a kind of dare to the 'good girl' female spectator, if not exactly to enter the sex trade, to examine her own self-division."[37] Annie makes this connection between all women and female porn stars and the presence of each in the same body at the end of her piece when she says: "Maybe there's a little porn star in you. Maybe not. But I can tell you from experience . . . there's a little of you in every porn star."[38]

The "Slut and Goddess Salon" takes this reunification of the patriarchal division of women into sluts and goddesses even further. Women explore both sides of these powerful archetypes, ending with a ritual to unite "the sluts and goddesses within you and within the world."[39] The Sluts and Goddesses flyer invites women to "Change your consciousness by changing your clothes":

> First explore your super-slut side by wearing your choice of corsets, wigs, rubber and leather lingerie, six inch spiked high heels, garter belts, false eye lashes, etc. . . . Replace the judgements you have about yourself and other women with acceptance and compassion. Learn the secrets, feel the power and enjoy the pleasures of sluthood. Next explore your Goddess side. We'll adorn ourselves in colorful, sparkly Goddess attire, choose new names, create a sacred temple-like space, chant, breathe, awaken our senses, belly dance, learn ancient Tantric/Taoist/Native American techniques to build and channel sexual energy, go into ecstacy and learn about full body orgasm.

Sprinkle, the hostess, who refers to herself as a "Tantric devotee . . . new age girl, performance artist, high priestess, prostitute . . . and teacher," personifies a postmodern recreation of Aspasia's Salon and the *hetairae* schools in ancient Greece. Describing the guided crossover into the spiritual, Sprinkle says:

> I put on this music of nature sounds. The whole place becomes a temple. When they open their eyes they are in the temple of the sacred prostitute. All the candles are lit . . . Then we start going into really sacred space and magic time. We stay in silence. Everyone gets into their goddess clothes: sparkly, colorful, very sexy.[40]

The goddess is a spiritual and a sexual being. Sprinkle, through the Slut/Goddess workshop, is recuperating for the goddess that which Western philosophy and religion has absented: the sexual. She is returning to the space of the ancient sacred prostitute.

"Pornstistics" is a short, humorous segment that reviews Annie's porno/prostitution career through the use of computer graph charts on slides with such titles as "Why I Did It: Advantages" and "Why I Did It: Disadvantages." These two pie graphs provide the following answers (in order of weightiness). Advantages: "Money, Didn't know what else I wanted to do, Love and Attention, Creative outlet, To rebel against society, Glamour, I don't know why, Sex, I liked the costumes,

To overcome shyness." Disadvantages: "I met some *horrible* people, Irreversable psychological damage, I hurt my parents, Not enough money, I didn't want to work, Social disapproval, Became sexually jaded and confused, Felt like an object, Physical danger, It was hard sometimes, Politics." Using a weigh scale Annie concludes that the "Pros seem to Outweigh the Cons." Noticeably, not by very much on the scale. By presenting both the good and the bad aspects of her life in "the life," Annie creates an ambiguity, an ambiguity most women feel when they think about these industries; she doubly removes herself from the victim position: the victim position of someone so identified with the prostitute persona that she can see nothing problematic and the victim position of someone who experiences her prostitute career in retrospect as nothing but a nightmare.

A bar graph depicts the "Amount of cock sucked" by juxtaposing a penis to the Empire State Building; placed end to end the former equals the latter minus the antenna. A second bar graph compares Annie's weekly income of $4,000 to an average American woman's monthly income of $1,500; the final bar graph makes the difference in income wider by comparing Annie's seventeen-hour workweek to the forty-hour workweek. Just when the audience is either beginning to think that the benefits of pornography/prostitution far outweigh the drawbacks or that Annie is absenting the negative, Annie enacts "100 Blow Jobs," in which she performs fellatio on a dozen dildos nailed to a board while male voices on a taped soundtrack make angry demands. The segment does not end with her humiliation, as one is led to expect, but rather, with Annie sitting at her makeup table and giving herself the Aphrodite Award for sexual service to the community. She expresses her life-sex philosophy: "we are ALL sexually abused just by virtue of the fact that we live in such a sex-negative society."[41] Part of Annie's approach in "Pornstistics" and "100 Blow Jobs" is to disrupt the audience's expectations moment to moment as they arise by a double displacement: the pros of prostitution/pornography outweigh the cons; sexual commerce is humiliating; prostitution is a dignified service and commercial sex in a sex-negative society is a benefit to humanity.

"Bosom Ballet" and "A Public Cervix" both function to deconstruct the meanings attached to two of the most fetishized parts of a woman's body: her breasts and her vagina. Annie, wearing evening gloves and mimicking the movements of classical ballet, jiggles, slaps, wiggles, shakes, twists, and pulls her breasts to Strauss's "Blue Danube Waltz." This parody of high-culture forms, ballet and classical music, in a low-culture striptease genre both undercuts the patriarchal division of the female form into high (the ballerina) and low (the stripper) cultural forms and makes fun of the conventional fetishization of large breasts. Annie quotes *High Performance* art magazine's commentary on "The Bosom Ballet": "Showing her tits spills over the limit of sexiness and exaggerates by analogy our exaggerated interest in seeing or having large breasts, until humor overtakes self-consciousness."[42] Sprinkle desexualizes her large breasts, much sought after in the pornography industry (she made 150 feature porn movies and 20 feature videos) by a carnivalized presentation. Annie has created a photo installation of the "Bosom Ballet" which consists of eighteen photos freezing the movements of the live presentation.

"A Public Cervix," in which Annie with the aid of a speculum and a flashlight invites spectators to view her cervix, narrows the line between performer and spectator to a participant/voyeur space: the voyeur is actively holding a light and looking and Annie is directly returning his/her gaze and dialoguing with the individual spectator about the beauty of the cervix; intermittently she encourages the voyeur to describe what she or he sees. "A Public Cervix" challenges the patriarchal fear and disgust with women's internal sexual organs— Annie is saying "isn't my cervix beautiful." The piece cuts through the very premise of pornography—the distanced and anonymous viewer appropriating the object of desire for (usually) his pleasure. Objectifying eroticism is stripped away and in its place is eroticism of the whole female sexual organ that belongs to the subject: Annie. The male gaze that traditionally objectified the external female genitalia and separated it from the internal reproductive part is confronted with the beauty of the inside, the neck of the womb through which everyone has passed. Annie begins the piece by showing charts of the female reproductive system; she tells the audience what to look for. Annie gives five reasons for doing this performance:

1. To demystify women's bodies.
2. To create a reality where there is no shame about genitalia.
3. Because the cervix is beautiful. . . .
4. Because it's fun. . . .
5. [I]t's a way of saying to some men, "You . . . want to see pussy . . . I'll show you more . . . than you ever wanted to see."[43]

What men see is not the fetishized external "pussy" of pornography; what they see is a unified female sexual/reproductive organ; and the exhibition is on Sprinkle's terms, not theirs.

The pieces of the second half of the show—"New Ancient Sex (Theory)" and "New Ancient Sex (Practice)"—mark a change in genre from deconstruction of the pornographic female body, the body of the porn industry, to presentation of the female body as a sacred temple and celebration of the ancient sacred prostitute. In the theory segment Annie tells the legend of the sacred prostitute, exposing society's degradation of the contemporary prostitute and disrespect for the sexual body. This is part of her reconstruction of the ancient legend:

> Once upon a time, a long, long time ago, in ancient cultures such as Sumeria, Mesopotamia, Egypt and Greece, there were no whorehouses or street walkers. . . . Instead at that time, there were Temples of the Sacred Prostitutes.
>
> The Sacred Prostitutes were highly respected members of society, considered by all people to be powerful healers, counselors and magicians. . . . They were taught everything there was to know about sacred sex by the elder priestesses; their well-tended bodies were trained to be channels for the Divine. . . . The most essential elements of their love-making sessions were prayer and ritual. Sex was their path to enlightenment, their creative and spiritual discipline.
>
> People went to a Sacred Prostitute to be cleansed, healed, nourished and pleasured. Her temple was breathtakingly beautiful. . . . [44]
>
> They would go into a state of sexual ecstasy because that was the best time to pray and to have visions and if there was a war or plague they could create miracles when they were in this state of sexual ecstasy.[45]

Here one can read a trace to Diotima, the sacred priestess of the *Symposium*, who postponed a plague on Athens through spells. Annie says "I am really connected with this legend of the sacred prostitute. I feel like I embody her."[46]

The practice segment of the "New Ancient Sex" is the re-creation of a masturbation ritual whose origin Annie attributes to the ancient sacred prostitutes. It is a participatory event: Annie describes it as "a ritual of participation rather than voyeurism."[47] Every spectator is given a rattle which she or he shakes to music made from Annie's sexual body sounds. As the audience provides auditory stimulation Annie, encircled by burning candles, breathes, undulates, and masturbates (using a vibrator) herself into an erotic trance and frequently to orgasm. She calls on an erotic tradition evoking the spirits and knowledge from ancient tantric and Taoist masters, Native American teachers, the Phoenix fireman and firewoman, the geishas, in addition to the spirit of the sacred prostitute. Annie combines the philosophy and physiology of sacred sex.

Post Porn Modernist is a transgression of the profane to the sacred and then a re-transgression from the spiritual to the flesh as Annie and the audience collectively produce a sexually aroused orgasmic body. One body becomes the other; the audience becomes a sexual partner; the sacred and the profane are united in Annie and the audience. Her performance transcends artspace and is, momentarily, as she indicates in the *Eye* interview, an act of healing oneself and the world.

Portrait of a Sexual Evolutionary: Veronica Vera

Bare Witness[48] evolved as a performance piece out of four origins: Vera's biographical segment in *Deep Inside Porn Stars*, a written text "Beyond Kink" (Vera describes her writing as the documentation of "life as performance art"),[49] her film *Portrait of a Sexual Evolutionary* (1987), and her testimony before a Senate Judiciary Committee (1985) that became part of the Meese Commission's report on pornography.[50] The dominant theme behind *Bare Witness*—a theme according to which Vera both narrates and montages her life (also a theme that is traceable through De Sade, Bataille, and Foucault)—is that the profane and the sacred are transcendences of one another; that is, the excess of one goes into the representation of the other. Veronica is saying:

> God is exciting! He introduced me to the forbidden. He is the intoxicating frankincense of benediction, the priest dressed in robes of silk brocade: purple for passion, green means hope, white for joy and red for suffering.[51]

This speech is accompanied by pictures of her nude body bound in strips of white silk (de)contextualized by Catholic church music. These are followed by two pictures of a golden Christ; in the first he is nailed on the cross and in the second he is dragging the cross. The latter is beside a Bible turned to the "Scourging of Christ"; this provides a religious trace for the later shots of Vera wearing white, red, and black sexual attire, arms raised and tied. The church music resumes with the Christ-like poses that Vera has adopted for these slides/photos. Vera links God, suffering, and sexuality: "Martyrs whose suffering brought them closer to God—who cleansed themselves of impurity each night [as] they whipped themselves to sleep."[52] Vera unites the spiritual and the sexual in precisely the same way Bataille does: "God is a whore exactly like other whores."[53] Vera presents sex as transgression and transgression both as "a continuous process of self-transcendence"[54] and the "incessant cross[ing] and re-cross[ing] of a line which closes up" as it is crossed;[55] in Vera's presentation the line between madonnas and whores closes up. Vera calls herself a "shady madonna": "shady madonna conveys the idea that a woman is not just a madonna or a whore. She is both of these at once and all points in between."[56] Vera's work is about the unification of what has been marked out and separated as good and bad; her other two representations of this closing of the line are the nuclear family/sadomasochism and the little girl/lusty woman.

Vera introduces her piece as a journey:

It is a journey in the quest of light on the other side—a place where the little girl joins hands with the lusty woman, a glorious place of understanding and self acceptance—beyond kink.

She begins with "Little Mary" who "always tried to do everything right"; here the viewer sees shots of Mary tap dancing with two other little girls at a dancing school recital and Mary playing house; Mary is in white. Veronica speaks an old nursery rhyme over the text:

There was a little girl
Who had a little curl right in the middle of her
forehead.
When she was good, she was very, very good.
And when she was bad, she was horrid.

The poem is accompanied by pictures of Veronica (Mary's confirmation name, we are informed) with wrists tied, body bound, and rope around her neck; the binding is all in white. The last line of the rhyme ends on Vera's pink vulva exposed through a slit in her panties, highlighting that the female sexual organ was the part that was "horrid."

Veronica links her sadomasochism to her childhood and her mother's chastisements: "S/M began with childhood yearnings and the confusion between painful punishments and tenderness following it." Here the viewer sees shots of Veronica being punished by her S/M mother, Mistress Antoinette. The narrative is of a childhood punishment and of the overlapping of pain and love:

> "Don't touch yourself down there," Mommy tells me. "God does not
> like it." Mommy . . . punishes me with Daddy's belt. It is a long black
> snake of a belt that lives in the loops of Daddy's pants. . . . The belt
> comes to life in her hand. The belt hurts my fingers, lashes out at my
> fanny. . . . The belt makes it all better. Mommy can love me again.

Part of Veronica's sexual evolution is from being Mistress Antoinette's
slave to being a mistress/mommy. Using the language of motherhood—"Don't cry sweetheart. Mommy will make you all better"—
Veronica shows shots of herself administering punishment. Veronica
hypothesizes that "a lot of fetishes began right in the womb" as the
spectator watches slides of her, clad from head to foot in black latex,
doing a rebirthing scene in a pool.

Vera intentionally crosses and recrosses the line between the sacred
(religion and the family) and the pornographic so many times that the
images and narrative are collaged, producing an intertext in which they
are inseparable. She shows slides from a series named "The Menstruation Photos" of herself smearing menstrual blood over her entire
body. She says, "My Mother told me something wonderful was going
to happen to me one day"; in the background is the song, "Momma
said there'll be days like this; there'll be days like this my Momma
said." Describing an experience in Catholic school when the nun
cleared the room of all the boys and told the girls "never to let a boy
touch us, our bodies were our temples," Vera says "I didn't understand
what she was talking about but I knew that the passion in her voice
got me very excited." She describes her work as "weaving like a tapestry," a tapestry of the ordinary and the forbidden, with the ordinary
producing and contextualizing the forbidden. Vera reverses the process
and uses the forbidden to recontextualize the ordinary and thus de-
territorializes both.

Vera makes a distinction between erotic presentation and the "pornography machinery." Saying "I prefer to make my own images, my
own statements," she continues with slides of herself in contemporary
erotic/pornographic costumes "recreating the Kama Sutra in the land
where these love positions were born"; her body is juxtaposed to sacred sexual engravings on Eastern religious temples. She produces this
image on postcard art, telling us how to read the image by rewriting
her teacher/nun's statement: "My Body Is a Temple" beneath it. Veronica informs her audience: "I create an image of myself that I can
cherish, an image that will unite me with all women through all

time." Her predominant statement is the unity of all women and all female body images.

Vera's work without her narrative could be read as a reproduction of the pornographic woman; that is, the visual images on their own do not act as critique in and of themselves, as much of Sprinkle's images do. It would be difficult, for example, to read photos of "The Bosom Ballet" as part of the more "standard" pornographic genre, while Vera's "Menstruation Photos" of a beautiful woman smearing her blood on her body possibly could be read this way. But Vera's aim, especially in *Beyond Kink*, is a closing of the line between art (presentation as critique) and pornography (representation). The art medium and the mode of presentation of the material displaces the pornographic meaning, but not entirely, and that is her point. Vera ends one version of *Bare Witness* with the following questions to her audience:

> Do you see the whore who wants to be punished?
> Do you see the little girl tied up by the Indians?
> Do you see the martyr about to have her nipples chopped?
> Do you see the woman, trussed up and ridiculous?
> Do you see the sex goddess, the fertility symbol?
> Do you see the bitch in heat who yearns to be touched?
> Do you see the sacred, shady Madonna?
> Do you see that little girl with her fingers in her underpants?
> Do you understand that what you see is not simple?
> Do you understand that all these women are me?[57]

Here Veronica collapses and collages binary female stereotypes: refusing to hold any one of them, she is all of these opposites: the whore/little girl; the martyr/woman trussed up, the sex goddess/fertility symbol, the sacred/shady madonna. She displaces the standard meanings through unification so that the dominant meanings are rewritten.

Merchants of Love and *HARDCORE*: Gwendolyn

Gwendolyn's two major performance pieces *Merchants of Love* and *HARDCORE* are overtly political. Gwendolyn uses her position as a sex worker (stripper and former prostitute) as a subject position from which to critique psychotherapy (*Merchants of Love*,) and the antiporn movement (*HARDCORE*).[58] Both pieces integrate films made by Gwendolyn. She narrates over the film segments, producing a different

1. Candida Royalle. From *Deep Inside Porn Stars*. Courtesy of Femme Productions.

2. Annie Sprinkle, "A Public Cervix," from *Post Porn Modernist*. Photo by Leslie Barany.

3. Veronica Vera, "Shady Madonna," from *Bare Witness*. Photo by Annie Sprinkle.

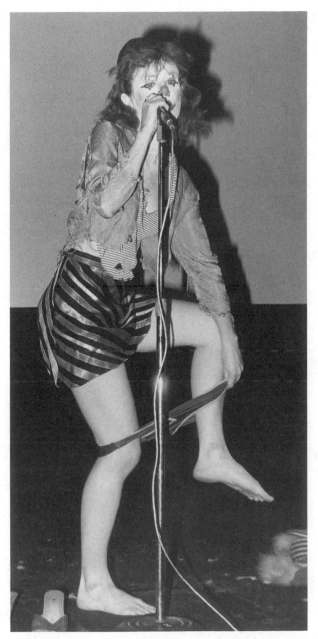

4. Gwendolyn in "Cardiac Arrest." Photo by K. Reich.

5. Janet Feindel as "Georgia Scott," from *A Particular Class of Women*, Lazara Publications, distributed by Blizzard Press (Canada) and Inland Book Co., Connecticut (U.S.). Photo by Leonard Moss.

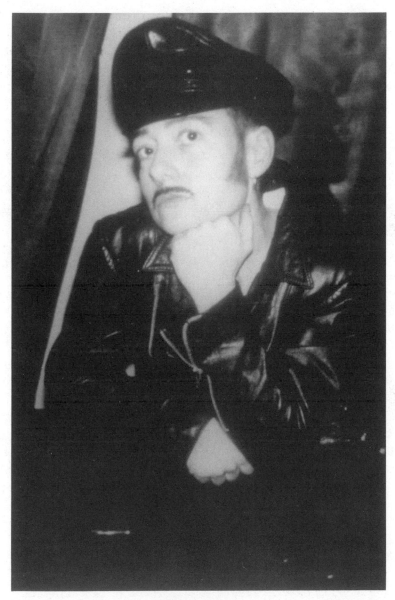

6. Shannon Bell as "Sam" in the Drag-King-for-a-Day Salon at the Sprinkle Salon. Photo by Annie Sprinkle.

text each showing. Her usual style is to disrobe, quite unerotically, either at the very beginning of her performances or close to the beginning; she narrates part of her text completely nude except for sneakers, then in a denim jacket; as the performance progresses Gwendolyn dresses herself in torn fishnets, a ripped tank top/muscle shirt, and a satin miniskirt. Visually, Gwendolyn is desexualizing her body, naturalizing her nudeness.

Merchants of Love is subtitled "A Sex Worker's Experiences in Therapy." Gwendolyn performs in a painted clown face. Interspersed are a couple of ball-juggling acts. She is providing a trace to burlesque theater where strippers, clowns, and jugglers shared a stage. This performance combines a couple of her jobs that are usually considered to be exclusionary: working as a clown at children's birthday parties and stripping at clubs and at adult male stags. In clown face complete with red clown nose (the nose later comes off) Gwendolyn plays with her lines: "Might as well tell ya, cause the truth will out. I am a professional bad girl. Painted lady. Could you tell?"[59] Gwendolyn links therapy and sex work as service industries, informing the audience/customer "if you're looking for love, call the fifty-minute hour, if you're looking for love, call the sliding-scale facilitators—counselors, therapists." She distinguishes her experience in each context: "There are two sides to the story: gettin' paid for bein' laid [prostitution] and the flip side—payin' somebody to fuck me over [therapy]."

Gwendolyn entered therapy always with a female therapist, usually a feminist therapist; she first started therapy at a time when the stripping industry in Toronto was changing and strippers were beginning to be subject to both police and club owner harassment. She shows *Choice Boredom*, a movie that she has made of her first therapist. The film text is a collage of paintings by Gwendolyn, a papier-mâché puppet with yellow twine hair (Gwendolyn informs us that Choice was a big husky blonde), a putty pig nose, and a large red mouth for eating the twenty-dollar bills Gwendolyn's hand feeds her. Gwendolyn is represented by her hand in the film. The film begins with Gwendolyn shaking her hand and saying (live), "Ow it hurts. It's okay I'll just slip on a bit of paint," and her hand paints her nails. The narrative of *Choice Boredom* begins: "She lived in the rich part of town, where money grows on trees." A picture of money pasted on painted trees is on the screen. The narrative continues: "she had a swimming pool in her backyard." A blond Barbie doll floats in a basin of water. "She liked

to drink tea with milk, no sugar." Gwendoln's hand pours milk into
a teacup and stirs.

Gwendolyn brings out one of her criticisms of therapists with the
implication that although both therapists and sex workers provide
"love" for money, therapists are hypocritical about the exchange.
Gwendolyn tells the audience: "Once I complained 'cause she was
away a lot. Like, how can you run a business if you're not there? She
said, 'I don't do this for the money.' " "Then why am I paying you?"
Gwendolyn asks. She tells the audience, "I know. I'll feel better if I
pay. It's more like real life." The hand feeds the devouring puppet
mouth more twenties.

Juxtaposing what was going on in her day-to-day life, Gwendolyn
says: "we were sucking up to bosses, and sucking off cops, to keep out
of trouble." In therapy Gwendolyn was talking about kindergarten and
her time on the street. Shots of hands writing with fingerpaint "I love
you" backward and a segment of Gwendolyn negotiating a trick follow.
She comments: "So you stay in the now, and talk about the past."
Following more shots of the hand feeding twenties to the *Choice Boredom* puppet, who bites it, the film ends with the image of a prettily
wrapped package. "Therapy is not a gift. You got to pay for it." "Pretty
package." The hands unwrap it to display an empty box. "That's it."

Accompanied by slides Gwendolyn decribes her addiction therapy
with a number of therapists. The message she conveys is how out of
touch middle-class "straight" therapists are with the reality of many
of their clients and how if a client is in the sex business their psychological problems, which they share with people in all professions, are
constructed by the therapist as determined by their sexual practices:

> One therapist said "you are a stripper and you are a drug addict. Sim-
> ple. Stop stripping. Then you won't need drugs. Anyone would take
> drugs if they had to face a crew of drunken brutes every night."

Gwendolyn disrupts this logic, which is premised on and perpetuates
the construction of the prostitute as different, as the female other,
with the fact that "There are chemically dependent people in every
walk of life. Maybe we should all stop working." Playing on the North
American anti-drug war she advises, "Just say no to the landlord."

Gwendolyn blends her attraction, love, resentment, anger, hurt, and
contempt for a particular therapist in her film *Katrinka*, but the particular moves into a general commentary on therapy as a discursive

practice which produces victims. The visual text shows Gwendolyn in a T-shirt and sweats, clutching a pillow, tossing and turning on a bare futon. She is fighting her hash addiction. Talking over the film, Gwendolyn tells how Katrinka broke her heart; Gwendolyn was "transferring her obsession with dope to Katrinka." Katrinka's insensitivity and lack of compassion is evident in her narration of her recent positive and pleasant dope experience to Gwendolyn. Many of Gwendolyn's sessions, we are informed, are taken up by Katrinka talking about her own sexual exploits. In an angry gesture Gwendolyn doesn't show for her session two weeks in a row. These are the only two sessions she's missed over a two-year period. Gwendolyn waits for a sign—a telephone call, a note—to show her that Katrinka cares about her as a person. Nothing. When Gwendolyn finally calls Katrinka's office, her secretary informs Gwendolyn that her space has been given to another client. Gwendolyn narrates her confrontation with Katrinka:

> I went to her house and I said, "I guess I am better off now, right?" At least I know now that you didn't care about me. . . . You didn't even think about me." Katrinka said, "But I did think of you. I heard of a woman found dead in a ditch, and I thought of you."

The film image is of Gwendolyn lying face down in a ditch. The film image shifts to Gwendolyn punching and beating the pillow she previously had been clutching. From beneath wooden floorboards Gwendolyn removes a large butcher knife and begins slashing and slashing the pillow; blood appears; Gwendolyn lies crying in the bath, clothes on, holding the blood-stained pillow. Talking over the images she asks questions directed to the audience. Her questions expose society's assumptions about prostitutes:

> Why would I be found dead in a ditch? Because I am a bad girl and I deserve to be punished? Or because sex workers are suppose to be victims? Why would I, an honest whore, be any more likely to be found dead in a ditch than you, a lazy, arrogant, incompetent quack of a doctor?

Gwendolyn has come under feminist criticism for the pillow-slashing scene; the claim is that it is a representation of violence against women. Gwendolyn tells the audience: "I figure it was violence against a pillow that kept me from violence against a particular woman." This difference between image/fantasy and reality is an issue that is central to her critique of antipornography.

Gwendolyn's collage of presentations—herself in clown face, periodically drinking from a silver flask (reproducing that old connection between prostitutes and alcohol), the roughly made, simple, and humorous images of *Choice Boredom*, the painful and violent images of *Katrinka*—produce a multilayered critique of the therapy business, making the business of prostitution look kinder by comparison. And this is precisely Gwendolyn's point.

HARDCORE is a collage of eleven narratives beginning with Adam and Eve and ending with Gwendolyn's much acclaimed short film *Prowling by Night* (1990). *Prowling by Night* is an entirely prostitute produced and narrated depiction of the Toronto Prostitute Safe Sex street project and of police harassment of both the safe-sex outreach workers and the women working. *Prowling by Night* is part of the *Five Feminist Minutes* program sponsored by the National Film Board of Canada. Subtitled "A Sex Worker Examines the Morality of the Anti-Porn Movement," *HARDCORE* interconnects religious profaning of the nude female image, antiporn feminist ideology, and police brutalization of prostitutes and strippers.

Gwendolyn begins the piece in a black vinyl raincoat; she opens it, revealing her nakedness; nude, she narrates the story of Adam and Eve. Gwendolyn polishes an apple on her pubic hair, pulling apart her vaginal lips to confront the spectators straight on. The spectator sees exactly what he or she would see of Gwendolyn's body in the strip club where she works, except that what is seen is filtered through both its location in artspace and Gwendolyn's narrative. Gwendolyn shakes the apple, shaking out her vaginal juices to the audience. "Mmmm, it's good,"[60] she says as she reenacts Eve's bite into knowledge. The visual text shifts to slides of Jesus out of a Sunday school primer and slides of children painting at a Sunday school class. Gwendolyn narrates her first experience of censorship:

My first experience of censorship was when I was a little girl in Sunday school. The teacher told us the story of Adam and Eve. I drew a picture of Eve bare naked. . . . Suddenly the teacher snatched Eve from my arms and tore her apart. Censorship: violence against pictures.

Playing on the language of antiporn feminism, Gwendolyn counters and displaces "pornography: violence against women" with "censorship: violence against pictures." Her intent, which becomes more pronounced later in the performance when she invites women to make their own porn, is to maintain a line between image and reality. She says: "write it down, make a picture, do a movie, because pornography is fantasy, not reality."

Gwendolyn narrates a history of the destruction of the strippers' union CABE (Canadian Association of Burlesque Entertainers). She shows slides of herself and union sisters dancing, protesting, and riding on a float in the annual Labor Day parade. Inside an intricate history of the particularity of the busting of CABE is a history of the destruction of the burlesque tradition.

> For those of you who were there and those of us who care to remember. We were part of a tradition—Burlesque. Strippers, comics, musicians, all on one stage. Took away the musicians, took away the comics. Now they have taken away the stage. Table dancing. Eighth wonder of the world. If you haven't seen it the table does not dance.

Gwendolyn actually is a postmodern burlesque performer—postmodern because the elements are mixed: she strips but is not doing a strip show; she is a comic and does clown acts. But what really marks her as a postmodern burlesque performer are these personas put together as a format for the purpose of presenting political analysis and documentary historical narratives. Her montage documentation of the bombing of porn stores in western Canada and Litton industry (which produced a part for the cruise missile) in Toronto by Direct Action, a Vancouver-based political/terrorist group, slides into an exposition of antiporn feminist persecution of sex workers. She shows a slide of her and her girlfriend doing a sex show at a stag for "some guys at Litton" the week after it was bombed. As she informs us that the stag was booked way in advance, we see slides of Gwendolyn and her friend on a stage spraying whipped cream on each others vaginas. The slides switch to pictures of Toronto's first "Take Back the Night March." Gwendolyn, connecting the sentiment that says it is acceptable to destroy visual representations (porno videos) with the hurting of human beings (Litton workers were hurt), tells of how antiporn feminists added to strippers' fears that their places of work might be attacked by Direct Action supporters:

> Just after all these explosions feminists here in Toronto marched down Yonge street in a thing called "Take Back the Night." They stopped in front of one of our strip clubs and demanded that it be closed. Said "stripping was pornography," "was violence against women." I remember a feminist screaming at a whore, "You make it impossible for women to walk down the streets." The girls inside were scared.

We were afraid some fool might plant a soothing comfy bomb in one of our clubs.

In one of the most incisive quips of the show, Gwendolyn counsels women to make their own images. Making fun of the division between pornography and erotica that has taken up much feminist energy, she says:

Pornography tells lies about women. . . . Tell the truth, make your own porn, or make erotica if that's what you are into. Erotica, the Noah's Ark of Sex: Two by two, side by side, nobody on top in my fantasy.

Gwendolyn shows a film excerpt of her and her cat Pumpkin "pleasuring each other." She refers to it as her "jerk-off" segment, explaining that a "good girl told her not to say 'jerk off.' Men jerk off." Gwendolyn asks the audience: "What do women do, fake it? Even when they are alone, lip gloss for the wet look?" The film excerpt is part of the longer film *Out of the Blue: A Cozy Porn and Variety Slut Show*. It was made by a group of strippers, prostitutes, and lesbian/gay activists as part of a series called "Toward an Erotic Film Language" sponsored by A Space, a Toronto gallery and performance space.

Gwendolyn educates the audience about the work Toronto sex workers are doing running Maggies, a government-sponsored, prostitute administered and run Prostitutes' Safe Sex Project. She doesn't so much provide safe-sex techniques (this is the subject of her prostitute produced sexually explicit film *Pedagogy* that is shown in alternate film venues) but lets the audience know that, as her button says, "Hos Are Safe Sex Pros."

The final segment in *HARDCORE* is a showing of *Prowling by Night*. There is a double play on the word "prowling." The film shows two Safe Sex outreach workers, Valerie Scott and Ryan Hotchkiss, distributing condoms and providing information on safe-sex techniques and on police harassment and prostitutes' rights to the women who are on the prowl for clients. They are constantly followed by a prowling police car and frequently stopped and harassed by the officers in the car. As Val and Ryan stroll the strip the working women tell them about the most recent episodes of police harassment. The film style is photo montage; the visual images are hand-produced drawings cut out and layered to produce a three-dimensional effect; each woman is represented by a hand-drawn cut-out. The narrative, completely dialogical, is constructed by the voices of twenty women who work and one male voice who does the cop role. The film is a documentation of police brutality: women tell of how cops demand blow jobs, destroy the women's condoms, refuse to use condoms for the forced oral sex they elicit from the women, and take the women's money. In a deconstruction of the Toronto police department's motto "To Serve and Protect," the film depicts a uniformed police officer, pants down, erect penis out directly in front of a woman on her knees; the woman is holding out money; the officer is motioning with his hands toward his penis. His buddy waits in the cruiser, a sign that this is a commonplace occurrence which does not need to be hidden. The last word of the police motto "protect" is visible on the car's front door. Written beneath the woman's knees are the words "He gets laid and paid." *Prowling by Night* rewrites the dominant cultural images of prostitutes as criminals and the police as the protectors of "good" society from these criminal elements; it displaces the idea that johns and pimps are the main abusers of prostitutes; and it shows prostitutes as safe-sex educators and practitioners.

Gwendolyn's work undermines the taken-for-granted societal preconceptions: those which automatically construct therapists as more noble than prostitutes; those which dissociate antipornography feminists from violence while seeing strippers as perpetuators of violence against women; and those which view the police as upholders of justice, prostitutes and pimps as criminals, and pimps and johns as by definition abusers.

A Particular Class of Women: Janet Feindel

As Feindel explains in her introduction, *A Particular Class of Women* evolved into a published play out of a series of monologue impressions, part mimicry, part parody, of women she worked with in the striptease business. The impressions grew, over a four-year period, into eight developed characters. Each character is a complete performance piece in itself. When Feindel performs more than one of the character pieces the continuity is maintained through onstage costume changes. Feindel's persona changes with each costume change. What the play performed in its totality produces is a typology of women in the striptease industry: Luv the young punk chick, Lil the retiring burlesque queen, Glynis the academic, Marky the sweet young woman, Pink

Champagne the obnoxious feature act, Petal Rose the ballerina cum stripper cum hooker, Angel the clown, and Georgia Scott the tough and mouthy mature woman.

The title of the play, *A Particular Class of Women*, under which the eight characters are collectively presented, is a political tactic Feindel has employed to deconstruct an Ontario judge's statement to a jury hearing a rape case in which the woman raped worked as a stripper: the judge informed the jury "she is from a particular class of women whose profession it is to incite lust." Feindel plays on class, showing the differences among the women working: educationally, economically, socially, ethnically, and in terms of sexual preference.

Combining the genres of monologue, drama, some mime, and striptease Feindel describes her work as "a kaleidoscope in which various issues are explored, through the unique perceptions of each character."[61] Unlike the other performance artists, Feindel is playing characters other than herself; these roles are not, however, removed from herself; they are her construction of women she has worked with. She presents the characters without distancing herself or reflecting on them in any way. Feindel poses as a mirror of each woman reflecting her individual life experience, creating a composite picture that is in constant flux. Each character speaks from the subject position of strip woman; one, "Petal Rose," from the additional subject position of prostitute woman.

Although this is only a subtheme in the work, the characters provide a documentation of the change in stripping from vaudeville through burlesque to table dancing. Two of the women—Lil and Georgia—have their performance roots in burlesque; both lament the changes which have reduced the stripper from an entertainer to "pure cunt."[62] Each of the women's acts presents a stage in the devolution of striptease as an art form: burlesque act, classic strip, stocking act, floor show, table dancing.

A Particular Class of Women is first and foremost a performance medium for presenting the "personal lives" of eight strip women. It is also a response to the feminist denial of feminist "identity" to sex workers in general and strippers in particular. Feindel informs the reader: "It has a strong feminist sentiment expressed not only through the camaraderie of the women, but also in their ability to articulate sexual issues which women are generally discouraged from doing."[63] Georgia's story of her inability to achieve orgasm is a good example of the intersection of both: the women jointly aid Georgia in reclaiming her sexual body. Georgia narrates to the audience:

> I can't come right. I always figured it was on account of the fact I was gang raped at sixteen. . . . I'm talking about the fact that I can't come. Next thing I know, I got my legs spread from here to Philadelphia, five broads looking up my snapper, checkin' out the problem. Turns out I got a hooded clit. Cu clux clit. Just had to rub lower.[64]

The work, in part and whole, has had a number of North American showings; excerpts have been performed in feminist cabarets and lesbian/gay performance events. Feindel performed "Petal Rose" at the 1985 "Feminist and Sex Workers Conference on Pornography and Prostitution." She did excerpts at Le Strip, a Toronto strip theater, recrossing the boundary between art and pornography; the art piece comes out of the pornographic genre, then returns there to reclaim the pornographic space as a medium in which the whole performer (body and life history) is on stage. As a spectator at Janet's performance of "Petal Rose" for the Prostitute and Feminist conference, one could feel the mixture or ambivalence of fear and desire that some of the women (and perhaps some of the few men there) had that Petal Rose would take her clothes off completely; she stopped at the G-string. This audience ambivalence was articulated the next day at one the conference's open forums. It had a lot to do with this being the first time a number of the women were in a striptease voyeur situation. In contrast, when Feindel performed "Luv" (who is a bisexual punk chick) for lesbian and gay audiences in Toronto (Cabaret for Pride Week) and New York (WOW Cafe), women and men removed black licorice from her leg garters with their teeth.[65]

The play has three areas: the kitchen, the dressing room, and the dance area, which is a lit runway that goes into the audience. There is a fluidity among the areas; the women's striptease does not always take place on the strip runway; the runway is intermittently used as the monologue space, thus breaking the spaces of speech and dance; this could be read as a conscious deconstruction of the representation of the stripper as nothing but a body/object. Each woman is announced "on" and "off" stage in strip club lingo by a male MC voice:

> MC: That's right Ladies and Gentlemen! We bring you the marvellous Marky, liquid fire in motion, the girl with the twenty-one jewel movements. Marky! Marky! Let's hear it for her Marky! . . .

MC: And that was Marky! The girl with the face of an angel and one devil of a body.[66]

As the female characters change and a new one "comes on," each disrupts the audience's expectation of their stripping: Marky strips before she speaks; Georgia Scott undresses out of her street clothes and dresses in her strip costume so that the audience sees her putting on her G-String rather than taking it off; the play closes with Lil, who has quit the business, walking out of the kitchen area and doing one last act, not coincidentally a classic strip act. The viewers are constantly in the dual position of drama theater spectators and strip theater spectators, unsure of when the boundaries of one medium will be crossed to the other. Petal Rose, who left the National Ballet to become a star at Marvin's, erases what she sees as the artificial line between the dance forms of ballet and stripping:

[S]tripping, ballet, it's all the same. Dancing is an addiction. . . . Besides, if you look up the word "ballet" in the Encyclopedia Britannica, say, 1905, it will say lewd, obscene dancing. Now ballet is acceptable and stripping is considered lewd and obscene.[67]

The women reflect politically on their own condition and displace the dominant cultural myths about strippers: for example, that most strippers and prostitutes are incest survivors and that the women in the business often do not get along and are jealous of one another. Angel, who performs a cross between a striptease and a clown act to "Girls Just Want to Have Fun," tells the audience about her stepfather's sexual abuse of her and her sister. Just as the audience is comfortably feeling that one of their presuppositions about strippers is being confirmed by women on the "inside," Angel begins to talk about her incest group:

I'm going to one of them incest groups. . . . People say, "You're a stripper. You must be an incest victim." They're so full of shit. There's ten of us in my group and I'm the only stripper.[68]

The friendship and respect among the women is evident in all the characters except for Pink Champagne, who doesn't view stripping as a job but rather is obsessed with her stardom. Reflecting on her twenty-two-year career as a stripper, Lil tells the audience:

I miss the girls. You know when I look back over my years in the business, that's the best thing about it; the girls. Great ladies. And strong. We had fun.[69]

Angel, talking to an absent Lil and the audience, says:

> I love my work. Every girl I ever worked with I like. Isn't one girl in
> this business I'd bad mouth. If there's a new girl, you help her out.
> Remember when Phebe started? We're telling her what costume to
> wear, what music to dance to[.][70]

Feindel undercuts the ridiculous fascination of the "straight" culture with "why" a woman would choose to strip. Glynis parodies the
standard questions strippers are asked in reference to her job as university cafeteria cashier (she informs the audience it takes her a week
to make the same amount of money she made in one night of stripping): "What's it like to be a cashier? How do you handle it? Of course
you must have been an incest victim."[71] Feindel through her character
Petal Rose displaces the belief that paid sex is somehow necessarily of
lesser worth and less intimate than sex in which money is not overtly
exchanged. Petal Rose says: "I enjoy sex more if I charge. The best
thing for me is to be in bed with a trick and eating! . . . I've trained a
lot of men to pay and now they prefer it."[72] Thus she undercuts the
dominant narrative according to which prostitutes by the nature of the
sexual exchange cannot have fun with their clients. She also displaces
mainstream feminism's position that the prostitute is the client's sexual slave.

Feindel doesn't ignore the undesirable side of working as a stripper.
In particular, she criticizes club owners demanding sexual favors and
trying to "rip the women off" for money. Two of the women—Luv
and Glynis—discuss their abusive relationships with their ex-hus-
bands; the abuse, however, is presented as abuse that women in all
occupations can experience from male companions in a patriarchal
society.

A Particular Class of Women alters the patriarchal and feminist
signification of the stripper; it disrupts the dominant heterosexual text
that reduces strip women to their sexual body parts and counters the
feminist construction/critique of the stripper as an extreme manifestation of "the objectified woman." Refusing both patriarchal and feminist texts, Feindel poses new multiple texts grounded in real strippers'
experience and sexuality.

Scarlot Harlot: Carol Leigh

Scarlot Harlot, Carol Leigh's alter ego, personifies/embodies the
postmodern prostitute performance artist. She is a clown, a burlesque

drag queen whore turned out in southern belle American flag attire, and she is a sexual healer and feminist activist. Leigh refers to herself as a life artist, an "autobiographical journalist . . . using myself and my life as an example, employing the image of whore in order to reclaim female sexual symbolism."[73] Carol Leigh is a writer, performer (stage and street), filmmaker, and television host. Her work spans five areas which stand individually and also come together in multimedia ensemble. These five areas include (1) her early one-woman show, *The Adventures of Scarlot Harlot;* (2) public acts of civil disobedience presented as guerrilla street perform-ins; (3) performance art/theater; (4) guerrilla cinematography; and (5) feminist activism and education.

Leigh's early show *The Adventures of Scarlot Harlot*[74] had its inception in 1980,[75] a time when prostitute performance art was beginning as a postmodern art genre. *The Adventures of Scarlot Harlot* is a personal narrative of what a woman experiences when she announces she is a prostitute; it is a coming-out story presented as stream of consciousness in which Leigh articulates her reflections on the pride and shame of being a whore and tells jokes.

The political aim barely below the surface in *The Adventures of Scarlot Harlot* is twofold: "to show the audience that most of the discomfort prostitutes suffer is a result of the stigma, rather than the sex or the sex-for-money"[76] and to enable "people to examine their prejudices about prostitutes."[77] Scarlot aims to get the audience to realize that prostitutes are just like them: "the person sitting next to you could be a prostitute. People think we're either rich or desperate; most of us are middle class."[78] Leigh substantiates this by disclosing that in her prostitute support group most of the women are college-educated: "a lawyer, elementary teacher and film historian are among the group."[79]

Deploying nudity as what will become a recurrent consciousness-raising technique, Scarlot undresses and dons pants and a T-shirt which reads "We're all prostitutes."[80] She then directly involves the audience with this human condition by questioning individual members about what they do for a living. The audience begins to participate as the other character in the play and the monologue becomes a dialogue about how they make their money and their assumptions about prostitutes.

Scarlot is known for protest performances and acts of civil disobedience; she takes her political messages onto the street, presenting short, spontaneous guerrilla pieces relating to prostitution, AIDS, and other feminist issues. Leigh's first action as Scarlot Harlot was to attend a NOW (National Organization of Women) meeting with a paper bag over her head, inscribed "This PAPER BAG symbolizes the ANO-NYMITY of PROSTITUTES." Leigh said in an interview, "I went around town with my paper bag"[81] —publicizing in one visual moment the shame and degradation that society visits upon the prostitute.

Scarlot has held public solicitations in busy downtown areas at peak pedestrian hours, most famously her 1990 public solicitation on Wall Street at lunch time. Leigh uses this tactic of guerrilla street theater to protest the soliciting laws and call for the decriminalization of pros-titution. Dressed in her American flag gown, Scarlot informs the crowd: "I provide safe sex for sale and I am offering intercourse with a condom for $200. . . . I have ultimate jurisdiction over my body. . . . I am protesting State Penal Code 230 and I am defiantly offering sexual services."[82] Scarlot carries this street act of solicitation into artspace, soliciting the audience as part of her performances:

> I would like to engage you in a little civil
> disobedience.
> You all know that it is against the law, it is a crime
> to solicit for the act of prostitution.
> I don't know if you know this but a few years ago they
> made a law that it is illegal to agree to engage in
> prostitution.
> First of all are there any cops in the audience?
> You have to tell me, otherwise it is entrapment.
> I am going to offer my sexual services, you just say
> yes.
> $200 for intercourse, of course with a condom.
> Now who agrees to engage in prostitution with me?
> Great.
> Thank-you so much for engaging in this act of civil
> disobedience.[83]

Scarlot has also staged a number of AIDS demonstration perform-ins protesting the lack of services and funding. For example, as part of a week of protests by AIDS Action Pledge, in full Scarlot dress—her American flag gown, red elbow-length gloves, red boots and tights, political buttons on each breast: "Just Say No to Mandatory Testing," "Sin Condom No Hay Amor"—Scarlot tied up a fellow protester in red tape to publicize and protest the red tape involved in getting public assistance for people with AIDS. At the Sixth International Conference on AIDS (1990) in San Francisco, Scarlot was taken into custody for protesting the exclusion of women from AIDS research.[84]

Responding to a papal fundraiser for the 1987 visit of Pope John Paul II, Scarlot organized a small group of protesters who, calling themselves the Whores of Babylon, sang a take-off on Madonna's "Papa Don't Preach":

Pope don't preach, you're in trouble deep.
Pope don't preach, I hope you are losing sleep.
But I made up my mind, I'm terminating my pregnancy.
I'm gonna terminate my pregnancy.[85]

Pope, Don't Preach, I'm Terminating My Pregnancy developed into a political music video.

What has evolved as Scarlot's uniquely postmodern approach is to stage a street perform-in/demonstration and to film the event, producing a guerrilla documentary film which she then uses as part of a new piece involving live performance, video, and discussion. In her recent two-part *All Purpose Bad Girl* events, Scarlot in Part I did a live performance piece of *Sunreich, Sunsetup* and *Pope, Don't Preach, I'm Terminating My Pregnancy*, showed her video *G.H.O.S.T.: Spiritual Warfare*, and engaged the audience in a discussion of the political implications the three pieces raise. *Sunreich, Sunsetup* is a short musical commentary on the war in the Persian Gulf, which is a part of Scarlot's series *Whore in the Gulf*. Wearing her famous flag attire Scarlot sings the following to the tune of "Fiddler on the Roof":

Is this the little war I hoped for?
Is this the GI Joes at play?
I don't remember bombing Basra,
When did they?

Why won't she grow to be a woman?
Why won't he grow to be a man?
Arabs were sacrificed in this war,
by Bush and Saddam.

Sunrise, Sunset, Sunrise, Sunset
Swiftly fall the bombs
People turn overnight to corpses
Didn't this happen back in Nam?

Sunrise, Sunset, Sunrise, Sunset
Swiftly flows the cash.
Chaos turns overnight to contracts.
Sucking the profit from the ash.[86]

Scarlot from her position as a prostitute critiqued the war; Leigh would go to the antiwar demonstrations every day and interview her fellow activists. She would intertext their comments with CNN cut-ups: shots of people suffering juxtaposed to official state commentary.

G.H.O.S.T.: Spiritual Warfare (1990) contains a documentation of a street performance Scarlot did as a protest against the three-day prayer fest organized by the televangelist Larry Lea and his Prayer Army. "G.H.O.S.T." is an acronym for Grand Homosexual Outrage at Sickening Televangelists. The video documents the confrontation between Larry Lea's prayer warriors and thousands of the San Francisco gay and alternative community on Halloween. Scarlot begins this twenty-minute video with footage from the protest: protestors in drag presenting high-camp images are juxtaposed to husbands and wives and religious lower-middle Americans going into the prayer meeting; gay men are holding a kiss-in in response to Lea's explicit homophobia. The film shifts to pre-demonstration footage of Leigh interviewing lesbian and gay activists, in various stages of getting dressed for Halloween, recording their messages to Larry Lea's people. One respondent says:

> We are your sons and daughters who came out to San Franscisco because it was kind of hard to be this way in Texas. . . . We are capable of loving each other just like you are capable of loving each other. We want your tolerance and acceptance. We want you to see us for what we are: happy, healthy people who know how to have fun.[87]

The remainder of the footage documents various verbal clashes between the protesters and the prayer warriors. Scarlot, Pink Jesus, and Sadie, Sadie, The Rabbi Lady lead the protesters in the recurrent chants of "Begone Bigots, Begone!" and "Larry Lea, Go Away, Racist, Sexist, Anti-Gay." Scarlot's perform-in commences with her shouting "Grab your makeup, fix your hair. Prostitutes are everywhere . . . whores, whores, whores!" Informing fellow protesters and prayer warriors "I am Scarlot Harlot. I represent the Great Whore Goddess," and exclaiming "here, I'll show you!" Scarlot tears off all her clothes except for a turquoise feather boa draped around her neck. She then declares: "I have been channeling the goddess. I had a vision, and in my vision Larry Lea comes out of the ministry and prostrates himself at my feet. He seeks the divine light of the Whore Goddess." Within seconds a fellow activist impersonating Lea does just that, declaring: "I believe in the goddess, take me into the folds of your love, take me into your church, I am your disciple. Take Me. I am yours, I take you as my saviour." Scarlot, playing on the commercialization of the great whore goddess, replies "Yes. Yes. But will it be Visa or MasterCard?"

At her second *All Purpose Bad Girl* show held the following week Scarlot focused on violence against women from the prostitute point of view: "To me, the laws against prostitution represent institutional-ized rape and sexual abuse; that is, if the police are sent to our bed-rooms to arrest us, that sounds like sexual abuse to me."[88] She per-forms an excerpt from her musical satire *Bad Laws*, which trashes the California State Legislature for passing mandatory HIV testing laws for prostitutes. With changing slides of vintage Scarlot protest footage and in the presence of two exotic dancers carrying placards which read "Keep Your Laws off My Body," "Whore Power," "No Mandatory Test-ing," "Support Prostitutes' Rights," "Decriminalize Prostitution," and "Prostitutes Use Condoms, Do You?" Scarlot sing/shouts:

> I'm talking about really, really bad laws,
> Bad Laws.
> I'm talking about horrible legislation,
> See them doing it in broad daylight,
> Hoping they don't catch the latest blight,
> They don't get laid,
> Cause their butts are too tight.
> You ask yourself, just who do they think they are?
> And while you are wondering, they make laws that are
> putting prostitutes in jail until they die.
>
> They make really bad laws.
> I am against any law that curtails my feedom of
> sexpression,
> And my freedom to do whatever I want with my body.
> They make really, really bad laws,
> Sad laws, bad laws, they make me mad laws,
> Bad laws.
> All they do is add laws.
>
> I tell you what I'm gonna do
> I'm gonna get myself a new tattoo
> Says "let your government die for you"
> Cause they make Bad Laws.[89]

At the end of her performance Scarlot provides the audience with a handout of her article "No Mandatory Testing! A Feminist Prostitute

Speaks Out," which analyzes the political and social consequences of mandatory testing.

This live performance is followed by a showing of two of Scarlot's feminist films: *Sex Workers Take Back the Night* (1991) and *Yes Means Yes, No Means No* (1992). In *Sex Workers Take Back the Night* Scarlot documents the diverse attitudes among pro-porn and antiporn feminists who are attending the 1990 Take Back the Night march. She focuses on what the women consider violence, their opinions on pornography and on the women who take part in it. The film opens and is contextualized by a marcher's identification of the Montreal massacre as one of the most dramatic instances of misogyny; she lists countless other misogynistic practices, from spousal battering, to discrimination against women in the legal system, to women earning sixty cents on the dollar, to denial of reproductive rights. This statement unites antiporn and pro-porn feminists in the face of the larger patriarchal acts of violence against women. Leigh carefully contains the division among women which she is documenting inside a concept of coalition politics. Scarlot asks her interviewees what issues are most important to them as they Take Back the Night. A young sex worker attending the march with a group of her sex worker friends says: "We don't believe that violence against women is perpetuated through pornography. Censorship in the name of protecting women isn't protection at all; a lot gets cut out, including women's sexual voices. There is a groundswell of female-produced and feminist-produced pornography that is also getting silenced by censorship."[90] Another sex worker says: "We came down here to say we are sex-positive sex workers, we are not coerced into it, we are not manipulated." A woman who identifies herself as a stripper says: "I don't believe that being naked in front of people is degrading. You have to allow yourself to be degraded in order to be degraded." At this point Scarlot, who is videotaping the interview, interjects: "I feel degraded constantly being a very big woman and I'm forty. Life is one big degradation, prostitution sometimes is degrading." Here Scarlot is consciously linking prostitution with other feminist issues like size and age and linking it to general degradation in our society. At one point Scarlot pulls her top down, displaying her breasts and holding a sign which reads WHOREPOWER, she tells those around her that "Take Back the Night has had a history of not doing outreach to prostitutes": she proudly announces "I was invited especially."

Scarlot questions another woman who has identified herself as a sex worker: "What about Taking Back the Night? Do you feel whores ought to be able to take back the night?" The woman responds that she has been dancing for two years and that it is one of best things she has ever done. She adds, "The hardest thing about dancing is when people say to me that it is degrading to women." Antiporn feminists are shown with a huge mobile installation entitled "Erotomisogynist speech incites femicide"; the installation is covered with pictures of nude women, battered women, and women in mainstream pornographic poses. An antiporn feminist at the installation tells Scarlot, "This stuff is hate literature." Scarlot asks her what she thinks should be done with it. She responds: "I think we should expose it wherever we go, like we are doing here." Scarlot then questions her as to what she thinks about the women who posed for the pictures. The woman says: "I think they are traitors to their sex." Scarlot doesn't confront her.

In another mini perform-in Scarlot, topless, is yelling, "I am exercising my right to freedom of speech." Later, as the march is under way, she connects her freedom of speech action to that of a woman who is ripping up a porn magazine. Scarlot asks her, "Are you exercising your freedom of speech on Haight Street?" The woman answers: "We oppose erotomisogynist literature." Scarlot is presenting both sides of the pornography debate and positions in between, such as that of a woman stating "Pornography is something to be talked about between us and among us, not to be fought about. It is to be fought with men about." As the march is winding up, a protester states: "I think it was a mistake for the feminist movement to take on an antiporn stance. What we need to do is reform or transform those images, not try to eliminate them in society."

Sex Workers Take Back the Night has been used as a consciousness-raising tool to initiate a dialogue between sex workers/pro-porn feminists and antipornography activists. In addition, Scarlot has organized and facilitated a four-part discussion and work group entitled *Taking Back the Night/Challenging Divisions* through Open Forum—A School of Collective Learning. The Open Forum flyer states: .

This is a woman's discussion group to bridge the gap between sex workers and anti-pornography activists. . . .

A facilitated discussion will create a safe space for women to express a variety of attitudes towards sexuality, and personal exploration

will enhance our understanding of stigma and social control.
Participants will consider strategies to resist divisions based on our
sexual experiences and preferences.[91]

Among the items on the agenda were "What do we want from other
women in regard to issues of sexual representation, sexual expression,
sexual communication?" "What are our various definitions of pornography, erotica, sexually explicit material, erotomisogyny?" "What stig-
mas have hurt you?" "How have you been oppressed by women?"
"What are your sexual rights? (Do they include the right to receive
payment for sexual services? The right to engage in safe sex if we are
HIV positive? The right to sell sexual services if we are HIV positive?
etc.)." "What sort of abuse did you experience as a young person?"[92]
These and other issues were explored in accordance with both consciousness-raising style (each woman speaking without interruption)
and discussion style. Scarlot, in an interview, says

> [T]he workshops were a big learning experience for everyone. I learned
> a lot about how to deal with and talk to anti-porn women. I . . . see
> them as warriors. I have always admired them. I myself need to have
> room to be who they are: the one who says no. I want to be that too,
> and I want to be this. There just has to be room for both.[93]

Leigh has made essential contributions to the construction of a new
postmodern role of performance educator; she has produced films on
prostitution, AIDS, and date rape as educational tools that promote
discussion among the groups that view them. *Outlaw Poverty, Not
Prostitution* records the 1989 World Whores' Summit in San Francisco.
Through a series of interviews and newspaper, television, and film
montages, Leigh documents the discussion of prostitutes' conditions
by prostitute activists from Thailand, Amsterdam, Brazil, and the
United States. Her 1990 video *Whores and Healers: Women Respond
to AIDS* documents the role of prostitutes and ex-prostitutes as healers
and teachers. It includes footage of CAL-PEP—the HIV prevention and
education program designed and implemented by prostitutes and ex-
prostitutes for prostitutes and IV drug users and their partners. Leigh
says, "We are trying to teach people in general about sex. We are sex
experts." She contends: "We want people to know that we are very
involved in safe sex education; we really care about our health, we care
about other people's health." "Sex workers are healing people."[94] Leigh
and performance artist Dee Russell recently produced *Yes Means Yes,*

No Means No, a date drama which begins with flowers and candy and ends in rape; the only soundtrack is the continuous singing of "That Old Black Magic" by Frank Sinatra. *Yes Means Yes, No Means No* is used as a training tape for service providers by the San Francisco Rape Crisis Center. It is also shown at performance events such as Scarlot's *All Purpose Bad Girl* show. All of her films are featured on her weekly television show *The Collected Works of Scarlot Harlot* on channel 29 in San Francisco.

Scarlot Harlot is a performance/protest artist, and a teacher/activist who narrows the boundaries between entertainment and education and performing and teaching.

Conclusion

In the introduction to this chapter, I suggested that prostitute performance art could be thematically structured around the overriding theme of breaking down the dichotomization of the female body into the sacred and the profane and that from the destabilization of this general division emanates an erosion of such equivalent couples as feminists/whores, good girls/bad girls, sluts/goddesses, porn stars/ordinary women, therapists/prostitutes. My intent has been to show how this theme is present and operative in each of the six performance texts and at the same time to present the integrity of each text; that is, to present the artists' voices and the artists own political projects. *Deep Inside Porn Stars* deconstructs the division between the pornographic and non-pornographic by giving the audience a glimpse into the non-pornographic side of well-known porn stars; Annie Sprinkle, on the other hand, shows that sluts and goddesses are sides of the same by uniting the slut and goddess in all women. Veronica Vera uses her own life to show that the dualities of sacred and profane are inseparable parts of a whole in which one readily becomes the other. Gwendolyn takes on two contemporary issues in her work, therapy and pornography, and shows that therapists can be more like what dominant culture has projected onto the whore—uncaring and money grabbing; that antiporn feminists in their construction of pornography and prostitution as violence against women condone violence against whores. Janet Feindel collapses the division of women into strippers and the non-strippers, non-prostitutes, good girls. Scarlot Harlot, the whore-clown, feminist, educator, and artist, collapses the worn boundary between performing and teaching. All of the artists claim feminist space for their work and for the prostitute in her various manifestations, from the sacred priestess in Annie's work to the stripper in Feindel's.

The shock value of aspects of the performances—aiding sacred prostitute priestess Annie Sprinkle to masturbate to orgasm in art-space; viewing sliding images of Veronica Vera and Christ, both bound; witnessing a film representation of Gwendolyn violently slashing a pillow substitute for a therapist who had imposed a different kind of violence on her while Gwendolyn herself is present in clown face— makes space for the audience, through identification with the artists, to experience disgust and indignation at dominant cultural represen- tations. Witnessing Scarlot Harlot, a very large full-figured woman, nude on the street, making a spectacle of herself, not only gives pros- titutes a presence—a face and a voice—but in the same instance shakes up the standardized image of the prostitute.

Taken together prostitute performance work destabilizes what has traditionally been considered theater and what is still considered the- oretical engagement. It broadens both theater and theory to include new areas of life and new political subjects. Prostitute performance artists have not only transgressed public space and academic space by bringing the pornographic, the carnivalesque, into these realms, but in so doing they have produced a new social identity—the prostitute as sexual healer, goddess, teacher, political activist, and feminist—a new social identity which can trace its genealogy to the ancient sacred prostitute.

CONCLUSION
From Aspasia's Salon
to the Sprinkle Salon

PHILOSOPHERS AS diverse as Alison Jaggar[1] and Lars Ericsson[2] have indicated the need for a philosophical theory of prostitution; neither, however, has thought to include prostitutes among the participating philosophers. This is, of course, not surprising: philosophy, until postmodernity, has been the "high," or what Irigaray names the "discourse on discourse," unapproachable without years of academic training and postsecondary achievements, the self-styled apex of all educated discourses. What has been occurring in postmodernity—the production of prostitute discourse(s) from the diverse subject positions and standpoints of prostitutes themselves has altered the discursive domain of prostitution. Ethically, there can no longer be a philosophy of prostitution in which there is an absence of prostitute perspectives and prostitute philosophers.

As a genealogy, the aim of *Reading, Writing, and Rewriting the Prostitute Body* has been to foreground "the prostitute," the marginalized other, within the categorical other: woman. As I indicated in chapter 1, this text could only be produced in this postmodern moment when prostitutes themselves are actively producing their own discourses and rewriting their own bodies. It is the "wordflesh" of politicized prostitute spokespersons and performance artists that catalyzed my recovery of the *hetairae* in ancient Greece as simultaneously sophistic philosophers and erotic teachers. Until this rereading, their philosophic presence in Western thought had been buried both by canon interpretations and by what I refer to in chapter 2 as feminist discourses of the womb. This project could not have been done ten or even five years ago; it could not have been accomplished until feminist philosophers such as Page du Bois, Wendy Brown, Susan Okin, Mary O'Brien, Jean Elshstain, and Arlene Saxonhouse recovered the feminine in Plato's texts; until prostitute philosophers and political activists started to reappropriate their own bodies and construct a positive prostitute identity; until prostitute performance artist Annie Sprinkle began her public recovery of the goddess in artspace. It is not that Sprinkle consciously knew the history of the sacred prostitute; she disclosed to me in an interview that "at the end of the show I tell the legend of the sacred prostitute . . . I made this . . . up, but then I found out later that it is real."[3] When I began my study of the *hetairae* in Plato's text, I was unfamiliar with Sprinkle's recovery of the sacred prostitute. Yet, our narratives—mine created from sketchy pieces of historical and philosophical knowledge buried as asides and casual allusions in other texts, and Annie's created from the collective goddess unconscious and her spiritual work with tantric and Taoist masters and Native American shamans—coincided.

It is the condition of postmodernity in which the canon readings of philosophy and political theory, taught and retaught in graduate courses, can be seen for what they are: merely some few among many possible interpretations. It is the postmodern insight, so elegantly pointed out by Jean-François Lyotard in *The PostModern Condition*,[4] that there is no longer a privileged site of knowledge, that in the coming together and collision of different knowledges, a space opens: an ethical space of otherness. And in this space fragments from different fields of knowledge—what Lyotard refers to as "little narratives"—can momentarily coalesce. This work is a coalescence of many little narratives: Sprinkle's *Post Porn Modernist*, Pateman's *The Sexual Contract*, Laclau and Mouffe's *Hegemony and Socialist Strategy: Towards a Radical Democratic Politics*, Plato's *Menexenus*, Parent-Duchatelet's *De la prostitution dans la Ville de Paris*, and Derrida's *Dissemination*, to name just a few. It is my hope that the reader will at least for a moment question whether a text such as Derrida's *Dissemination* must be considered any more philosophical than Sprinkle's *Post Porn Modernist*, and will reflect on a pedagogical system that privileges one over the other.

One aim of my text has been to destabilize the boundaries between what are traditionally considered "high" and "low" sites of discourse. The ruse in my text has been to appropriate the pedagogues of postmodern theory for the project of validating prostitutes' voices and knowledges. Or has it been the opposite: the appropriation of the pedagogues of prostitute knowledge and voices for the validation of postmodern theory? Or perhaps, rather, it has been a dual project—a careful holding together of both projects to stave off any "danger of appropriating the other by assimilation."[5]

This text has been a tracing of a female other doubly disprivileged: inside the feminine and by the hegemonic masculine discourses. After disentombing ancient prostitute voices in chapter 2, I examined "The Making of the Modern Prostitute Body" in chapter 3. This is a crucial moment in marking the lineage of the contemporary prostitute on two accounts. First, it is in modernity that woman is fully dichotomized into madonna/whore and such equivalent couples as good girl/bad girl, normal/abnormal, licit/illict. Second, it is the medical-moral-legal discourses of modernity that have produced the various inscriptions of the prostitute as the profane body which have dominated our image of the prostitute and which feminists and prostitutes have sought to redress. In chapter 4, I examined four contemporary feminist theorists' writings of the prostitute body. The selection of Carole Pateman, Catharine MacKinnon, Luce Irigaray, and Gayle Rubin was made in the interests of one of the major aims of my text, which is to show that even counter-hegemonic, critical discourses, which problematize the modern image of the prostitute within the more general context of a feminist project, appropriate the other through assimilation. That is to say, modernist feminists enclose the prostitute body within a theorized totality which leaves no space for the prostitute herself as speaking subject. By simply inverting the masculine/feminine dichotomy and privileging its negative side, they reproduce this dichotomization. As I argued in chapter 4, it is only postmodern feminism which, due to its commitment to a multiplicity of difference, can open a space for prostitutes to speak. Although Irigaray, inadvertently, I contend, opens a space for the prostitute as speaking subject, this space is still constrained within an external or foreign discourse. It is Rubin who, due to her concept of radical sexual pluralism, can open theoretical space for prostitutes and all sexual others to write their own bodies and produce their own discourses. In chapter 5, I showed that prostitute discourse itself is a contested terrain that reproduces the dichotomization of the prostitute as a powerful sexual being and a disempowered sexual victim. WHISPER seizes on one side of this dichotomy: the prostitute as sexual victim. Rights groups, I suggest, hold the tension between both poles of the dichotomization. They accomplish this by constructing a new prostitute identity which has traces to the ancient sacred prostitute. The movement recognizes the positive possibilities of prostitution and the positive roles prostitutes play as sexual teachers and healers, but presents these as being undermined by the negativity that is associated with commercial sex in our

patriarchal society and by laws that criminalize prostitution and stig-
matize the prostitute.

Drawing on her clown performance persona, Gwendolyn describes
the holding of both sides of the empowerment/victimization dichotomy in her political work and in her performance art as a "balancing
act"

> I am doing this balancing act. I'm really torn between my commit-
> ment to the movement for prostitutes' rights making positive propa-
> ganda against seeing us as victims and at the same time wanting to
> be true to myself and process all that I know. The stereotype can ring
> true. Everything isn't all right. Some people are in very desperate
> straits. They aren't working the street by choice—they are living with
> addiction, poverty or abuse. But we all should be respected for the
> work we do instead of getting fucked over by bad laws. . . . Our big-
> gest problem is that society sees prostitution as deviant behavior.[6]

What Gwendolyn describes as a balancing act is made extremely vivid
in the performance medium; so I have contended in chapter 6, which
presented the texts of six prostitute performance artists—Gwendolyn,
Annie Sprinkle, Veronica Vera, Janet Feindel, Scarlot Harlot, and Candida Royalle—around the common theme that these texts themselves
disclose: each work balances the presentation of the prostitute body as
an abused body and as an empowered body, refusing any bifurcation.
In so doing, the broader binary division of women into femi-
nist/mother/good girl and male-identified/slut/bad girl has been destabilized. It is in this destabilized space, the space in which the
male-defined division of woman into madonna/whore is already deconstructed, that any new philosophical theory of prostitution needs
to find its point of departure.

Aspasia, as I pointed out in chapter 2, conducted a salon for prostitutes, philosophers, and statesmen. Jess Wells, in *A Herstory of Prostitution in Western Europe*, suggests that Aspasia's salon was, in addition, a meeting place not only for prostitute women but also for
married women. She says:

> In a society where women were totally sequestered and deprived of all
> intellectual and cultural activities, taught not to speak or be seen
> when discussions took place, Aspasia's home was a woman's ref-
> uge[.][7]

Annie Sprinkle conducts a salon in artspace to educate the general
public about prostitution, pornography, sexuality, spirituality, and goddess power; she also hosts Sprinkle salons at her home, for women

only. Here women learn how to recognize themselves as both sluts and goddesses, and to unite these archetypes; women also learn what it is like to go out into the world as a man by creating a male persona at the "Drag King for a Day Salon." Annie holds monthly salons for female-to-male transsexuals and cross-dressers; she offers workshops on "Sacred Sex" and "Sexual Healing" for both women and men. Like Aspasia's salon, the Sprinkle salon is a refuge for erotic, philosophical, and spiritual learning. And so my text comes full circle, tracing a genealogy from the philosophical clitoris of ancient Greece to the philosophical clitoris of postmodernity.

NOTES

1. Reading, Writing, and Rewriting the Prostitute Body

1. Michel Foucault, *Discipline and Punish*, trans. Alan Sheridan (New York: Vintage Books, 1979), p. 31.

2. There is debate over whether postmodernism came into being in the 1950s, 1960s, or 1970s. The term "postmodernism" gained wide currency in the 1970s. I would say, following the Frankfurt School critics Adorno and Horkheimer's meditations in *The Dialectic of Enlightenment*, that the liberal humanist project culminated and was eclipsed in Auschwitz; that the 1950s were a period of transition in which the ideology of the Enlightenment/humanist project was fiercely clung to as it imploded, yet new ideologies and subjects did not emerge until the 1960s: the student revolts, the antiwar protests, the counterculture of the hippies, seeds of the women's movement, the black power movement, beginnings of decolonization, and gay/lesbian liberation.

3. This definition of postmodernism has been developed from my interaction with a number of sources: Steven Best and Douglas Kellner, *Postmodern Theory: Critical Interrogations* (New York: Guilford Press, 1991); David Harvey, *The Condition of Postmodernity* (Oxford: Blackwell, 1989); Dick Hebdige, *Hiding in the Light* (London: Routledge, 1988); Susan Hekman, *Gender and Knowledge: Elements of a Postmodern Feminism* (Cambridge: Polity Press, 1990); Andreas Huyssen, *After the Great Divide: Modernism, Mass Culture, Postmodernism* (Bloomington: Indiana University Press, 1986); Fredric Jameson, *Postmodernism: The Logic of Late Capitalism* (Durham: Duke University Press, 1991); Arthur Kroker, *The Possessed Individual* (Montreal: New World Perspectives, 1992); Scott Lash, *The Sociology of Postmodernism* (London: Routledge, 1990); Andrew Ross, ed., *Universal Abandon? The Politics of Postmodernism* (Minneapolis: University of Minnesota Press, 1988); Neville Wakefield, *Postmodernism: The Twilight of the Real* (London: Pluto Press, 1990).

4. Jacques Derrida, *Of Grammatology*, trans. Gayatri Chakravorty Spivak (Baltimore: Johns Hopkins University Press, 1974), "Translator's Preface," p. xlix.

5. Original will be hereafter placed in quotation marks.

6. Jacques Derrida, *Dissemination*, trans. Barbara Johnson (Chicago: University of Chicago Press, 1981), p. 355.

7. Ibid., p. 355.

8. Terry Eagleton, *Literary Theory: An Introduction* (Minneapolis: University of Minnesota Press, 1983), p. 141.

9. Jacques Derrida, *Dissemination*, trans. Barbara Johnson, "Translator's Introduction," p. x.

10. Eve Tavor Bannet, *Structuralism and the Logic of Dissent* (Houndmills, UK: MacMillan, 1989), p. 204.

11. Ibid., p. 205.

12. Bannet explains:

> By following the traces of a word both "in" the text and "outside" it, and by
> re-marking the word as it appears "in" a text with its various meanings, differential
> relations, associations, and contexts "outside" that text, articulation joins the "in-
> side" of a text to its "outside". It joins the word or meaning which is "present" in
> the text to words, meanings and associations which are "absent" in the text but
> implied by the word's chain of associations of differential relations. (p. 212)

Articulation, by locating and connecting the traces of a word from one text to
other texts and to contexts outside the text, dissolves the boundaries of the text
and grafts all texts onto each other. Articulation decenters the text: "the 'text'
with its own 'proper' meaning or meanings is no longer either its own centre or at
the centre of the critical discourse" (p. 213).

13. Ibid., p. 216.

14. Ibid., pp. 220–21.

15. The historiography of Foucault combined with the defining postmodern
assumptions provide the backbone for "new historicism," the most recent branch
of postmodern scholarship. The assumptions of new historicists are that there is
no transhistorical or universal human essence; that human subjectivity is culturally constructed, there is no objectivity, the world is experienced in language; and
that the reader's historical and cultural position informs her or his representations
of the world and reading of texts and events. Judith Newton, "History as Usual?:
Feminism and the New Historicism," *Cultural Critique*, Spring 1988, provides a
good summary of new historicism and its relevance to the many voices and sites
of power that traditional history overlooks.

16. Michel Foucault, "Two Lectures," *Power/Knowledge*, ed. Colin Gordon,
trans. Colin Gordon, Leo Marshall, John Mepham, Kate Soper (New York: Pantheon
Books, 1980), p. 81.

17. Ibid., p. 83.

18. Michel Foucault, *The History of Sexuality*, Volume I: *An Introduction*,
trans. Robert Hurley (New York: Vintage Books, 1980), p. 18.

19. Ibid., p. 149.

20. Michel Foucault, "Nietzsche, Genealogy, History," *Language, Counter-Memory, Practice*, ed. Donald F. Bouchard, trans. Donald F. Bouchard and Sherry Simon
(Ithaca: Cornell University Press, 1977), p. 148.

21. Ibid.

22. I argue in "Feminist Ejaculations," *The Hysterical Male: New Feminist
Theory*, eds. Arthur Kroker and Marilouise Kroker (London: St. Martin's Press,
1991), that ejaculation is a biological possibility for the female body which has been
socially denied, pathologized, and restricted.

23. Susan Rubin Suleiman, ed., "Introduction," *The Female Body in Western
Culture* (London: Harvard University Press, 1986), p. 2.

24. Michel Foucault, *The History of Sexuality*, Vol. I., pp. 151–52.

25. Ibid., p. 105.

26. Ibid., pp. 105–106.

27. According to Foucault, it was the codification of sex that distinguished Victorian sexuality from that of earlier epochs.

Foucault identifies four strategies of knowledge production which constitute
what he terms "the deployment of sexuality" in the modern period: the hysteriza-
tion of the female body, the sexualization of children, the pathologization/psy-
chiatrization of the pervert, and the regulation of the population. The prostitute
body is the site of the intersection of three of these strategies; four if one includes

child prostitutes. The deployment of sexuality "engenders a continual extension of areas and forms of control" (Michel Foucault, *The History of Sexuality*, Vol. 1, p. 106). The deployment of sexuality arose out of the earlier deployment of alliance—the system governing marriages and kinship relations. While the deployment of alliance had the function of maintaining the social body through reproduction and the provision of a system of rules defining the permitted and the forbidden, the function of the deployment of sexuality is to proliferate, innovate, annex, create and penetrate bodies in an increasingly detailed way and to control populations in an increasingly comprehensive way (pp. 106–107).

Foucault argues that the deployment of sexuality was governed by the endeavor to expel from reality the forms of sex that were not amenable to the economy of reproduction, placing sex in a binary system—licit and illicit—defining sexual activities, and producing sexualities.

28. Ibid., p. 61.

29. Michel Foucault, *Discipline and Punish*, p. 27.

30. This is Michel Pecheux's concept. *Language, Semantics and Ideology: Stating the Obvious*, trans. Harbans Nagpal (London: MacMillan, 1982). Foucault allows for reversals, reverse discourses, and counter-identifications but not dis-identification, at least not explicitly.

31. Chantal Mouffe, "Radical Democracy: Modern or Postmodern?" trans. Paul Holdengraber, *Universal Abandon? The Politics of Postmodernism*, ed. Andrew Ross, p. 42.

32. Ernesto Laclau and Chantal Mouffe, *Hegemony and Socialist Strategy: Towards a Radical Democratic Process*, trans. Winston Moore and Paul Cammack (London: Verso, 1985), p. 181.

33. Chantal Mouffe, "Hegemony and New Political Subjects: Toward a New Concept of Democracy," trans. Stanley Gray, *Marxism and the Interpretation of Culture*, eds. Geoff Bennington and Brian Massumi (Urbana: University of Illinois Press, 1988), p. 90.

2. Reading the *Hetairae* in Plato's Texts

1. A textual interconnection has already been made between Diotima and Aspasia by David Halperin in his article "Why Is Diotima a Woman?" Halperin reads Diotima as the spiritualized "surrogate for Aspasia" (Halperin, "Why Is Diotima a Woman?" *One Hundred Years of Homosexuality* [New York and London: Routledge, 1990], p. 129). Plato replaced Aspasia with Diotima in the *Symposium*, according to Halperin, to distinguish his discourse about eros from that of Aeschine, who had written a now almost completely lost dialogue entitled *Aspasia* on the same subject. In Halperin's reading Diotima is not a prostitute. In fact, Halperin reads the replacement of Aspasia with Diotima as a sign that Plato excludes the sexual from his erotics (Ibid., p. 124). I read both Diotima and Aspasia as *hetairae* whose genealogy traces to the sacred prostitute.

2. A sophist is a teacher, a disseminator of different knowledges. Of course Plato designated them—for all time, he hoped—as false philosophers. Sophistic philosophy addresses the same themes that Socrates and Plato treated: wisdom, justice, virtue, love, the good. What distinguishes sophistic teaching, in its many diversified forms, from Plato's teaching is the absence of the Ideas of universal truth, fixed rules of conduct, preexisting principles, and the rationality of nature.

3. Jane Gallop, *The Daughter's Seduction: Feminism and Psychoanalysis* (Ithaca: Cornell University Press, 1982), p. 48.

4. Gayatri Chakravorty Spivak, "Feminism and Critical Theory," *In Other Worlds: Essays in Cultural Politics* (London: Methuen, 1987), p. 82.

5. Mikhail Bakhtin represents forms such as the mimic tradition, the dialogue, and the symposium as carnivalization. Bakhtin, *Rabelais and His World*, trans. Helen Iswolsky (Cambridge, MA: M.I.T. University Press, 1968), p. 98.

6. Gayatri Chakravorty Spivak, "Feminism and Critical Theory," p. 152. The emphasis is mine.

7. Feminist philosophers employing the discourse of the womb include, among others, Susan Okin's *Women in Western Political Thought* (Princeton: Princeton University Press, 1979); Mary O'Brien's *The Politics of Reproduction* (Boston: Routledge & Kegan Paul, 1981); Jean Elshstain's *Public Man, Private Woman: Women in Social and Political Thought* (Princeton: Princeton University Press, 1981); Arlene Saxonhouse's *Women in the History of Political Thought: Ancient Greece to Machiavelli* (New York: Praeger, 1985); and Eva Keuls, *The Reign of the Phallus: Sexual Politics in Ancient Athens* (New York: Harper & Row, 1985).

8. Wendy Brown, "Supposing Truth Were a Woman . . . Plato's Subversion of Masculine Discourse," *Political Theory*, vol. 16, no. 4 (1988).

9. Wendy Brown, *Manhood and Politics. A Feminist Reading in Political Theory* (New Jersey: Rowman & Littlefield, 1988).

10. Plato, *The Republic of Plato*, trans. Allan Bloom (New York: Basic Books, 1968), 495b–496a. I use Bloom's translation of the *Republic* throughout my text.

11. Page du Bois, *Sowing the Body: Psychoanalysis and Ancient Representations of Women* (Chicago: University of Chicago Press, 1988).

12. "A trace is a track, a path, a mark or a sign left behind by someone or something that has passed" (Eve Tavor Bannet, *Structuralism and the Logic of Dissent*, p. 192).

13. Plato, *Theaetetus*, trans. F. M. Cornford, *The Collected Dialogues of Plato*, ed. Edith Hamilton and Huntington Cairns (New York: Bollingen Foundation, 1961), 149d.

14. The use of information compiled by William Sanger is in no way a sign of support for the anti-prostitute and sexist ideology underpinning his historical and empirical study.

15. William Sanger, *The History of Prostitution* (New York: Harper and Brothers, 1869), p. 63.

16. David Halperin, "Why Is Diotima a Woman?" p. 114.

17. Ibid., p. 117.

18. Ibid., p. 142.

19. Ibid., p. 145.

20. Historical information on sacred prostitution and the *hetairae, auletrides,* and *dicteriades* is from my reading of four sources: Paul Brandt (Hans Licht), *Sexual Life in Ancient Greece,* (London: George Routledge & Sons, Ltd., 1932); Fernando Henriques, *Prostitution and Society*, Vol. I, *Primitive, Classical and Oriental* (London: MacGibbon and Kee, 1962); William Sanger, *The History of Prostitution* (New York: Harper and Brothers, 1869); and Jess Wells, *A Herstory of Prostitution in Western Europe* (Berkeley, CA: Shameless Hussy Press, 1982).

21. Fernando Henriques, *Prostitution and Society*, Vol. I, p. 35.

22. Jess Wells, *A Herstory of Prostitution in Western Europe*, pp. 6–7.

23. Plato, *Symposium*, trans. Michael Joyce, *The Collected Dialogues of Plato*, ed. Edith Hamilton and Huntington Cairns (New York: Pantheon Books, 1966), 191e.

24. It is quite likely that there was a fluid movement between these two categories of prostitutes, especially in the direction from *auletrides* to *hetairae*.

25. Alciphron, Letter XIII, "Megara to Bacchis," *Letters from the Country and the Town of Fisherman, Farmers, Parasites and Courtesans*, trans. F. A. Wright (London: George Routledge & Sons, 1922), pp. 194–95.

26. Sappho, "To Hera, the Great Goddess, who succoured Agamemnon, a prayer for a safe journey," *Sappho of Lesbos: Her Works Restored*, trans. Beram Saklatvala (London: Charles Skilton, 1968), p. 31.

27. Ibid.

28. Paul Brandt, *Sexual Life in Ancient Greece*, p. 319.

29. Plato, *Symposium*, 201d.

30. Robin May Schott, *Cognition and Eros* (Boston: Beacon Press, 1988), p. 14.

31. Nye points out that "[t]he root meaning of 'host' is a physical body on whose flesh parasites feed." Andrea Nye, "The Hidden Host: Irigaray and Diotima at Plato's Symposium," *Hypatia* vol. 3, no. 3 (Winter 1989): 45.

32. Ibid., p. 57.

33. Ibid., p. 55.

34. Arlene Saxonhouse, *Women in the History of Political Thought*, p. 52.

35. Fernando Henriques, *Prostitution and Society*, Vol. I, p. 33.

36. Plato, *Symposium*, 201d.

37. Fernando Henriques, *Prostitution and Society*, Vol. I, p. 33.

38. Eva Keuls, *The Reign of the Phallus: Sexual Politics in Ancient Athens*, pp. 205–206.

39. Paul Brandt (Hans Licht), *Sexual Life in Ancient Greece*, p. 39.

40. Ibid., p. 340.

41. Plato, *Symposium*, 202e.

42. Ibid., 203d.

43. Plato, *Symposium*, trans. Walter Hamilton (Middlesex: Penguin Books, 1951), 203d. Michael Joyce, upon whose translation of the *Symposium* I rely, translates the same inscription as "a lifelong seeker after truth."

44. I will refer to the speech delivered by Socrates in the *Symposium* henceforth as Diotima's speech; Socrates begins by referring to it as "her teaching" (201d) and ends the speech stating "This . . . gentlemen—was the doctrine of Diotima" (212b).

45. Ibid., 201d.

46. Irigaray has described this movement toward the middle as Diotima's dialectic. Diotima's dialectic

. . . does not work by opposition to transform the first term into the second, in order to arrive at a synthesis of the two. . . . [S]he establishes the intermediary and she never abandons it as a mere way or means. Her method is not, then, a propaedeutic of the destruction or destructuration of two terms in order to establish a synthesis which is neither one nor the other. She presents, uncovers, unveils the existence of a third that is already there[.]

Luce Irigaray, "Sorcerer Love: A Reading of Plato's Symposium," trans. Eleanor H. Kuykendall, *Hypatia*, vol. 3, no. 3, (Winter 1989): 32.

47. Plato, *Symposium*, 206b.

48. Ibid., 208e–209a.

49. Ibid., 210a–d.

50. In his last conversation Socrates talks about the release of the "pure" soul

which "carries with it no contamination of the body, because it has never willingly associated with it in life, but has shunned it and kept itself separate as its regular practice[.]" Plato, *Phaedo*, trans. Hugh Tredennick, *The Last Days of Socrates* (New York: Penguin Books, 1969), 80a.

51. The passage reads: "pure were we from the pollution of the walking sepulchre which we call a body, to which we are bound like an oyster to its shell." Plato, *Phaedrus*, trans. Walter Hamilton (New York: Penguin Books, 1973), 250.

52. Ibid., 209c–d.

53. Xenophon, *Memorabilia and Oeconomicus, Symposium and Apology*, trans. E. C. Marchant (London: William Heinemann, 1923, rpt. 1968), III, xi, 16.

54. Leo Strauss, *Xenophon's Socrates* (Ithaca: Cornell University Press, 1972), p. 89.

55. Mary Ellen Waithe, ed., *A History of Women Philosophers*, Vol. I, *600 BC–500 AD*, (Dordrecht: Martinus Nijhoff Publishers, 1987), introductory plate.

56. Alciphron, Letter VI, "Thais to Euthydemus," p. 175.

57. Arlene Saxonhouse, *Women in the History of Political Thought*, p. 55.

58. R. E. Allen, "Comment," *The Dialogues of Plato*, Vol. I, *Translation and Analysis* (New Haven: Yale University Press, 1984), p. 55.

59. Plato, *Menexenus*, trans. B. Jowett, *The Collected Dialogues of Plato*, ed. Edith Hamilton and Huntington Cairns (New York: Bollingen Foundation, 1961), 235e.

60. Nicole Loraux, *The Invention of Athens: The Funeral Oration in the Classical City*, trans. Alan Sheridan (Cambridge, MA: Harvard University Press, 1986), p. 304.

61. Ibid., p. 325.

62. Ibid., p. 311.

63. Loraux states: "[T]here is not a single element that Plato does not borrow from Aristophanes" (ibid.).

64. Ibid., p. 323.

65. Ibid.

66. Ibid.

67. R. E. Allen, "Comment," *The Dialogues of Plato*, Vol. I, p. 321.

68. Plato, *Menexenus*, 236a–b.

69. Nicole Loraux, *The Invention of Athens*, p. 323.

70. Wendy Brown, "Supposing Truth Were a Woman," p. 597.

71. Plato, *Menexenus*, 236c.

72. Ibid., 249d.

73. Ibid.

74. Ibid., 249e.

75. Arlene Saxonhouse, *Women in the History of Western Political Thought*, p. 56.

76. Thucydides, "Pericles' Funeral Oration," *The Peloponnesian War*, trans. Rex Warner (Middlesex: Penguin Books, 1954), 36, p. 145.

77. Plato, *Menexenus*, 237b–238a.

78. Arlene Saxonhouse, *Women in the History of Political Thought*, p. 56.

79. Plato, *Menexenus*, 237c.

80. H. S. Versnel, "Wife and Helpmate: Women of Ancient Athens in Anthropological Perspective," Josine Blok and Peter Mason, eds., *Sexual Asymmetry: Studies in Ancient Society* (Amsterdam: J. C. Gieben, 1987), p. 77.

81. Thucydides, "Pericles' Funeral Oration," 43, p. 149.

82. Ibid.

83. Plato, *Menexenus*, 247a.

84. Ibid., 246c.

85. Thucydides, "Pericles' Funeral Oration," 46, p. 151.

86. This view is implied by Arlene Saxonhouse, *Women in the History of Political Thought*, p. 56.

87. Sarah Pomeroy, *Goddesses, Whores, Wives and Slaves: Women in Classical Antiquity* (New York: Schocken Books, 1975), p. 90.

88. Plato, *Menexenus*, 249d. Pericles' speech says "as the law demanded" (46, p. 151).

89. Allan Bloom, a well-known Straussian, marks Book V as

preposterous. . . . Socrates expects it to be ridiculed. It provokes both laughter and rage in its contempt for convention and nature, in its wounding of all the dearest sensibilities of masculine pride and shame, the family, and statemanship and the city.

Allan Bloom, "Interpretive Essay," *The Republic of Plato*, p. 380.

90. Plato, *Republic*, 455d–e.

91. I am not arguing that Plato is simply an advocate of gender equality. Plato's sexism in Book V of the *Republic* is more than evident in his repeated marking of guardian women as weaker than guardian men (455e, 456a, 457a), his reference to female guardians as "their [male guardians'] women" (454e), and his statement that "All these women are to belong to all these men in common" (457d).

92. Plato, *Republic*, 458e.

3. The Making of the Modern Prostitute Body

1. Leah Lydia Otis, *Prostitution in Medieval Society: The History of an Urban Institution in Languedoc* (Chicago: University of Chicago Press, 1985), p. 69. Leah Otis traces a progression from acceptance and toleration of prostitution in the twelfth and thirteenth centuries to its institutionalization in the fourteenth and fifteenth centuries to repression and exclusion of the prostitute beginning in the sixteenth century.

2. " '[S]exuality'. . . . The term itself did not appear until the beginning of the nineteenth century." Michel Foucault, *The Use of Pleasure*, Vol. II, *The History of Sexuality*, trans. Robert Hurley (New York: Vintage Books, 1985), p. 3.

3. Lynda Nead, *Myths of Sexuality* (Oxford: Blackwell, 1988), p. 94.

4. Peter Stallybrass and Allon White, *The Politics and Poetics of Transgression* (London: Methuen, 1986), p. 4.

5. Ibid., p. 193.

6. Ibid., p. 202.

7. Walter Benjamin, "Central Park," *New German Critique*, Vol. 34 (Winter 1985): 52–53.

8. Angelika Raunch, "The Trauerspiel of the Prostituted Body, or Woman as Allegory of Modernity," *Cultural Critique* (Fall 1988): 81.

9. Charles Baudelaire, *Intimate Journals*, trans. Christopher Isherwood (San Francisco: City Light Books, 1983), p. 3.

10. Charles Baudelaire, "Allegory," *Les Fleurs Du Mal*, trans. Richard Howard (Boston: Godine, 1982), p. 132.

11. Jill Harsin, *Policing Prostitution in Nineteenth Century Paris* (Princeton: Princeton University Press, 1985), p. 102.

12. Ibid.

13. Judith R. Walkowitz, *Prostitution and Victorian Society: Women, Class, and the State* (Cambridge: Cambridge University Press, 1980), pp. 36–37.

14. Alain Corbin, *Women for Hire*, trans. Alan Sheridan (Cambridge, MA: Harvard University Press, 1990), p. 7.

15. Alexander John Baptiste Parent-Duchatelet, *De la Prostitution dans la Ville de Paris* (Paris: J. B. Bailliere, 1836), Vol. I, p. 14. The translations are my own unless otherwise indicated.

16. Ibid., pp. 190–96.

17. This information is calculated from Parent-Duchatelet's table on page 95 of his study.

18. This would support the claim that the Social Purity Movement's emphasis later in the century on child prostitution as extensive was a moral panic that did not reflect reality.

19. This information is calculated from Parent-Duchatelet's statistical table on age on pages 91 and 92 of his study.

20. Judith Walkowitz, *Prostitution and Victorian Society*, p. 3.

21. Parent-Duchatelet, *De la Prostitution dans la Ville de Paris*, pp. 67–68.

22. Ibid., p. 83.

23. Sander Gilman, "The Hottentot and the Prostitute," *Difference and Pathology: Stereotypes of Sexuality, Race, and Madness* (Ithaca: Cornell University Press, 1985), p. 94.

24. Parent-Duchatelet, *De la Prostitution dans la Ville de Paris*, p. 6; translated by Jill Harsin, *Policing Prostitution in Nineteenth Century Paris*, p. 108.

25. Parent-Duchatelet, *De la Prostitution dans la Ville de Paris*, pp. 219–23.

26. Ibid., p. 42.

27. Ibid., p. 205.

28. Ibid., pp. 205–206.

29. Ibid., p. 206.

30. Ibid., p. 209.

31. Ibid.

32. Ibid., p. 233.

33. Ibid., p. 234.

34. Ibid., p. 186.

35. Ibid., p. 135.

36. Ibid., pp. 187–88.

37. Ibid., p. 121.

38. Ibid., p. 141.

39. Ibid.

40. Ibid., p. 586.

41. Ibid., p. 522.

42. Ibid., p. 103.

43. Ibid., p. 99.

44. Ibid.

45. Ibid.

46. Judith Walkowitz, *Prostitution and Victorian Society*, p. 47.

47. William Acton, *Prostitution Considered in Its Moral, Social, and Sanitary Aspects* (London: Frank Cass, 1870), reprint 1972, p. v.

48. Judith Walkowitz, *Prostitution and Victorian Society*, p. 44.

49. William Acton, *Prostitution Considered in Its Moral, Social, and Sanitary Aspects*, p. 49.

50. Ibid.
51. Ibid., p. 73.
52. Ibid., p. viii.
53. Walkowitz, *Prostitution and Victorian Society*, p. 13.
54. Acton, *Prostitution Considered in Its Moral, Social, and Sanitary Aspects*, p. 24.
55. Ibid., p. 39.
56. Ibid., p. 24.
57. Ibid., p. 27.
58. Ibid.
59. Ibid.
60. Ibid., p. 28.
61. Ibid.
62. Ibid., pp. 29–30.
63. Ibid., p. 29.
64. Ibid., p. 30.
65. Ibid.
66. Ibid., pp. 31–32.
67. Ibid., p. 178.
68. Ibid.
69. M. Jeanne Peterson, "Dr. Acton's Enemy: Medicine, Sex and Society in Victorian England," *Victorian Studies*, vol. 29, no. 4 (Summer 1986), denies that Acton was the spokesperson for Victorian medical views of sexuality, citing the work of Sir James Paget, a Victorian medical practitioner, who inscribed the Victorian female as sexual. Notwithstanding, I would argue that Acton's construction contributed strongly to the discursive creation of the stereotypical depiction of the asexual woman.
70. William Acton, *Prostitution Considered in Its Moral, Social, and Sanitary Aspects*, p. 32.
71. Ibid., p. 33.
72. Ibid., p. 39.
73. Ibid., p. 34.
74. Ibid., p. 38.
75. Ibid.
76. Ibid., p. 39.
77. Ibid., p. 40.
78. Ibid.
79. Ibid., p. 74.
80. Ibid., p. 73.
81. Ibid., p. 166.
82. Ibid., p. 162.
83. Ibid.
84. Ibid., p. 167.
85. Ibid., p. 168.
86. Ibid., p. 180.
87. Ibid., p. 177.
88. Ibid.
89. *Report of the Royal Commission upon the Administration and Operation of the Contagious Diseases Acts* (London: George Edward Eyre and William Spottiswood, 1871), p. 13.
90. Ibid., p. 4.

91. Ibid., p. 6.

92. Ibid.

93. Ibid., pp. 4–5.

94. Ibid., p. 4.

95. Frank Mort, *Dangerous Sexualities: Medical-Moral Politics in England since 1830* (London: Routledge & Kegan Paul, 1987), p. 81.

96. This includes the Acts themselves, the Medical Committee's Report (1866), the House of Lords Select Committee Minutes and Report (1868), the House of Commons Select Committee Minutes and Report (1869), and the host of briefs and speeches arguing for the extension or for the repeal of the Acts.

97. *Minutes of Evidence Taken before the Royal Commission*, p. 568, para. 16,076.

98. Ibid., p. 571, para. 16,118.

99. Ibid., p. 571, para. 16,121.

100. *The Royal Commission Report*, p. 17.

101. Ibid.

102. *Minutes of the Royal Commission*, p. 107, para. 3456.

103. Ibid., p. 112, para. 3652.

104. Ibid., p. 107, para. 3458.

105. Ibid., p. 102, para. 3306.

106. *The Royal Commission Report*, p. 8.

107. Pickthorn was the visiting surgeon to the Devonport district.

108. *Minutes of the Royal Commission*, p. 46. para. 1485.

109. Ibid., p. 475, para. 13,684.

110. Ibid., p. 476, para. 13,703.

111. Ibid., p. 479, para. 13,748.

112. Ibid., p. 484, para. 13,796–97.

113. Ibid., pp. 484–85, para. 13,809.

114. Ibid., p. 487, para. 13,861.

115. *The Royal Commission Report*, p. 11.

116. *Minutes of the Royal Commission*, p. 251, para. 7728.

117. Ibid., p. 251, para. 7753.

118. Ibid., p. 252, para. 7766.

119. Ibid., p. 253, para. 7809.

120. Marianna Valverde, "The Love of Finery," *Victorian Studies*, vol. 32, no. 2 (Winter 1989): 175.

121. Ibid., 187.

122. *Minutes of the Royal Commission*, p. 226, para. 9540.

123. Ibid., p. 327, para. 9581.

124. Ibid., p. 325, para. 9514.

125. Ibid., p. 326, para. 9554.

126. Josephine Butler exposes police denial of clandestine prostitution as a fallacy. She verifies the existence of clandestine prostitutes and indicates why it is that the police believe there are none: she says, "I have found several cases of clandestine prostitutes who have confessed to me that they had been practising clandestinely, but who certainly would not confess that to one of the policemen because the policemen are the last persons in the world they would tell it to" (*Minutes of the Royal Commission*, p. 446, para. 13,013).

127. Ibid., p. 5, para. 122.

128. Ibid., p. 8, para. 216.

129. Judith Walkowitz, *Prostitution and Victorian Society*, p. 146.

130. *Minutes of the Royal Commission*, p. 437, para. 12,851.

131. Ibid., p. 426, para. 12,555.

132. Ibid., p. 426, para. 12,552.

133. Ibid., p. 426, para. 12,555.

134. Ibid., p. 426, para. 12,574.

135. Ibid., p. 427, para. 12,587.

136. Ibid., p. 428, para. 12,601.

137. Ibid., p. 428, para. 12,602.

138. Ibid., p. 427, para. 12,587.

139. Ibid., p. 429, para. 12,619.

140. Ibid., p. 429, para. 12,620.

141. Ibid., p. 429, para. 12,620.

142. Ibid., p. 429, para. 12,622.

143. Ibid., p. 427, para. 12,626.

144. Ibid., p. 437, para. 12,851.

145. Ibid., p. 442, para. 12,932.

146. Ibid., p. 438, para. 12,869.

147. Ibid., p. 438, para. 12,869.

148. Ibid., p. 438, para. 12,869.

149. Ibid., p. 439, para. 12,878.

150. Ibid., p. 441, para. 12,921.

151. Ibid., p. 441, para. 12,921.

152. Ibid., p. 443, para. 12,944.

153. Ibid., p. 448, para. 13,074.

154. Ibid., p. 448, para. 13,074.

155. Paul Robinson, *The Modernization of Sex*, (New York: Harper & Row, 1976), p. 3.

156. Ibid., "Preface," p. v.

157. Havelock Ellis, *Sex in Relation to Society: Studies in the Psychology of Sex*, Vol. VI (Philadelphia: F. A. Davis, 1910), p. 218.

158. Ibid., p. 223.

159. Ibid., p. 266.

160. Ibid., p. 267.

161. Ibid.

162. Ibid.

163. Ibid., p. 218.

164. Havelock Ellis, *Sexual Inversion: Studies in the Psychology of Sex*, Vol. I, second edition (Philadelphia: F. A. Davis, 1908), p. 150.

165. Sheila Jeffreys, "The Invention of the Frigid Woman," chapter 9, *The Spinster and Her Enemies: Feminism and Sexuality, 1880–1930* (London: Pandora Press, 1985), pp. 165–85.

166. Havelock Ellis, *Sex in Relation to Society*, p. 272.

167. Ibid., pp. 272–73.

168. Ibid., p. 273.

169. Ibid.

170. Ibid., p. 150.

171. Havelock Ellis, *Sexual Inversion*, pp. 140–43.

172. Havelock Ellis, *Sex in Relation to Society*, p. 312.

173. Havelock Ellis, *Analysis of the Sexual Impulse, Love and Pain, the Sexual Impulse in Women: Studies in the Psychology of Sex*, Vol. III (Philadelphia: F. A. Davis, 1908), p. 69.

174. Margaret Jackson, "Facts of Life or the Eroticization of Women's Oppression: Sexology and the Social Construction of Heterosexuality," *The Cultural Construction of Sexuality*, ed. Pat Caplan (London: Tavistock Publications, 1987), p. 58.

175. Havelock Ellis, *Sex in Relation to Society*, p. 273.

176. Ibid., p. 277.

177. Ibid.

178. Ibid., p. 280.

179. Ibid., p. 311.

180. Ibid., p. 315.

181. Ibid., p. 316.

182. Sigmund Freud, "Infantile Sexuality," *On Sexuality: Three Essays on the Theory of Sexuality and Other Works*, trans. and ed. James Strachey (Middlesex: Penguin Books, 1953), p. 109.

183. Ibid.

184. Ibid.

185. Ibid.

186. Ibid.

187. Sigmund Freud, "A Special Type of Object Choice Made by Men" (1910), *Sexuality and the Psychology of Love*, ed. Phillip Rieff (New York: Collier Books, 1972).

188. Ibid., p. 64.

189. Ibid.

190. Ibid., p. 51.

191. Ibid., p. 54.

192. Ibid., p. 55.

193. Ibid.

4. Writing the Prostitute Body

1. Alison Jaggar provides a clear-cut and useful summary of these in her article "Prostitution," first published in *Philosophy of Sex*, ed. Alan Soble (Totowa, New Jersey: Littlefield, Adams, 1980), and republished in a feminist collection *Women and Values*, ed. Marilyn Pearsall (Belmont, CA: Wadsworth, 1986).

2. Jacques Derrida and Christie V. McDonald, "Choreographies," *Diacritics*, vol. 12 (1982): 68.

3. Ibid., 76.

4. Carole Pateman, *The Sexual Contract* (Cambridge: Polity Press, 1988), p. 4.

5. Ibid., p. 1.

6. Ibid., p. 2.

7. Carole Pateman, "The Fraternal Social Contract," *The Disorder of Women: Democracy, Feminism, and Political Theory*, (Cambridge: Polity Press, 1989), pp. 36–37.

8. Carole Pateman, *The Sexual Contract*, p. 5.

9. Pateman critiques prostitution in chapter 7 ("What's Wrong with Prostitution?") of her book *The Sexual Contract* and in her article "Defending Prostitution: Charges against Ericsson," *Feminism and Political Theory*, ed. Cass R. Sunstein (Chicago: University of Chicago Press, 1990).

10. Carole Pateman, *The Sexual Contract*, p. 17.

11. Ibid., p. 194.

12. Carole Pateman, "Defending Prostitution: Charges against Ericsson," p. 205.

13. Quoted by Carole Pateman, *The Sexual Contract*, p. 202.

14. Ibid.

15. Ibid., p. 203.

16. Ibid., p. 191.

17. Karl Marx, *The Economic and Philosophic Manuscripts, Karl Marx Early Writings*, trans. Rodney Livingstone and Gregory Benton (New York: Vintage Books, 1975), p. 350.

18. Carole Pateman, *The Sexual Contract*, p. 203.

19. Ibid.

20. Ibid., p. 259n.33.

21. Carole Pateman, "Defending Prostitution: Charges against Ericsson," p. 203. This was written before her book *The Sexual Contract* but I contend that belief underpins her writing of the sexual contract and is responsible for the inconsistencies.

22. Laurie Shrage, "Should Feminists Oppose Prostitution?" *Feminism and Political Theory*, ed. Cass R. Sunstein (Chicago: University of Chicago Press, 1990), p. 197.

23. Ibid.

24. Annie Sprinkle, perhaps the most well-known prostitute in North America, says this about her clients: "I was deeply in love with almost everyone who came to me. . . . I loved them all. I really loved them" (Shannon Bell, "Ejaculator Meets Slut Goddess! Or, Deep Inside Annie Sprinkle's Mind, Heart and Pussy . . . " *Spectator: California's Weekly Sex News and Review*, vol. 27, no. 9 [Nov. 1991]: 16). Annie also dispels the belief that there is no commitment and responsibility in commercial sex. She says: "Samuel is my favorite trick. I have been seeing him for seventeen years now and we are still going strong. . . . Samuel has helped me out in several emergencies. . . . My relationship with Samuel is by far the longest relationship I've had with a man." Annie Sprinkle, *Post Porn Modernist* (Amsterdam: Torch Books, 1991), p. 14.

25. Catharine MacKinnon, *Toward a Feminist Theory of the State* (Cambridge, MA: Harvard University Press, 1989), p. 3.

26. Ibid., p. 109.

27. Ibid., p. 243.

28. Ibid., p. 168.

29. Ibid., p. 125.

30. Catharine MacKinnon, "Desire and Power," *Feminism Unmodified: Discourses on Life and Law* (Cambridge, MA: Harvard University Press, 1987), p. 59.

31. Ibid.

32. Catharine MacKinnon, *Toward a Feminist Theory of the State*, p. 118.

33. Ibid., p. 113.

34. Andrea Dworkin, *Intercourse* (New York: Free Press, 1987), p. 122.

35. Laurie Shrage, "Should Feminists Oppose Prostitution?" p. 194.

36. Catharine MacKinnon, *Toward a Feminist Theory of the State*, p. 121.

37. Ibid., p. 109.

38. Ibid.

39. Ibid.

40. Catharine MacKinnon, "Desire and Power," *Feminism Unmodified*, p. 49.

41. Ibid., p. 61.

42. Ibid.

43. Catharine MacKinnon, *Toward a Feminist Theory of the State*, p. 153.

44. Ibid.

45. Ibid., p. 149.

46. Catharine MacKinnon, "Desire and Power," *Feminism Unmodified*, p. 60.

47. Ibid., p. 49.

48. Karl Marx, *Capital*, Vol. I, p. 149.

49. Joan Cocks, in her analysis of the hegemonizing impetus of radical feminism as it counters the masculine/feminine regime, suggests that

Between the rule of masculine/feminine and the triumph of the rule, perversities, insurgencies, and overturnings always are able and likely to occur—not merely for those who break with heterosexual desire but for those who receive pleasure from it.

Joan Cocks, *The Oppositional Imagination: Feminism, Critique and Political Theory* (London: Routledge, 1989), p. 140.

50. Jon Stratton, *Writing Sites* (New York: Harvester/Wheatsheaf, 1990), p. 199.

51. Catharine MacKinnon, "Desire and Power," *Feminism Unmodified*, p. 59.

52. Ibid., p. 50.

53. Ibid.

54. Jacques Derrida and Christie V. McDonald, "Choreographies," p. 71.

55. William Simon and John H. Gagnon, "Sexual Scripts," *Theories of Human Sexuality*, ed. James Greer and William T. O'Donohue (New York: Plenum Press, 1987), pp. 364–67.

56. Gad Horowitz, "The Renunciation of Bisexuality," *Repression* (Toronto: University of Toronto Press, 1977), p. 87.

57. Ibid., p. 93.

58. Susan Hekman, *Gender and Knowledge: Elements of a Postmodern Feminism* (Boston: Northeastern University Press, 1990), p. 185.

59. Ibid., pp. 189–90.

60. Luce Irigaray, "Questions," *This Sex Which Is Not One*, trans. Catherine Porter (Ithaca: Cornell University Press, 1985), p. 164. Following citations for Irigaray are from *This Sex Which Is Not One*. The names of the essays will be given.

61. Luce Irigaray, "The Power of Discourse," p. 74.

62. Ibid.

63. Luce Irigaray, "This Sex Which Is Not One," p. 24.

64. Elizabeth Grosz, *Sexual Subversions: Three French Feminists* (Sydney: Allen & Unwin, 1989), p. 116.

65. Luce Irigaray, "This Sex Which Is Not One," p. 24.

66. Ibid.

67. Ibid., p. 25.

68. Ibid.

69. Ibid., p. 33.

70. Luce Irigaray, "Women on the Market," p. 186.

71. Ibid., p. 184.

72. Ibid., p. 175.

73. Ibid.

74. Ibid., p. 177.

75. Ibid., p. 180.

76. Ibid., p. 172.

77. Ibid., p. 185.

78. Ibid., p. 186.

79. Ibid., p. 186.

80. Ibid.

81. Ibid., p. 187.

82. Luce Irigaray, "Commodities among Themselves," p. 192.

83. Ibid., p. 172.

84. Luce Irigaray, "The Power of Discourse," pp. 84–85.

85. Janet Feindel, "The Whore/Madonna Complex," p. 8 (unpublished paper available at the Prostitute's Archives, the Canadian Women's Movement Archives, Toronto).

86. Luce Irigaray, "Women on the Market," p. 177.

87. Gayle Rubin, "Thinking Sex: Notes for a Radical Theory of the Politics of Sexuality," *Pleasure and Danger: Exploring Female Sexuality*, ed. Carole S. Vance (Boston: Routledge & Kegan Paul, 1984), p. 283.

88. Ibid., p. 301.

89. Ibid., p. 284.

90. Ibid., p. 279.

91. Ibid., pp. 180–81.

92. Ibid., p. 283.

93. Ibid.

94. Ibid.

95. Ibid., p. 282.

96. Ibid., p. 302.

97. Ibid., p. 286.

98. Ibid., pp. 286–87.

99. Ibid., p. 289.

100. Ibid., p. 293.

101. Ibid., p. 302.

102. Ibid.

103. Ibid., p. 308.

5. Rewriting the Prostitute Body

1. L. A. Kauffman, "The Anti-Politics of Identity," *Socialist Review*, vol. 20, no. 1 (1990): 75.

2. Tom Keenan, "The 'Paradox' of Knowledge and Power: Reading Foucault on a Bias," *Political Theory*, vol. 15, no. 1 (Feb. 1987): 28.

3. Michel Foucault, "Two Lectures," *Power/Knowledge*, ed. Colin Gordon, trans. Colin Gordon, Leo Marshall, John Mepham, Kate Soper (New York: Pantheon Books, 1980), p. 108.

4. Ibid.

5. Mary Wollstonecraft, *A Vindication of the Rights of Woman*, ed. Miriam Kramnick (New York: Penguin Books, 1975), p. 165.

6. Gail Pheterson, ed., *A Vindication of the Rights of Whores* (Seattle: Seal Press, 1989), p. 29.

7. Jane Sawicki, "Identity Politics and Sexual Freedom: Foucault and Feminism," *Feminism and Foucault*, ed. Irene Diamond and Lee Quinby (Boston: Northeastern University Press, 1988), p. 188.

8. Annie Sprinkle, *Post-Porn Modernist*, p. 13, and Scarlot Harlot, "Whores and Healers" (educational video), 1990.

9. Ernesto Laclau and Chantal Mouffe, *Hegemony and Socialist Strategy*, p. 158.

10. Chantal Mouffe, "Radical Democracy: Modern or Postmodern?" p. 36.

11. Tracy Quan, "Books about Our Business," *PONY X-Press*, vol. 1, no. 1 (1990): 19.

12. "A Brief History of Our Life and Times," *PONY X-Press*, vol. 1, no. 1 (1990): 3.

13. Veronica Vera, "P.O.N.Y. Tales," mimeograph, 1990, p. 2.

14. "Turning out the Charter at the First World Whores' Congress," *A Vindication of the Rights of Whores*, p. 38.

15. "Human Rights: Simple Human Respect," *A Vindication of the Rights of Whores*, p. 80.

16. "A Brief History of Our Life and Times," *PONY X-Press*, vol. 1, no. 1 (1990): 3.

17. Veronica Vera, "P.O.N.Y. Tales," mimeograph, 1990, p. 2.

18. Gail Pheterson, "Not Repeating History," *A Vindication of the Rights of Whores*, p. 3.

19. Ibid.

20. Ibid., p. 28.

21. Ibid.

22. There are many other prostitutes' rights groups that are members of ICPR. For a listing of these groups see Gail Pheterson, "Not Repeating History," *A Vindication of the Rights of Whores*, pp. 4–8.

23. Margo St. James, "The Reclamation of Whores," *Good Girls/Bad Girls: Sex Trade Workers and Feminists Face to Face*, ed. Laurie Bell (Toronto: The Women's Press, 1987), p. 82.

24. Gail Pheterson "Not Repeating History," *A Vindication of the Rights of Whores*, p. 4.

25. "Statement on Prostitution and Feminism," *A Vindication of the Rights of Whores*, pp. 193–94.

26. Ibid., p. 194.

27. "Statement of Purpose," *PONY X-Press*, vol. 1, no. 1 (1990): 1.

28. Interview with Veronica Vera, New York, April 1991.

29. Ibid.

30. Veronica Vera, "P.O.N.Y. Tales," p. 7.

31. Tracy Quan, "The Vox Fights," interview, *Vox* (Winter 1991): 35.

32. Ibid.

33. Shannon Bell, "Ejaculator Meets Slut Goddess!" p. 16.

34. Annie Sprinkle, *Post Porn Modernist*, p. 13.

35. Ibid.

36. Shannon Bell, "Ejaculator Meets Slut Goddess!" p. 16.

37. Interview with Veronica Vera, New York, April 1991.

38. Shannon Bell, "Ejaculator Meets Slut Goddess!" p. 16.

39. Conversation with Valerie Scott, November 1990.

40. *Statement on Prostitution and Feminism, A Vindication of the Rights of Whores*, p. 194.

41. Ibid.

42. Priscilla Alexander, "Prostitution: A Difficult Issue for Feminists," *Sex Work: Writings by Women in the Sex Industry*, ed. Frederique Delacoste and Priscilla Alexander (Pittsburgh: Cleis Press, 1987), pp. 196–97.

43. Ibid., p. 188.

44. Valerie Scott, Peggy Miller, and Ryan Hotchkiss, "Realistic Feminists," *Good Girls/Bad Girls*, p. 207.

45. Christine Sypnovich, *The Concept of Socialist Law* (Oxford: Clarendon Press, 1990), p. 85.

46. *World Charter for Prostitutes' Rights, A Vindication of the Rights of Whores*, p. 40.

47. *Statement on Prostitution and Human Rights, A Vindication of the Rights of Whores*, p. 103.

48. Carol Leigh, *Outlaw Poverty, Not Prostitutes*, video, 1990.

49. Ibid.

50. The *Statement* points out that throughout the world the murder of prostitutes commonly occurs without penalty; that the physical liberty of prostitutes is restricted by state and city regulations which establish curfews and prohibit prostitutes' presence in certain areas or at certain times; and that forced prostitution denies a person's right to liberty and security of her or his person. As an example of forced prostitution it cites the common transport of Third World women, under false pretenses, to the West to work in prostitution. The *Statement* points out that prostitutes do not receive the same police protection as other citizens; that forced medical testing denies liberty to prostitutes; and that forced or pressured registration with the police stigmatizes prostitutes and violates their liberty to change professions if they wish (*Statement on Prostitution and Human Rights, A Vindication of the Rights of Whores*, p. 104).

51. Ibid., p. 106.

52. Ibid., p. 108.

53. Ibid., pp. 103–108.

54. COYOTE, "National Task Force on Prostitution," *Sex Work*, p. 291.

55. *World Charter for Prostitutes' Rights, A Vindication of the Rights of Whores*, p. 40.

56. Gail Pheterson, *A Vindication of the Rights of Whores*, p. 33.

57. *Statement on Prostitution and Feminism, A Vindication of the Rights of Whores*, p. 194.

58. Gail Pheterson, *A Vindication of the Rights of Whores*, p. 34.

59. *Statement on Prostitution and Human Rights, A Vindication of the Rights of Whores*, p. 107.

60. Ibid.

61. *World Charter for Prostitutes' Rights, A Vindication of the Rights of Whores*, p. 40.

62. Ibid., p. 41.

63. Ibid.

64. Ibid., p. 40.

65. Valerie Scott, "C-49: A New Wave of Oppression," *Good Girls/Bad Girls*, pp. 102–103.

66. *World Charter for Prostitutes' Rights, A Vindication of the Rights of Whores*, p. 41.

67. *Statement on Prostitution and Feminism, A Vindication of the Rights of Whores*, p. 195.

68. Dolores French, *Working: My Life as a Prostitute* (New York: E. P. Dutton, 1988), p. 161.

69. Ibid., pp. 161–62.

70. Margo St. James, "From the Floor," *Good Girls/Bad Girls*, p. 129.

71. Interview with Priscilla Alexander, San Francisco, April 1989.

72. Carol Smart, *Feminism and the Power of Law* (London: Routledge, 1989), p. 5.

73. Ibid., p. 162.

74. Norma Jean Almodovar, "Prostitution and The Criminal Justice System— Part VII," *Spectator: California's Weekly Sex News and Review* (June 1991): 3. Norma Jean Almodovar is a spokesperson for L. A. COYOTE, a former Los Angeles police traffic officer, and the author of *Cop to Call Girl*. Almodovar did a seven-part series on prostitution for *Spectator*.

75. Ibid.

76. WHORE*CORP* pamphlet.

77. *Statement on Prostitution and Feminism, A Vindication of the Rights of Whores*, p. 192.

78. Ibid.

79. Ibid.

80. Margo St. James, "The Reclamation of Whores," *Good Girls / Bad Girls*, p. 85.

81. "Feminism: Crunch Point," *A Vindication of the Rights of Whores*, p. 144.

82. *Statement on Prostitution and Feminism, A Vindication of the Rights of Whores*, p. 193.

83. "Feminism: Crunch Point," *A Vindication of the Rights of Whores*, p. 150.

84. Ibid.

85. " 'The Big Divide': Feminist Reactions to the Second World Whores' Congress," *A Vindication of the Rights of Whores*, p. 177.

86. Disclosed by West German representative Pieke Biermann, "Feminism: Crunch Point," *A Vindication of the Rights of Whores*, p. 156.

87. Shannon Bell, "Ho'ing, Sex and Power," *Rites Magazine: For Lesbian and Gay Liberation*, vol. 6, no. 6 (November 1989): 7.

88. Joan Nestle, "Lesbians and Prostitutes: A Historical Sisterhood," *Sex Work*, p. 233.

89. Ibid., p. 243.

90. Ibid., p. 232.

91. "Statement on Prostitution and Feminism," *A Vindication of the Rights of Whores*, p. 196.

92. Ibid., p. 194.

93. "Health: Our First Concern," *A Vindication of the Rights of Whores*, p. 123.

94. Ibid.

95. *Statement on Prostitution and Health, A Vindication of the Rights of Whores*, p. 142. It identifies separate policies for prostitutes as discrimination.

96. "Health: Our First Concern," *A Vindication of the Rights of Whores*, p. 124.

97. Ibid.

98. Ibid., p. 116.

99. Ibid., p. 131.

100. Interview with Priscilla Alexander, San Francisco, April 1989.

101. Ibid.

102. "Prostitutes and AIDS," *PONY X-Press*, vol. 1, no. 1 (1990).

103. Tom Keenan, "The 'Paradox' of Knowledge and Power: Reading Foucault on a Bias," p. 30.

104. Sarah Wynter, "Confronting the Liberal Lies about Prostitution," *WHISPER Newsletter*, vol. 2, No. 2 (1987): 1.

105. Susan G. Cole, "Whispering Out Loud," *Broadside*, vol. 10, no. 4 (Feb. 1989): 3.

106. Sarah Wynter, "Empowering Women to Escape Prostitution," mimeograph, 1987.

107. Sarah Wynter, "WHISPER: Women Hurt in Systems of Prostitution Engaged in Revolt," *Sex Work*, p. 266.

108. Sarah Wynter, "Confronting the Liberal Lies about Prostitution," *WHISPER Newsletter*, vol. 2, no. 2 (1987): 10.

109. Evelina Giobbe, "When Sexual Assault Is a Job Description," *WHISPER Newsletter*, vol. 4, no. 3 (1990): 4.

110. Sarah Wynter stated this at a training session she led in Toronto with women working in battered-women's shelters to improve the services that shelters provide for prostitutes, cited by Susan Cole, "Whispering Out Loud," p. 3.

111. Evelina Giobbe, "The Vox Fights," interview, *Vox* (Winter 1991): 32.

112. Ibid.

113. Evelina Giobbe, "Prostitution: Sexual Commerce or Sexual Abuse?" *WHISPER Newsletter*, vol. 5, no. 1 (1991): 4.

114. Kathleen Barry, "UNESCO Report Studies Prostitution," *WHISPER Newsletter*, vol. 1, no. 3 (1986–87): 1.

115. Ibid.

116. Evelina Giobbe, "When Sexual Assault Is a Job Description," Violence Against Women Supplement, *Women and Foundations*, National Network of Women's Funds, Spring 1991.

117. Susan Cole, "Whispering Out Loud," p. 3.

118. Charlotte Davis Kasl, *Women, Sex, and Addiction* (New York: Ticknor & Fields, 1989), p. 256.

119. Evelina Giobbe, "Prostitution: Sexual Commerce or Sexual Abuse?" p. 4.

120. Ibid., p. 6.

121. Ibid., p. 4.

122. Evelina Giobbe, "Empowering Women to Escape Prostitution," mimeograph, 1987.

123. Susan Cole, "Whispering Out Loud," p. 3.

124. Evelina Giobbe, "Prostitution: Sexual Commerce or Sexual Abuse?" p. 4.

125. Priscilla Alexander, "Prostitution: A Difficult Issue for Feminists," *Sex Work*, p. 189.

126. Evelina Giobbe, "Prostitution: Sexual Commerce or Sexual Abuse?" p. 4.

127. Susan Cole, "Whispering Out Loud," p. 3.

128. Evelina Giobbe, "Prostitution: Sexual Commerce or Sexual Abuse?" p. 4.

129. Ibid., p. 5.

130. "1990 N. C. A. S. A. Resolution on Prostitution," *WHISPER Newsletter*, vol. 4, no. 3 (Winter 1990): 5.

131. June Levine and Lyn Madden, *Lyn: A Story of Prostitution* (London: The Women's Press, 1987).

132. Shannon Bell, Review of *Lyn: A Story of Prostitution*, by June Levine and Lyn Madden, "The Review Issue," *Resources for Feminist Research*, vol. 18, no. 1 (1989): 30–31.

133. Evelina Giobbe, "The Vox Fights," p. 35.

134. Susan Cole, "Whispering Out Loud," p. 3.

135. Evelina Giobbe, "The Vox Fights," p. 35.

136. Ibid., p. 29.

137. Ibid.
138. Susan Cole, "Whispering Out Loud," p. 3.
139. Kathleen Barry, "UNESCO Report Studies Prostitution," p. 1.
140. Ibid.
141. Ibid.
142. WHISPER, "Progress Report, 1985–1989," p. 1.
143. Ibid.
144. Norma Jean Almodovar, "Prostitution and the Criminal Justice System—Part I," *Spectator* (April 12–18, 1991): 4.
145. Evelina Giobbe, "Prostitution: Sexual Commerce or Sexual Abuse?" p. 4.
146. *World Charter for Prostitutes' Rights, A Vindication of the Rights of Whores*, p. 41.
147. The spokesperson for New York Prostitutes Anonymous does not wish to have her name used in adherence with the eleventh tradition which explicitly states: "we need always maintain personal anonymity at the level of press, radio and films" (*The Twelve Traditions*, mimeograph).
148. Prostitutes Anonymous flyer.
149. Prostitutes Anonymous, *The Twelve-Steps.*
150. Prostitutes Anonymous, "Opening Statement," mimeograph.
151. Prostitutes Anonymous, "Why We Are Here," mimeograph.
152. Prostitutes Anonymous, "Opening Statement," mimeograph.
153. Ibid.
154. Charlotte Davis Kasl, *Women, Sex, and Addiction*, p. 110.
155. Interview with New York Prostitutes Anonymous spokesperson, September 1990.
156. Adam Gelt, "Third Degree, René LeBlanc: Prostitutes Anonymous," *CHIC* (August 1989): 28.
157. Ibid.
158. Ibid., p. 13.
159. Ibid., p. 14.
160. Prostitutes Anonymous, "Opening Statement."
161. Prostitutes Anonymous, "Who Is a Prostitute?" mimeograph.
162. Ibid.
163. Prostitutes Anonymous, "What Is Prostitutes Anonymous?" mimeograph.
164. Interview with New York Prostitutes Anonymous spokesperson, September 1990.
165. Prostitutes Anonymous, *The Twelve Traditions.*
166. Adam Gelt, "Third Degree, Rene LeBlanc: Prostitutes Anonymous," p. 14.
167. Ibid.
168. Interview with New York Prostitutes Anonymous spokesperson, September 1990.

6. Prostitute Performances

1. Jean-François Lyotard, "Lessons in Paganism," *The Lyotard Reader*, ed. Andrew Benjamin (London: Basil Blackwell, 1989), p. 132.
2. Interview with Candida Royalle, New York, May 1991.
3. Steven Conner, *Postmodernist Culture* (Oxford: Basil Blackwell, 1989), p. 144.
4. Catherine Elwes, "Floating Feminity: A Look at Performance Art by Wom-

en," *Women's Images of Men*, ed. Sarah Kent and Jacqueline Morreau (London: Pandora 1990), pp. 172–73.

5. Ibid., p. 172.

6. Steven Connor, *Postmodernist Culture*, p. 141.

7. Regis Durand, "Theatre/SIGNS/Performance," *Innovation/Renovation: New Perspectives in the Humanities*, ed. Ihab Hassan and Sally Hassan (Madison: University of Wisconsin Press, 1983), p. 220.

8. Ibid., p. 218.

9. Jeanie Forte, "Women's Performance Art: Feminism and Postmodernism," *Theatre Journal*, vol. 40, no. 2 (May 1988): 218.

10. Ibid.

11. Ibid.

12. Ibid., p. 220.

13. Catherine Elwes, "Floating Femininity: A Look at Performance Art by Women," p. 164.

14. Jeanie Forte, "Women's Performance Art: Feminism and Postmodernism," p. 225.

15. Elinor Fuchs, "Staging the Obscene Body," *The Drama Review* (May 1990): 33.

16. Mary Russo, "Female Grotesques: Carnival and Theory," *Feminist Studies/Critical Studies* (Bloomington: Indiana University Press, 1986), p. 219.

17. Peter Stallybrass and Allon White, *The Politics and Poetics of Transgression*, p. 9.

18. Mary Russo, "Female Grotesques: Carnival and Theory," p. 217.

19. Ibid., p. 213.

20. George Bataille, *Erotism*, trans. Mary Dalwood (San Francisco: City Lights Books, 1986), p. 269.

21. Here Foucault writes "sole"; I have replaced "sole" with "a" to indicate a plurality of possibilities.

22. Michel Foucault, "A Preface to Transgression," *Language, Counter-Memory, Practice*, ed. Donald F. Bouchard (Ithaca: Cornell University Press, 1977), p. 30.

23. Catherine Elwes, "Floating Feminity: A Look at Performance Art by Women," p. 174.

24. Ibid.

25. Interview with Candida Royalle, New York, May 1991.

26. Carnival Knowledge program, 1984.

27. Interview with Candida Royalle, New York, May 1991.

28. Working script for *Deep Inside Porn Stars*.

29. Her first solo performance piece was part of "The Prometheus Project" at the Performing Garage. The Performing Garage, Franklin's Furnace, The Kitchen, P.S. 122, and the Pyramid are all alternative New York performance spaces. Annie has performed at all of these. The piece Annie did as part of "The Prometheus Project" was originally part of her sex performance in a strip club on Forty-Second Street. Annie had begun to parody strip theater in the venue of strip clubs and make the men laugh at themselves. "Pornsticks," originally part of "The Prometheus Project," is part of her *Post Porn Modernist* show. Annie continues to perform vignettes from the *Post Porn Modernist* show; in January 1991 she performed (with Veronica Vera) "The Temple of the Sacred Prostitute," which constitutes the latter part of her *Post Porn Modernist*, at the Pyramid; in February 1991 she performed a number of the pieces ("Bosum Ballet," "Pink Shots," "Annie's

Tits on Your Head Photos") for a P.S. 122 benefit which she hosted; I attended the latter event. During the summer and fall of 1991 she performed the entire show in Berlin, London, and Scandanavia. In February 1992 Annie performed *Post Post Porn Modernist* in Toronto, where I saw the entire show many times.

30. The term was originated by Veronica Vera as the *Post Porn Modernist Manifesto*; it has been popularized by Annie Sprinkle to such an extent that she is taken to be the embodiment of the post-porn modernist.

31. Shannon Bell, "The Ejaculator Meets the Slut Goddess!" p. 4.

32. Noah Cowan, "Calling All Slut/Goddesses," *Eye* (Feb. 13, 1992): 22.

33. Annie Sprinkle, *Post Porn Modernist*, p. 85.

34. Annie Sprinkle and Maria Beatty have produced a fifty-minute video workshop entitled *The Sluts and Goddesses Video Workshop; or, How to Be a Sex Goddess in 101 Easy Steps* (1992). The aim of the video is "to give ordinary women greater access to these arcane or stigmatized sources of female power, and to stop us from thinking of them as dichotomous." Carol Queen, "This Way to the Goddess," *Spectator*, vol. 28, no. 16 (July 10–16, 1992).

35. I document one such salon in my article "Finding the Male Within and Taking Him Cruising: Drag King-For-A-Day," *The Last Sex: Feminism and Outlaw Bodies*, ed. Arthur Kroker and Marilouise Kroker (New York: St. Martin's Press), pp. 91–97.

36. Ibid., p. 91.

37. Elinor Fuchs, "Staging the Obscene Female Body," p. 52.

38. Annie Sprinkle, *Post Porn Modernist*, p. 91.

39. Sluts and Goddesses flyer.

40. Shannon Bell, "The Ejaculator Meets the Slut Goddess!" p. 5.

41. Annie Sprinkle, *Post Porn Modernist*, p. 13.

42. Ibid., p. 67.

43. Ibid., p. 109.

44. Annie Sprinkle, *Post Porn Modernist*, program.

45. Annie narrated some of the story for me when I interviewed her, "Ejaculator Meets the Slut Goddess!" p. 4.

46. Ibid.

47. Annie Sprinkle, *Post Porn Modernist*, p. 114.

48. Vera has presented versions and segments of *Bare Witness* in performance spaces in New York, Tallahassee, and San Francisco and she has produced art gallery installations consisting of photos and video footage of herself and friends taken in collaboration with some of the top erotic photographers in the United States and Holland, including Robert Mapplethorpe. These, in slide form, are part of her performance piece. Her recent photo exhibition, March and April 1991 at Torch Gallery in Amsterdam, was entitled "Madonnas and Whores." I recently saw Vera perform a piece she called *Bright Lights, Big Titties* (December 1991) which included parts of her *Bare Witness* show and a screening of *Portrait of a Sexual Evolutionary*.

49. Interview with Veronica Vera, New York, April 1991.

50. The committee, chaired by Arlen Spector, was created to respond to proposals by Dworkin and MacKinnon that more laws be created around pornography.

51. All quotations are either from "Beyond Kink" or the film *Veronica Vera: Portrait of a Sexual Evolutionary*.

52. Ibid.

53. Georges Bataille, *Erotism*, p. 269.

54. Gad Horowitz, "The Foucaultian Impasse: No Sex, No Self, No Revolution," *Political Theory*, vol. 15, no. 1 (February 1987): 77.

55. Michel Foucault, "Preface to Transgression," p. 34.

56. Interview with Veronica Vera, New York, April 1991.

57. Veronica Vera, *Beyond Kink*.

58. Gwendolyn performed *Merchants of Love* (1989) at the Toronto Fringe (drama and performance) Festival, and in Ottawa and England. *HARDCORE* was performed at the 1990 Toronto Fringe Festival. Gwendolyn has also performed excerpts from both pieces at many Toronto alternative film and performance events.

59. All quotations from *Merchants of Love* are either from a published version in *Phoenix Rising: The Voice of the Psychiatrized*, vol. 8, nos. 3/4 (July 1990): S19–S25, or from a performance of excerpts for her film/performance show "Raunch Bouquet," Pleasure Dome series at the Cinecycle, Toronto, June 1991.

60. All quotations from *HARDCORE* are either from the original performance (Toronto Fringe Festival, 1990) or a performance of excerpts for Gwendolyn's film/performance show "Raunch Bouquet."

61. Janet Feindel, "Introduction," *A Particular Class of Women* (Vancouver: Lazara Publications, 1988).

62. Janet Feindel, *A Particular Class of Women*, p. 50.

63. Janet Feindel, "Introduction," *A Particular Class of Women*.

64. Janet Feindel, *A Particular Class of Women*, p. 51.

65. The complete play has been performed as a one-woman show in Toronto, Ottawa, Calgary, Edmonton, Victoria, Buffalo, and New York. It was performed in Vancouver and Cleveland in spring and summer 1992. *A Particular Class of Women* was produced in the fall of 1992, again in New York; this was the first time that the show was performed by nine actors, rather than as a one-woman show. The play, published by Lazara Press, is distributed by Blizzard Press in Canada and Inland Book Company in the United States.

66. Ibid., pp. 18 and 20.

67. Ibid., p. 24.

68. Ibid., p. 37.

69. Ibid., p. 59.

70. Ibid., p. 37.

71. Ibid., p. 44.

72. Ibid., p. 25.

73. Janet Ghent, "Festival should be red-letter event for the 'Scarlot Harlot,' " *Tribune*, Oakland, California, Nov. 2, 1989.

74. Carol Leigh published ten chapters of Scarlot's adventures in *Sex Work: Writings by Women in the Sex Industry*, ed. Frederique Delacoste and Priscilla Alexander. *The Adventures of Scarlot Harlot* is on video.

75. As well as playing around San Francisco, *The Adventures of Scarlot Harlot* was featured at the National Festival of Women's Theatre in Santa Cruz in 1983.

76. Murry Frymer, "Leigh calls her act 'The Scarlot Harlot,' " *San Jose Mercury News*, May 1983.

77. Ibid.

78. Thea Johnson, "First National Festival of Women's Theater," *Plexus: San Francisco Bay Area Women's Newspaper*, May 1983.

79. Hunter Drohojowska, "A happy Hooker goes on stage: Practicing prostitute performs comedy as Scarlot Harlot," *Los Angeles Herald Examiner*, March 7, 1984.

80. Carol Leigh, *The Adventures of Scarlot Harlot*, video.

81. Interview with Carol Leigh, San Francisco, July 1992.

82. "Art, Prostitution, Free Speech Form a Bizarre Brew at a Rally," *New York City Tribune*, May 25, 1990.

83. Performance which I attended at the Freedom of Sexpression Forum, sponsored by the National Writers Union, San Francisco, July 7, 1992.

84. She presented her music video *Safe Sex Slut* as part of a seminar on performance and social change at the Fifth International Conference on Aids (1989) in Montreal. She sings in the video:

I won't become disease infected
Me, I'll be so well protected
I always pay my income tax
I eat granola for my snacks
Safe sex, safe sex.

At the movies, in a car,
In a bathroom at a bar
Safe sex, safe sex.

Scarlot Harlot, *Safe Sex Slut*, video, 1987.

85. Charles Linebarger, "Papal Protesters Picket Dianne's Fundraiser," *San Francisco Sentinel*, July 31, 1987.

86. *The Scarlot Letter*, March 1990.

87. Carol Leigh, *G.H.O.S.T.: Spiritual Warfare*, 1990. The following quotations are from the video.

88. Carol Leigh, *Personal Statement of Purpose*, Taking Back the Night/Challenging Divisions, November 1991.

89. I saw Scarlot perform this piece at the Freedom of Sexpression Forum, sponsored by the National Writers Union, San Francisco, July 7, 1992.

90. This and following quotes are from Carol Leigh, *Sex Workers Take Back the Night*, 1991.

91. Open Forum—A School of Collective Learning (Spring 1992), flyer.

92. Carol Leigh, Taking Back the Night / Challenging Divisions, discussion group agenda.

93. Interview with Carol Leigh, San Francisco, July 1992.

94. Scarlot Harlot, *Whores and Healers*, 1990.

Conclusion

1. Alison Jaggar, "Prostitution," *The Philosophy of Sex*, ed. Alan Soble, pp. 348–68.

2. Lars Ericsson, "Charges against Prostitution: An Attempt at a Philosophical Assessment," *Ethics*, vol. 90 (April 1980): 335–66.

3. Shannon Bell, "Ejaculator Meets Slut Goddess!" p. 4.

4. Jean-François Lyotard, *The Postmodern Condition: A Report on Knowledge*, trans. Geoff Bennington and Brian Massumi (Manchester: Manchester University Press, 1984).

5. Gayatri Chakravorty Spivak, "Can the Subaltern Speak?" *Marxism and the Interpretation of Culture*, ed. Cary Nelson and Lawrence Grossberg (Urbana: University of Illinois Press, 1988), p. 308.

6. Kim Derko, "A High-Heeled Point of View: An Interview with Gwendolyn," *The Independent Eye* (May 1990): 7.

7. Jess Wells, *A Herstory of Prostitution in Western Europe*, pp. 7–8.

BIBLIOGRAPHY

Acton, William. (1870) *Prostitution Considered in Its Moral, Social, and Sanitary Aspects*. London: Frank Cass.

Alciphron. (1922) *Letters from the Country and the Town of Fishermen, Farmers, Parasites and Courtesans*, trans. F. A. Wright. London: George Routledge & Sons Ltd.

Alexander, Priscilla. (1987) "Prostitution: A Difficult Issue for Feminists," *Sex Work. Writings by Women in the Sex Industry*, ed. Frederique Delacoste and Priscilla Alexander. Pittsburgh: Cleis Press.

Allen, R. E., trans. and analysis. (1984) *The Dialogues of Plato*, Vol. I. New Haven: Yale University Press.

Almodovar, Norma Jean. (1991) "Prostitution and the Criminal Justice System—Part I and Part VII," *Spectator: California's Weekly Sex News and Review*, April and June.

Bakhtin, Mikhail. (1968) *Rabelais and His World*, trans. Helen Iswolsky. Cambridge, MA: M.I.T. University Press.

Bannet, Eve Tavor. (1989) *Structuralism and the Logic of Dissent*. London: MacMillan Press Ltd.

Barry, Kathleen. (1986–87) "UNESCO Report Studies Prostitution," *WHISPER Newsletter*, vol. 1, no. 3.

Bataille, George. (1986) *Erotism*, trans. Mary Dalwood. San Francisco: City Lights Books.

Baudelaire, Charles. (1983) *Intimate Journals*, trans. Christopher Isherwood. San Francisco: City Lights Books.

Baudelaire, Charles. (1982) *Les Fleurs Du Mal*, trans. Richard Howard. Boston: David R. Godine.

Bell, Shannon. (1991) "Ejaculator Meets Slut Goddess! Or, Deep Inside Annie Sprinkle's Mind, Heart and Pussy," *Spectator: California's Weekly Sex News and Review*, vol. 27, no. 9, November.

Bell, Shannon. (1991) "Feminist Ejaculations," *The Hysterical Male: New Feminist Theory*, eds. Arthur Kroker and Marilouise Kroker. New York: St. Martin's Press.

Bell, Shannon. (1989) "Ho'ing, Sex and Power," *Rites Magazine for Lesbian and Gay Liberation*, vol. 6, no. 6.

Bell, Shannon. (1989) "Review of *Lyn: A Story of Prostitution*, by June Levine and Lyn Madden." The Review Issue, *Resources for Feminist Research*, vol. 18, no. 1.

Benjamin, Walter. (1985) "Central Park," *New German Critique*, no. 34, Winter.

Best, Steven, and Douglas Kellner. (1991) *Postmodern Theory: Critical Interrogations*. New York: Guilford Press.

du Bois, Page. (1988) *Sowing the Body: Psychoanalysis and Ancient Representations of Women*. Chicago: University of Chicago Press.

Brandt, Paul (Hans Licht). *Sexual Life in Ancient Greece*. London: George Routledge & Sons Ltd.

Brown, Wendy. (1988) "Supposing Truth Were a Woman . . . Plato's Subversion of Masculine Discourse," *Political Theory*, vol. 16, no. 4.

Brown, Wendy. (1988) *Manhood and Politics: A Feminist Reading in Political Theory*. Totowa: Rowman & Littlefield.

Cocks, Joan. (1989) *The Oppositional Imagination: Feminism, Critique and Political Theory*. London: Routledge.

Cole, Susan G. (1989) "Whispering Out Loud," *Broadside*, vol. 10, no. 4.

Conner, Steven. (1989) *Postmodern Culture*. Oxford: Basil Blackwell.

Corbin, Alain. (1990) *Women for Hire*, trans. Alan Sheridan. Cambridge, MA: Harvard University Press.

Cowan, Noah. (1992) "Calling All Slut/Goddesses," *Eye*, Feb. 13.

Derko, Kim. (1990) "A High-Heeled Point of View: An Interview With Gwendolyn," *The Independent Eye*, May.

Derrida, Jacques. (1981) *Dissemination*, trans. Barbara Johnson. Chicago: University of Chicago Press.

Derrida, Jacques. (1974) *Of Grammatology*, trans. Gayatri Chakravorty Spivak. Baltimore: Johns Hopkins University Press.

Derrida, Jacques, and Christie McDonald. (1982) "Choreographies," *Diacritics*, vol. 12.

Durand, Regis. (1983) "Theatre/SIGNS/Performance," *Innovation/Renovation: New Perspectives in the Humanities*, ed. Ihab Hassan and Sally Hassan. Madison: University of Wisconsin Press.

Dworkin, Andrea. (1987) *Intercourse*. New York: Free Press.

Eagleton, Terry. (1983) *Literary Theory: An Introduction*. Minneapolis: University of Minnesota Press.

Ellis, Havelock. (1908) *Analysis of the Sexual Impulse, Love and Pain, the Sexual Impulse in Women: Studies in the Psychology of Sex*, Vol. III. Philadelphia: F. A. Davis.

Ellis, Havelock. (1910) *Sex in Relation to Society: Studies in the Psychology of Sex*, Vol. VI. Philadelphia: F. A. Davis.

Ellis, Havelock. (1908) *Sexual Inversion: Studies in the Psychology of Sex*, Vol. I, Second edition. Philadelphia: F. A. Davis.

Elshstain, Jean. (1981) *Public Man, Private Woman: Women in Social and Political Thought*. Princeton: Princeton University Press.

Elwes, Catherine. (1990) "Floating Feminity: A Look at Performance Art by Women," *Women's Images Of Men*, ed. Sarah Kent and Jacqueline Morreau. London: Pandora.

Ericsson, Lars. (1980) "Charges against Prostitution: An Attempt at a Philosophical Assessment," *Ethics*, vol. 90, April.

Feindel, Janet. (1988) *A Particular Class of Women*. Vancouver: Lazara Publications.

Feindel, Janet. (1983) "The Whore/Madonna Complex," unpublished paper, Prostitute Archives, The Canadian Women's Movement Archives, Toronto.

Forte, Jeanie. (1988) "Women's Performance Art: Feminism and Postmodernism," *Theatre Journal*, vol. 40, no. 2.

Foucault, Michel. (1979) *Discipline and Punish*, trans. Alan Sheridan. New York: Vintage Books.

Foucault, Michel. (1980) *The History of Sexuality. An Introduction*, Vol. I, trans. Robert Hurley. New York: Vintage Books.

Foucault, Michel. (1977) *Language, Counter-Memory, Practice*, ed. Donald F. Bouchard, trans. Donald F. Bouchard and Sherry Simon. Ithaca: Cornell University Press.

Foucault, Michel. (1980) *Power/Knowledge*, ed. Colin Gordon, trans. Colin Gordon, Leo Marshall, John Mepham, Kate Soper. New York: Pantheon Books.

Foucault, Michel. (1985) *The Use of Pleasure. The History of Sexuality*, Vol. II, trans. Robert Hurley. New York: Vintage Books.

French, Delores. (1988) *Working: My Life as a Prostitute*, with Linda Lee. New York: E. P. Dutton.

Freud, Sigmund. (1910) "A Special Type of Object Choice Made by Men," *Sexuality and the Psychology of Love*, (1972), ed. Phillip Rieff. New York: Collier Books.

Freud, Sigmund. (1953) "Infantile Sexuality," *On Sexuality: Three Essays on the Theory of Sexuality and Other Works*, trans. and ed. James Strachey. Middlesex: Penguin Books.

Fuchs, Elinor. (1990) "Staging the Obscene Body," *The Drama Review*, May.

Gallop, Jane. (1982) *The Daughter's Seduction: Feminism and Psychoanalysis*. Ithaca: Cornell University Press.

Gelt, Adam. (1989) "Third Degree, René LeBlanc: Prostitutes Anonymous," *CHIC*, August.

Gilman, Sander. (1985) *Difference and Pathology. Stereotypes of Sexuality, Race, and Madness*. Ithaca: Cornell University Press.

Giobbe, Evelina. (1987) "Empowering Women to Escape Prostitution," mimeograph.

Giobbe, Evelina. (1991) "Prostitution: Sexual Commerce or Sexual Abuse?" *WHISPER Newsletter*, vol. 5, no. 1.

Giobbe, Evelina. (1990) "When Sexual Assault is a Job Description," *WHISPER Newsletter*, vol. 4, no. 3.

Giobbe, Evelina. (1991) "The Vox Fights," interview, *Vox*, Winter.

Grosz, Elizabeth. (1989) *Sexual Subversions: Three French Feminists*. Sydney: Allen & Unwin.

Gwendolyn. (1987) *Choice Boredom*, film.

Gwendolyn. (1990) *HARDCORE*.

Gwendolyn. (1987) *Katrinka*, film.

Gwendolyn. (1989) *Merchants of Love*.

Gwendolyn. (1989) *Pedagogy*, film.

Gwendolyn. (1990) *Prowling by Night*, film.

Halperin, David. (1990) *One Hundred Years of Homosexuality*. New York: Routledge.

Harsin, Jill. (1985) *Policing Prostitution in Nineteenth Century Paris*. Princeton: Princeton University Press.

Harvey, David. (1989) *The Condition of Postmodernity*. Oxford: Basil Blackwell.

Hebdige, Dick. (1988) *Hiding in the Light*. London: Routledge.

Hekman, Susan. (1990) *Gender and Knowledge: Elements of a Postmodern Feminism*. Cambridge: Polity Press.

Henriques, Fernando. (1962) *Prostitution and Society*, Vol. I, *Primitive, Classical and Oriental*. London: MacGibbon and Kee.

Horowitz, Gad. (1987) "The Foucaultian Impasse: No Sex, No Self, No Revolution," *Political Theory*, vol. 15, no. 1.

Horowitz, Gad. (1977) *Repression*. Toronto: University of Toronto Press.

Huyssen, Andreas. (1986) *After the Great Divide: Modernism, Mass Culture, Postmodernism*. Bloomington: Indiana University Press.

Irigaray, Luce. (1985) *This Sex Which Is Not One*, trans. Catherine Porter. Ithaca: Cornell University Press.

Jackson, Margaret. (1987) "Facts of Life or Eroticization of Women's Experience/Sexology and the Social Construction of Heterosexuality," *The Cultural Construction of Sexuality*, ed. Pat Caplan. London: Tavistock Publishers.

Jaggar, Alison. (1980) "Prostitution," *Philosophy of Sex*, ed. Alan Soble. Totowa, New Jersey: Littlefield, Adams.

Jameson, Fredric. (1990) *Postmodernism: The Logic of Late Capitalism*. Durham: Duke University Press.

Jeffreys, Sheila. (1985) *The Spinster and Her Enemies: Feminism and Sexuality, 1880–1930*. London: Pandora Press.

Kasl, Charlotte Davis. (1989) *Women, Sex, and Addiction*. New York: Ticknor & Fields.

Kaufman, L. A. (1990) "The Anti-Politics of Identity," *Socialist Review*, vol. 20, no. 1.

Keenan, Tom. (1987) "The 'Paradox' of Knowledge and Power: Reading Foucault on a Bias," *Political Theory*, vol. 15, no. 1.

Keuls, Eva. (1985) *The Reign of the Phallus: Sexual Politics in Ancient Athens*. New York: Harper & Row.

Kroker, Arthur. (1992) *The Possessed Individual*. Montreal: New World Perspectives.

Kroker, Arthur and Marilouise Kroker. (1991) *The Hysterical Male: New Feminist Theory*. New York: St. Martin's Press.

Laclau, Ernesto and Chantal Mouffe. (1985) *Hegemony and Socialist Strategy: Towards a Radical Democratic Process*, trans. Winston Moore and Paul Cammack. London: Verso.

Lash, Scott. (1990) *The Sociology of Postmodernism*. London: Routledge.

Leigh, Carol. (1983) *The Adventures of Scarlot Harlot*, video.

Leigh, Carol. (1990) *G.H.O.S.T.: Spiritual Warfare*, video.

Leigh, Carol. (1990) *Outlaw Poverty, Not Prostitution*, video.

Leigh, Carol. (1987) *Safe Sex Slut*, video.
Leigh, Carol. (1991) *Sex Workers Take Back the Night*, video.
Leigh, Carol. (1990) *Whores and Healers*, video.
Leigh, Carol. (1992) *Yes Means Yes, No Means No*, video.
Levine, June and Lyn Madden. (1987) *Lyn: A Story of Prostitution*. London: The Women's Press.
Loraux, Nicole. (1986) *The Invention of Athens: The Funeral Oration in the Classical City*, trans. Alan Sheridan. Cambridge, MA: Harvard University Press.
Lyotard, Jean-François. (1989) "Lessons in Paganism," *The Lyotard Reader*, ed. Andrew Benjamin. London: Basil Blackwell.
Lyotard, Jean-François. (1988) *The Postmodern Condition: A Report on Knowledge*, trans. Geoff Bennington and Brian Massumi. Manchester: Manchester University Press, 1984.
MacKinnon, Catharine. (1987) *Feminism Unmodified: Discourses on Life and Law*. Cambridge, MA: Harvard University Press.
MacKinnon, Catharine. (1989) *Toward a Feminist Theory of the State*. Cambridge, MA: Harvard University Press.
Marx, Karl. (1977) *Capital*, Vol. I, trans. Ben Fowkes. New York: Vintage Books.
Marx, Karl. (1975) *The Economic and Philosophic Manuscripts, Karl Marx Early Writings*, trans. Rodney Livingstone and Gregory Benton. New York: Vintage Books.
Minutes of Evidence Taken before the Royal Commission. (1871) London: George Edward Eyre and William Spottiswood.
Mort, Frank. (1987) *Dangerous Sexualities: Medical-Moral Politics in England since 1830*. London: Routledge & Kegan Paul.
Mouffe, Chantal. (1988) "Radical Democracy: Modern or Postmodern?" trans. Paul Holdengraber. In *Universal Abandon?* ed. Andrew Ross. Minneapolis: University of Minnesota Press.
Mouffe, Chantal. (1988) "Hegemony and New Political Subjects: Towards a New Concept of Democracy," trans. Stanley Gray. In *Marxism and the Interpretation of Culture*, ed. Geoff Bennington and Brian Massumi. Urbana: University of Illinois Press.
Nead, Lynda. (1988) *Myths of Sexuality*. Oxford: Basil Blackwell.
Nestle, Joan. (1987) "Lesbians and Prostitutes: A Historical Sisterhood," *Sex Work: Writings by Women in the Sex Industry*, ed. Frederique Delacoste and Priscilla Alexander. Pittsburgh: Cleis Press.
Newton, Judith. (1988) "History as Usual?: Feminism and the New Historicism," *Cultural Critique*, Spring.
Nye, Andrea. (1989) "The Hidden Host: Irigaray and Diotima at Plato's Symposium," *Hypatia*, vol. 3, no. 3.
O'Brien, Mary. (1981) *The Politics of Reproduction*. Boston: Routledge and Kegan Paul.
Okin, Susan. (1979) *Women in Western Political Thought*. Princeton: Princeton University Press.
Otis, Leah Lydia. (1985) *Prostitution in Medieval Society. The History of*

an *Urban Institution in Languedoc*. Chicago: University of Chicago Press.

Parent-Duchatelet, Alexander John Baptiste. (1836) *De la Prostitution dans la Ville de Paris*, Vol. I.

Pateman, Carole. (1990) "Defending Prostitution: Charges against Ericsson," *Feminism and Political Theory*, ed. Cass R. Sunstein. Chicago: University of Chicago Press.

Pateman, Carole. (1988) *The Sexual Contract*. Cambridge: Polity Press.

Pateman, Carole. (1989) *The Disorder of Women: Democracy, Feminism, and Political Theory*. Cambridge: Polity Press.

Pecheux, Michel. (1982) *Language, Semantics and Ideology: Stating the Obvious*, trans. Harbans Nagpal. London: MacMillan.

Peterson, M. Jeanne. (1986) "Dr. Acton's Enemy: Medicine, Sex and Society in Victorian England," *Victorian Studies*, vol. 29, no. 4, Summer.

Pheterson, Gail, ed. (1989) *A Vindication of the Rights of Whores*. Seattle: Seal Press.

Plato. (1968) *The Republic of Plato*, trans. Allan Bloom. New York: Basic Books Inc.

Plato. (1951) *Symposium*, trans. Walter Hamilton. Middlesex: Penquin Books.

Plato. (1966) *Symposium*, trans. Michael Joyce, *The Collected Dialogues of Plato*, ed. Edith Hamilton and Huntington Cairns. New York: Pantheon Books.

Plato. (1961) *Menexenus*, trans. B. Jowett, *The Collected Dialogues of Plato*, ed. Edith Hamilton and Huntington Cairns. New York: Bollingen Foundation.

Plato. (1961) *Theaetetus*, trans. F. M. Cornford, *The Collected Dialogues of Plato*, ed. Edith Hamilton and Huntington Cairns. New York: Bollingen Foundation.

Pomeroy, Sarah. (1975) *Goddesses, Whores, Wives and Slaves: Women in Classical Antiquity*. New York: Schocken Books.

Prostitutes Anonymous, "Opening Statement," mimeograph.

Prostitutes Anonymous, "What Is Prostitutes Anonymous?" mimeograph.

Prostitutes Anonymous, "Who Is a Prostitute?" mimeograph.

Prostitutes Anonymous, "Why We Are Here," mimeograph.

Prostitutes Anonymous, *The Twelve Steps*, mimeograph.

Prostitutes Anonymous, *The Twelve Traditions*, mimeograph.

Quan, Tracy. (1990) "Books about Our Business," *PONY X-Press*, vol. 1, no. 1.

Quan, Tracy. (1991) "The Vox Fights," interview, *Vox*, Winter.

Raunch, Angelika. (1988) "The *Trauerspiel* of the Prostituted Body, or Woman as Allegory of Modernity," *Cultural Critique*, Fall.

Report of the Royal Commission upon the Administration and Operation of the Contagious Diseases Acts. (1871) London: George Edward Eyre and William Spottiswood.

Robinson, Paul. (1976) *The Modernization of Sex*. New York: Harper & Row.

Ross, Andrew, ed. (1988) *Universal Abandon! The Politics of Postmodernism*. Minneapolis: University of Minnesota Press.

Royalle, Candida. (1984) *Deep Inside Porn Stars*, working script.

Rubin, Gayle. (1984) "Thinking Sex: Notes for a Radical Theory of the Politics of Sexuality," *Pleasure and Danger: Exploring Female Sexuality*, ed. Carole S. Vance. London: Routledge & Kegan Paul.

Russo, Mary. (1986) "Female Grotesques: Carnival and Theory," *Feminist Studies/Critical Studies*, ed. Teresa De Lauretis. Bloomington: Indiana University Press.

St. James, Margo. (1987) "The Reclamation of Whores," *Good Girls/Bad Girls. Sex Trade Workers and Feminists Face to Face*, ed. Laurie Bell. Toronto: The Women's Press.

Sanger, William. (1869) *The History of Prostitution*. New York: Harper and Brothers.

Sawicki, Jane. (1988) "Identity Politics and Sexual Freedom: Foucault and Feminism," *Feminism and Foucault*, ed. Irene Diamond and Lee Quinby. Boston: Northeastern University Press.

Saxonhouse, Arlene. (1985) *Women in the History of Political Thought: Ancient Greece to Machiavelli*. New York: Praeger.

Schott, Robin May. (1988) *Cognition and Eros*. Boston: George Routledge & Sons Ltd.

Scott, Valerie. (1987) "C-49: A New Wave of Oppression," *Good Girls/Bad Girls: Sex Trade Workers and Feminists Face to Face*, ed. Laurie Bell. Toronto: The Women's Press.

Scott, Valerie, Peggy Miller, and Ryan Hotchkiss. (1987) "Realistic Feminists," *Good Girls/Bad Girls: Sex Trade Workers and Feminists Face to Face*, ed. Laurie Bell. Toronto: The Women's Press.

Shrage, Laurie. (1990) "Should Feminists Oppose Prostitution?" *Feminism and Political Theory*, ed. Cass R. Sunstein. Chicago: University of Chicago Press.

Simon, William, and John H. Gagnon. (1987) "Sexual Scripts," *Theories of Human Sexuality*, ed. James Greer and William T. O'Donohue. New York: Plenum Press.

Smart, Carol. (1989) *Feminism and the Power of Law*. London: Routledge.

Spivak, Gayatri Chakravorty. (1988) "Can the Subaltern Speak?" *Marxism and the Interpretation of Culture*, ed. Cary Nelson and Lawrence Grossberg. Urbana: University of Illinois Press.

Spivak, Gayatri Chakravorty. (1987) *In Other Worlds: Essays in Cultural Politics*. London: Methuen.

Sprinkle, Annie. (1991) *Post Porn Modernist*. Amsterdam: Torch Books.

Stallybrass, Peter, and Allon White. (1986) *The Politics and Poetics of Transgression*. London: Methuen.

Stratton, Jon. (1990) *Writing Sites*. New York: Harvester/Wheatsheaf.

Strauss, Leo. (1972) *Xenophon's Socrates*. Ithaca: Cornell University Press.

Suleiman, Susan Rubin, ed. (1986) *The Female Body in Western Culture*. Cambridge, MA: Harvard University Press.

Sypnovich, Christine. (1990) *The Concept of Socialist Law*. Oxford: Clarendon Press.

Thucydides. (1954) "Pericles' Funeral Oration," *The Peloponnesian War*, trans. Rex Warner. Middlesex: Penguin Books.

Valverde, Marianna. (1989) "The Love of Finery," *Victorian Studies*, vol. 32, no. 2.

Vera, Veronica. (1988) *Beyond Kink*.

Vera, Veronica. (1990) "P.O.N.Y. Tales," mimeograph.

Vera, Veronica. (1987) *Veronica Vera: Portrait of a Sexual Evolutionary*, video.

Versnel, H. S. (1987) "Wife and Helpmate: Women of Ancient Athens in Anthropological Perspective," *Sexual Asymmetry: Studies in Ancient Society*, ed. Josine Blok and Peter Mason. Amsterdam: J. C. Gieben.

Waithe, Mary Ellen, ed. (1987) *A History of Women Philosophers*. Vol. I, *600 BC–500 AD*. Dordrecht: Martinus Nijhoff Publishers.

Wakefield, Neville. (1990) *Postmodernism: The Twilight of the Real*. London: Pluto Press.

Walkowitz, Judith. (1980) *Prostitution and Victorian Society. Women, Class, and the State*. Cambridge: Cambridge University Press.

Wells, Jess. (1982) *A Herstory of Prostitution in Western Europe*. Berkeley, CA: Shameless Hussy Press.

WHISPER. (1989) "Progress Report, 1985–1989."

Wollstonecraft, Mary. (1792) *A Vindication of the Rights of Woman*. Rpt. 1975, ed. Miriam Kramnick. New York: Penguin Books.

Wynter, Sarah, aka Evelina Giobbe. (1987) "Confronting the Liberal Lies about Prostitution," *WHISPER Newsletter*, vol. 2, no. 2.

Wynter, Sarah, aka Evelina Giobbe. (1987) "Empowering Women to Escape Prostitution," mimeograph.

Wynter, Sarah, aka Evelina Giobbe. (1987) "WHISPER: Women Hurt in Systems of Prostitution Engaged in Revolt," *Sex Work: Writings by Women in the Sex Industry*, ed. Frederique Delacoste and Priscilla Alexander. Pittsburgh: Cleis Press.

Xenophon. (1968) *Memorabilia, Oeconomicus, Symposium and Apology*, ed. E. H. Warmington, trans. E. C. Marchant. London: William Heineman Ltd.

INDEX

Shannon Bell is a postmodern *hetaira*: a political and sexual feminist philosopher. She teaches classical political theory, feminist theory, and postmodern theory. She received her Ph.D. in Political Science from York University.